Charles Burnham

Centennial proceedings and other historical facts and incidents

relating to Newfane,

The county seat of Windham County, Vermont

Charles Burnham

Centennial proceedings and other historical facts and incidents relating to Newfane,
The county seat of Windham County, Vermont

ISBN/EAN: 9783337871703

Printed in Europe, USA, Canada, Australia, Japan

Cover: Foto ©ninafisch / pixelio.de

More available books at **www.hansebooks.com**

1774—1874.

CENTENNIAL PROCEEDINGS

AND OTHER

HISTORICAL FACTS

AND INCIDENTS

RELATING TO

NEWFANE,

The County Seat of Windham County.

VERMONT.

BRATTLEBORO:
D. LEONARD, STEAM JOB PRINTER.
1877.

VOTE AUTHORIZING THE PUBLICATION OF THE HISTORY OF NEWFANE.

At a town meeting, held at School House Hall, in Williamsville, on the 7th day of March, A. D. 1876, it was voted to have seven hundred copies of the "History of the Town and Church" published, together with the proceedings at the Centennial Celebration; and that one copy be furnished, free, to each family in town, the excess to be sold and the proceeds paid into the town treasury.

VOTED, To have a committee of three appointed to prepare and publish the aforesaid history at the expense of the town. Chose as said committee: J. J. Green, Rev. Charles Burnham and J. H. Merrifield.

D. A. DICKINSON,
Town Clerk.

PRELIMINARY OBSERVATIONS.

In the preparation of this volume, old records have been consulted not only, but thoroughly searched. Some things before in doubt have been settled. Where authorities apparently equally trustworthy have disagreed, we have adopted that view which seemed to have the best evidence in its favor, after diligently comparing and sifting the statements made. Notwithstanding all this, it will doubtless come to pass that some, as they read these pages, will say of certain things here recorded, "I do not believe that, I know that is not so." If the question should be asked, why you so believe, and how you know? perhaps you would say, "We have often heard the old people state these circumstances very differently." True, we have heard all these stories, and, after careful consideration, have reached the results set forth in this volume.

To illustrate, one writer says there were but six families in town when the church was organized; while the biographer of the Morse family sets the number at twenty. A careful examination of all the conflicting traditions, indicates beyond a reasonable doubt that there were at least fourteen families here in June, 1774, and perhaps twenty.

We cannot close these remarks without returning our sincere thanks to the descendants of the early pioneers and all those who, by their hearty co-operation in this enterprise, have rendered invaluable aid in the researches that have been necessary to complete this volume.

JOSEPH J. GREEN,
CHARLES BURNHAM, } Committee.
JOHN H. MERRIFIELD,

CONTENTS.

PART I.

	PAGE.
Record of Proceedings Preparatory to the Centennial Anniversary, &c.,	9
Historical Address,—C. K. Field,	15
Biographical Sketches,—C. K. Field,	34
Toasts and Responses,	98
Historical Notes,	105
"The Vermont Free Press,"	113
The Sleeping Beauty,	117
Centennial Discourse,	123
Sketch of Proceedings,	142

PART II.

Original Charter,	151
First Town Officers,	154
Family Genealogies,	155
Sawtell Family Sermon,	177
Longevity, Long Married Life, &c.,	185
Roads and Bridges,	186
Extracts from first Town Records, &c.,	188
School Districts and Schools,	190
Pondville Baptist Church,	194
First Universalist Church,	198
Methodism in Newfane,	201
Cemeteries,	202
Fayetteville,	205
Williamsville,	211
Pondville,	220
War Record,	225
Sons of Newfane Murdered in Louisiana,	243
Town Officers, 1774–1876,	245
Grand List, 1874,	250

PART I.

RECORD

OF THE PROCEEDINGS PREPARATORY TO THE CENTENNIAL ANNIVERSARY OF NEWFANE. JULY 4, 1874.

FAYETTEVILLE, VT., May 18, 1874.—Agreeable to a notice given out by the acting pastor of the Congregational Church, Rev. Charles Burnham, on the previous Sabbath, the citizens assembled at the vestry of said church, to take into consideration the subject of a Centennial celebration of the organization of the town of Newfane, also of the church, and organized by choosing Rev. Charles Burnham, Chairman, and F. O. Burditt, Secretary.

VOTED, To hold a town and church celebration. O. T. Ware and J. J. Green were appointed a committee to consult with citizens in the south part of the town, and invite them to be present and participate at the next meeting.

VOTED, To adjourn until the evening of the 26th inst., at 7 o'clock.

A true record.   F. O. BURDITT, Sec'y.

May 26, 1874.—Met agreeable to adjournment, and the meeting was called to order by the Chairman. The report of the proceedings of the last meeting was read by the Secretary; also heard the report of the committee appointed at the former meeting to consult with the citizens of the south part of the town. In response to the call of the Chairman, remarks were made by B. E. Morse, S. W. Bowker, D. D. Dickinson, E. P. Wheeler, A. J. Morse and Alexander Fairbanks in favor of, and heartily endorsing a centennial celebration.

VOTED. To celebrate the centennial anniversary of the organization of the town on some day to be determined hereafter.

VOTED. To appoint a committee of arrangements to consist of ten persons.

VOTED. That a committee of five be appointed to nominate permanent officers, and the committee of arrangements. The nominating committee was constituted as follows, viz: A. J. Morse, S. W. Bowker, D. D. Dickinson, O. T. Ware and B. E. Morse. After consultation, the committee reported as permanent officers the following list:

President of the Day—A. J. Morse.

Vice Presidents—B. E. Morse and Austin Birchard.

Secretary—F. O. Burditt.

Committee of Arrangements—S. W. Bowker, J. J. Green, D. D. Dickinson, B. E. Morse, O. T. Ware, W. T. Bruce, A. B. Franklin, W. A. Stedman, S. P. Miller and S. G. Brown.

The report was accepted and adopted.

VOTED. That the ladies present form themselves into a committee of the whole, and nominate a committee of arrangements from among themselves. The following nominations were made and confirmed:

Mrs. D. D. Dickinson,
" S. F. Whitney,
" D. A. Dickinson,
" F. O. Burditt,
" S. W. Bowker,
" O. T. Ware,
" C. E. Park,
" W. H. Goodnow,
" Frank Moore,
" D. S. Sabin,
" Nathaniel Higgins,

Mrs. Samuel Morse,
" W. T. Bruce,
" O. L. Sherman,
" G. B. Johnson,
" Hazelton Rice,
" Amherst Morse,
Miss Fanny Newton,
" Jessie M. Miller,
" E. E. Morse,
" Mary R. Birchard,

Floral Committee—Mrs. F. A. Fish and Mrs. Henry Cowan.

VOTED. That the celebration be held at Fayetteville on the 4th of July next.

VOTED. That a committee, consisting of one lady and one gentleman from each section of the town, be appointed to solicit subscriptions to pay necessary expenses.

Mrs. F. O. Burditt and Mr. O. T. Ware, Mrs. O. L. Sherman and Mr. D. D. Dickinson were appointed said committee.

VOTED. That the committee of arrangements meet at S. W. Bowker's to-morrow evening at 7:30, P. M.

VOTED, That when this meeting adjourns, it do so subject to the call of the committee of arrangements.

VOTED, To adjourn.

A true record.   F. O. BURDITT, Sec'y.

WEDNESDAY EVENING, May 27, 1874.—The committee of arrangements met at S. W. Bowker's, at 7:30 o'clock, and proceeded to business as follows:

VOTED. That a committee of three be appointed to make arrangements with the hotel keepers to furnish dinners on the day of celebration. S. W. Bowker, A. J. Morse and O. T. Ware were chosen such committee.

VOTED, That S. W. Bowker be the committee to consult the Hon. C. K. Field. and procure his services to deliver a historical address at the celebration. Should circumstances prevent his acceptance of the trust, then to procure some other person to perform that service.

VOTED, That the ladies take charge of the arrangements for costumes, and also for the singing.

VOTED, That the hour for the address be 11 o'clock.

VOTED, To have three Marshals, and S. W. Bowker. Col. A. B. Franklin and Samuel Morse were elected to those positions.

VOTED, That we meet at 9 o'clock, A. M., at or near the school house in Fayetteville, and form the procession.

William T. Bruce was appointed a committee to engage a band for the occasion.

J. J. Green was appointed a committee to furnish notices of the celebration and procure their insertion in the county papers.

VOTED, That when we adjourn, it be to meet at Bowles' Hotel two weeks from this evening, (June 9th), at 7 o'clock. Should it be a stormy evening, then to meet on the first pleasant evening after. Adjourned.

A true record.   F. O. BURDITT, Sec'y.

June 9th.—Met at Bowles' Hotel, at 7 o'clock, p. m. Meeting called to order by S. W. Bowker, Chairman. The report of the last meeting was read by the Secretary.

Voted. That B. E. Morse and Rev. Charles Burnham be appointed Toast Masters.

Voted, That S. W. Bowker appear in Continental costume, as one of the Marshals.

Voted. That a committee of three be appointed to prepare a programme for the day, and J. J. Green, O. T. Ware and F. O. Burditt were elected said committee.

Voted. That a committee of five be appointed to procure costumes, and make all necessary arrangements connected therewith. Mrs. D. A. Dickinson, Mrs. Wm. H. Goodnow, Mrs. S. W. Bowker, Mrs. O. T. Ware and Mrs. D. D. Dickinson were appointed such committee.

Voted, That F. O. Burditt and wife, and D. A. Dickinson and wife be a committee to arrange for the singing.

Voted, That the committee on costumes be requested to send for twenty male and twenty female costumes.

Voted. To adjourn the meeting for two weeks from this evening, to S. W. Bowker's Hotel, at 7 o'clock, p. m.

A true record.   F. O. Burditt, Sec'y.

June 23d, 1874.—The Committee of Arrangements met, according to adjournment, at S. W. Bowker's, at 7 o'clock, p. m. The meeting was called to order by the Chairman, and the proceedings of the last meeting were read by the Secretary.

On motion, a committee of three was chosen to procure lumber, build a platform, prepare seats, and make the general arrangements for the accommodation of speakers, invited guests, and the public in general. S. G. Brown, F. O. Burditt and D. A. Dickinson were appointed said committee.

Voted, To adjourn without day.

I certify the foregoing to be a true record of the proceedings in relation to the celebration of the centennial anniversary of the organization of the town of Newfane.

[Attest.]   F. O. Burditt, Sec'y.

The following is a copy of the circular letter of invitation issued, and published in the newspapers of the day:

1774.   1874.

CENTENNIAL

Of the Town of Newfane, Vt.

A. J. MORSE,
President.

AUSTIN BIRCHARD,   BENJ. MORSE.
Vice Presidents.

DEAR SIR :—This is the centennial year of the charter and organization of the Town and Congregational Church of Newfane, and we feel it not only a duty but a pleasure to do honor to the memory of those brave Fathers and noble Mothers who, facing all the perils and suffering the hardships incident to pioneer life, wended their way into this, then pathless forest, and built for themselves homes that soon echoed to the music from the cradle and the busy hum of the great wheel and the little wheel, and the wild free song of the girl at the loom

> As she fashioned the wool and the tow,
> For wear and not for show.

The settlement of the town was commenced in May, 1766, by Jonathan Park, Nathaniel Stedman and Ebenezer Dyer, from Worcester County, Mass.

The town was organized in 1774, and we feel that the appropriate day of the year to honor its founders, is that day which has crowned the work of all our fathers with honor and glory among the nations of the earth.

Therefore, we do earnestly and cordially invite you and yours to come and join with us in celebrating the Town Centennial, on the 4th of July, 1874.

Yours truly,   S. W. BOWKER,
Chairman of Com. of Arrangements.

NEWFANE, VT., June 1, 1874.

1774. 1874.

NEWFANE CENTENNIAL.

July 4th, 1874.

PROGRAMME OF THE DAY.

At 9 o'clock, A. M., the Procession will be formed in the following order:

1st. Ye ancient Marshal, S. W. BOWKER, will appear in the Military Uniform of Continental times, assisted by Marshals Col. A. B. Franklin and Samuel Morse, arrayed in the Military styles of the present day.

2d. Brattleboro Cornet Band.

3d. Settlers of 1766 moving into town.

4th. Parson Taylor's goodly people on their way to church, in the Sunday-go-to-meeting garb of a hundred years ago.

5th. Young America and My Lady of the Period.

The line of march will be through the Streets and around the Square.

At 11 o'clock, Prayer by the Rev. CHAS. BURNHAM.

AN ADDRESS OF WELCOME.

Music by the Choir - - - Auld Lang Syne.
Music by the Band.
Historical Address by the Hon. CHAS. K. FIELD.
Music by the Choir - - - Ode to Science.
Music by the Band.
Dinner at 12 1-2 o'clock.

———o———

2 o'clock, P. M., Music by the Choir - - Old Liberty.
Music by the Band.

2d. Voluntary Speeches, Sentiments, Responses, &c.
An Original Poem written for the occasion.

MUSIC.

———o———

Sunday, July 5. The morning service will be devoted to a SPECIAL HISTORICAL SKETCH OF THE CHURCH.

HISTORICAL ADDRESS

OF THE

HON. CHARLES K. FIELD:

Delivered at the Centennial Anniversary of the organization of the Church and Town of Newfane, July 4th, 1874.

NEWFANE, the shire town of Windham County, is situated eleven miles west of Connecticut river, and is bounded north by Townshend, east by Dummerston, Putney and Brookline, west by Wardsboro and Dover, and south by Marlboro. The township contained originally within its chartered limits thirty-six square miles; but, in 1820, that part of the town lying northeast of West river was annexed to Brookline, which materially reduced the chartered area of the town. The original charter of the town was granted in 1753, by Benning Wentworth, governor of New Hampshire, to Abner Sawyer and others, by the name of Fane. There was a current tradition, seventy years ago, that it was called Fane after Thomas Fane, one of the "men of Kent" who was engaged in an insurrectionary movement under Sir Thomas Wyat, in 1554, during the reign of Queen Mary, for the purpose of elevating Lady Jane Grey to the throne, in consequence of the odious Spanish match which Mary had formed with Philip 2d. Abner Sawyer and sixty-five others were the original grantees of Fane. Their names were as follows:

Abner Sawyer, John Milling, Ebenezer Morse, Vespasian

Millar, Joseph Baker, Thomas Adams, James Ball, John Ball, Samuel Brown, Jabez Beaman, John Hazeltine, Ross Wyman, John Young, John Adams, Charles Bridgham, Joseph Dyer, Jr., John Chadack, Barnet Wait, Ebenezer Taylor, Ebenezer Prescott, Isaac Temple, Edward Goodale, John Holland, Phineas Wilder, Joshua Houghton, Asa Boucher, David Osgood, Jonathan Osgood, Asa Whitcomb, Samuel Bayley, Thomas Sawyer, Saul Houghton, Ezekiel Kendall, Samuel Kendall, Daniel Allen, Ebenezer Taylor, Jr., Joseph Bayley, Nathaniel Houghton, John McBoide, Philip Goss, Joseph Glazier, Jacob Pike, Benjamin Glazier, Abner Wilder, Josiah Wilder, William Densmore, Barzillai Holt, John Glazier, Nathaniel Bexby, Rueben Moore, Aaron Newton, Peter Larkin, Matthias Larkin, Samuel Moore, Jonathan Wilder, Tille Wilder, Ezra Sawyer, Ezra Sawyer, Jr., John Stone, Fortunatus Taylor, Hy. Sherburne, Theodore Atkinson, Richard Wibird, Samuel Smith, John Downing, Samuel Solley, Sampson Sheaffe, Daniel Warner, and John Wentworth, Jr.

In 1761 the charter was returned to Gov. Wentworth, and a new one issued to Luke Brown and his associates, containing the same provisions that are embraced in the original charter. The 11th day of May, 1772, the governor of New York made a grant of this township, by the name of Newfane, to Walter Franklin and twenty others, most of whom resided in the city of New York. This New York charter is a literal copy of the original charter granted by Gov. Wentworth. The 12th of May, 1772, Walter Franklin and his associates, the grantees named in the New York charter, assigned and conveyed all their right in said township to Luke Knowlton and John Taylor, Esqs., of Worcester County, Mass. The titles to the lands in said township are derived directly from the New York charter. The township was surveyed in 1772, and duly organized May 17, 1774. The town was first settled in 1766, by Jonathan Park, Nathaniel Stedman and Ebenezer Dyer, who emigrated from Worcester County, Mass. The first clearing was made by Park and Stedman on the Nathan Merrifield farm, north of the Newfane Hill Common, in the spring of 1766. In 1774, Judge Knowlton, one of the original proprietors under the New York charter, was allotted some 300 or 400 acres in and about the present site of Fayetteville.

Deacon Park's clearing covered the old common on Newfane Hill and the Knowlton Farm. Judge Knowlton exchanged his lands in and about Fayetteville with Deacon Park for his clearing of eighty acres and a log cabin thereon. The deacon went down and cleared up the land in and about Fayetteville. In 1787, the judge succeeded in removing the shire from Westminster to Newfane Hill; but in 1824—thirty-seven years thereafter—the shire was removed from the Hill to Fayetteville. Had Judge Knowlton made his pitch upon the lots originally allotted to him on Smith's Brook, and contributed as liberally towards the growth and prosperity of a village where Fayetteville now is, it would have changed materially the destiny of Newfane. Starting, a hundred years ago, a settlement where Fayetteville now stands, with no rival villages near, it would have secured such a concentration of wealth and business as would have made it one of the most important villages in the county. For several years the early settlers suffered all the hardships and privations incident to the settlement of a new country. Without roads, or teams, or any of the ordinary means of transportation, they were under the necessity of conveying, by their own personal efforts, all their provisions and farming tools from Hinsdale, N. H.,—a distance of twenty miles—through an unbroken forest. At that early day there was no road or pathway up the valley of the West river, from Brattleboro; but they were obliged to cross Wicopee Hill, in Dummerston, by marked trees. Elizabeth, a child of Jonathan Park, was the first child born in town,—February 20th, 1768.

INDIANS.

The early settlers of Newfane were never molested by the Indians, for the reason that no permanent settlements were made in this town until after the storming and taking of Quebec by Wolf, in 1759, and the capitulation of Montreal in 1760, when the French lost their control over the Indian tribes in the Canadas. June 27, 1748, before any settlement was commenced, a battle was fought in the south part of this town or north part of Marlboro: the precise place of the battle cannot be fixed. Capt. Humphrey Hobbs, with 40 men, was ordered from Charlestown, No. 4, through the forest to Fort Shirly, in Heath, one of the frontier posts in Massachusetts. The march was made without interruption until Hobbs arrived at a point about twelve miles northwest of Fort Dummer, " on a low piece of ground covered with alders intermixed with larger trees, and watered by a rivulet," where he halted to give his men an opportunity to refresh themselves. A large body of Indians, commanded by a half-breed of the name of Sackett, who was said to have been a descendant of a captive taken at Westfield, Mass., discovered Hobbs' trail, and endeavored to cut him off. Hobbs had carefully posted a guard on his trail, and, while his men were refreshing themselves, the enemy came up and drove in the guard. Hobbs then arranged his men for action, each man selecting his tree for a cover. The enemy rushed forward, and received a well-directed fire from Hobbs' men, which checked their progress. A severe conflict ensued. Sackett and Hobbs were well known to each other, and both were distinguished for their intrepidity and courage. Sackett could speak English, and frequently called upon Hobbs to surrender, threatening to sacrifice his men with the tomahawk if he refused. Hobbs, in a loud voice, returned a defiant answer, and dared his enemy to put his threat in execution. The action continued about four hours, each party retaining their original position. During the fight the enemy would approach Hobbs' line, but were immediately driven back. Sackett, finding his men had suffered severely, retreated, carrying off his dead and wounded. Hobbs lost only three of his men —Ebenezer Mitchell, Eli Scott and Samuel Green; and three were wounded. The loss of the enemy was supposed to be greater. In all battles the Indians made extraordinary efforts to conceal their loss, and to effect this would incur greater exposure than in actual combat. When one fell, the nearest comrade was accustomed to crawl up and, under cover of the trees and brush, fix a "tump line" to the dead body and cautiously drag it to the rear. Hobbs' men stated that in this action they often saw the dead bodies of the Indians sliding along the ground as if by enchantment. As late as the year 1810, a large number of graves were visible on the lower portion of the Robinson flats, so-called, under a cluster of chestnut trees, near the South Branch below Williamsville, where the bodies of the Indians who were killed in this fight were supposed to have been buried: at least, such was the current tradition for fifty years or more among the early settlers of Newfane. Stevens, in his Journal, states that Capt. Hobbs started for Fort Shirly from Charlestown, No. 4, with forty-two men, officers included, on Thursday, June 23, 1748, and camped the first night at Bellows Falls, and the next day marched for West River, which they reached Saturday, 25th; "then traveled down the river and came to the South Branch, then traveled up the Branch two miles and camped, then traveled six miles southwest, and came to a small brook, where we boiled our kettles, and just as we began to eat, the enemy came upon us." The late General Field, who furnished a sketch of Newfane for Thompson's Gazetteer, about fifty years ago, was evidently misled by the prevailing traditions in relation to the fight with the Indians by Melvin's party for he fixed the scene of the battle at the mouth of the South Branch, in Newfane; and Belknap, in his history of New Hampshire, and Beckley, in his history of Vermont, adopt the same error. The publication of Capt. Melvin's journal, in the New Hampshire historical collections, fixes the place of the fight with Melvin's party in Jamaica, some seventeen miles above the mouth of the South

Branch in Newfane, and about four miles below the mouth of Winhall river, which, during the old French wars, was regarded as the upper fork of West river, and the South Branch in Newfane as the lower fork thereof. After the fight with Hobbs, Sackett retreated and passed down the Wantastiquet to its mouth, and, crossing the Connecticut, marched down to a point opposite Fort Dummer, where they ambuscaded a party of seventeen men, who were marching from Hinsdale to the fort, under command of Ensign Thomas Taylor, and killed four of the party. Four escaped, and the remainder, with Ensign Taylor, were taken prisoners. Ensign Taylor, in a journal describing his march to Canada, which he wrote after his return, describes his route to Crown Point, on Lake Champlain, as follows: " Crossed the Connecticut at a place called ' Catts-bane,' two or three miles above the mouth of West river, which we fell in with at the *lower fork;* thence proceeded up that river, part of the way on the flats, over the ground where Capt. Melvin's affair happened, three or four miles below the *upper fork;* thence to the source of the river." This would seem to settle the question conclusively, that the fight with Melvin's party took place some two hundred rods northeast of Jamaica village, on the banks of the West river. At the commencement of this century, the graves on the Robinson meadow, about one hundred rods below Williamsville, near the left bank of the South Branch, were plainly to be seen; and the writer of this remembers when a boy, as late as 1812, two graves were distinctly visible on Newfane Hill, and the current tradition was that two scouts from Fort Dummer were at one time engaged in shooting salmon at the mouth of the South Branch, and, being driven by the Indians to the summit of Newfane Hill, were killed, and afterwards buried about sixty rods northwest of the site of the old Court House. The theories of Beckley, Belknap, and others, in relation to the origin of the graves on the Robinson meadow and on Newfane Hill, are all contradicted by the journals of Melvin and Stevens. The ploughshare has long since rudely obliterated every trace of their existence.

RELIGIOUS SOCIETIES.

There are three religious societies in town, Baptist, Congregational and Universalist. The Congregational is the most numerous. Their place of worship is at Fayetteville. The Universalists have occasional preaching at Williamsville, and the Baptists worship at Pondville, in the extreme south part of the town.

A Congregational Church was organized in 1774, when there were but fourteen families residing in the town; it consisted of nine members, and Rev. Hezekiah Taylor was ordained and assumed the pastoral charge of it on the day of its organization.

RIVERS.

The Wantastiquet, commonly called West River, rises in Weston, Windsor County, and, passing through Newfane, empties into the Connecticut at Brattleboro. The South Branch, so-called, rises in Dover, and, after receiving a number of tributary streams, passes through the southerly part of the town and empties into the West River near the eastern boundary line of said town. Baker's Brook, a tributary of the South Branch, rises in Wardsboro, and empties into the South Branch at Williamsville. Smith's Brook rises in Wardsboro, and, running through the entire northerly part of the town, empties into West River, two miles below Fayetteville. These streams afford many eligible mill sites and water privileges.

FOREST TREES.

The original growth of forest trees is principally rock maple, beech, birch, spruce and hemlock; but the recent growth on the eastern and southern hillsides is oak and hickory, and in the south part of the town, on the intervals and hill sides near Williamsville, the chestnut grows abundantly. In no other town in Windham County, outside of the valley of the Connecticut, is the chestnut found growing.

SOIL.

The intervals afford excellent tillage land, and the uplands are inferior to none in the state for grazing. The town is diversified with high hills and deep valleys; but there are no elevations that deserve the name of mountains; there is little or no broken or waste land that is unsuitable for cultivation.

GEOLOGY AND MINERALOGY.

The geological character of the town is uniformly primitive; few continuous ranges can be traced with certainty. The rocks in place are principally mica slate and hornblende. Granite is by no means an uncommon rock; boulders and rolled masses of granite are scattered in profusion over every part of the town, and sometimes they are found on the summits of the highest hills which are composed entirely of mica slate. These boulders, by skillful splitting, are wrought into fence-posts and building-stone. Hornblende is a very common rock; it forms a range which extends through the entire town. It is the variety called hornblende slate, and is often curiously curved and twisted, and occasionally passes into primitive greenstone and greenstone porphyry. Mica slate is the most common rock in town, yet no connected range can be traced. It forms the summits and frequently the sides of the hills, and in the valleys it is a common rock; but hornblende is constantly thrusting itself from underneath the mica slate, and interrupting the continuity of its ranges. In the north part of the town are extensive strata of mica slate, which are occasionally quarried and wrought into flagging stones. Talcose slate better deserves the name of a range than any other in town. It traverses the whole county, passing through Whitingham, Wilmington, Marlboro, Newfane, Townshend, Windham, Athens and Grafton. In Grafton, Athens and Townshend it is extensively quarried, and wrought into fire-jambs, etc. There is an extensive bed of this rock in the west part of Newfane, bordering on Wardsboro and Dover, which, at some future day, will be successfully wrought, whenever the railroad facilities shall be such as to furnish a cheap mode of conveyance to market. Serpentine associated with talcose slate forms a range extending four or five miles on the western border of the town, presenting perpendicular precipices in some places forty or fifty feet in height. The crystalline appearance of this rock demonstrates it to be of the most primitive kind. Its texture is close, and it is extremely tough and hard, though in some cases it is easily broken on account of the fissures that pass through it. Chloride slate occurs in this town, in which is embedded splendid specimens of garnet. A nugget of native gold, weighing eight and one-half ounces, was found in this town in 1827, about one hundred rods east of the village of Williamsville. It was of a conical shape, and there were adhering to it a number of small crystals of quartz. It was found in alluvion consisting of thin strata of sand, clay and water-worn stones. The rocks *in situ* are all of a primitive class, consisting of hornblende, hornblende slate and greenstone porphyry, which are often found alternating with mica slate. At the time this mass of gold was found, it was supposed to have been a piece that was accidentally lost by a band of counterfeiters, who formerly resided in the immediate neighborhood, although their operations were confined exclusively to the counterfeiting of silver coin. Gold at that time had not been discovered elsewhere in New England; but since then its discovery at Somerset, Plymouth, Bridgewater, and other places in Vermont, seemed to favor the theory that it existed originally in the bed of serpentine and talcose slate in the west part of the town, near the head waters of the South Branch, and was swept out of place by some freshet and deposited in the alluvion some six miles below. All the gold which has thus far been found in Vermont has been associated with the serpentine and talcose slate range, which extends from Massachusetts north line to Canada. This town probably furnishes the richest and most extensive variety of minerals of any town in the State.

THE BURNING OF THE SAWTELL FAMILY.

A melancholy catastrophe occurred in this town on the night of the 2d of February, 1782, in the burning of the log house of Henry Sawtell, which created great sorrow, bordering upon terror, in the minds of the inhabitants of the vicinity, for the house was not only burned, but Mr. and Mrs. Sawtell and five children were consumed therein. The morning after the fire the neighbors saw a cloud of smoke gathered over the Sawtell place, and smelt an unusual odor in the air like burning flesh and clothing. The site of the house was hidden from the view of all the neighboring inhabitants, being situated in a deep valley; but as they approached the ruins they discovered, to their great horror and astonishment, the Sawtell house in ashes. Some of the larger logs were still burning, and the charred bodies of

Mr. and Mrs. Sawtell and five of their children were smouldering in the ruins. They gathered up, with pious care, the charred remains of the family, placed them in a coffin, and a public funeral was holden at the center of the town on the fourth, when a great crowd of people from the town and vicinity were assembled, and an appropriate sermon was preached by Rev. Hezekiah Taylor, the pastor of the church. From an old copy of his sermon, in the possession of the writer of this sketch, it appears that he exhorted his hearers not to construe this painful and violent death of a whole family as a judgment of God by reason of any great or unusual wickedness, for the manner of a person's death was no evidence of his righteousness or sinfulness before God. He appealed in pathetic and eloquent terms to the neighbors and townsmen of the deceased family, to take warning by this terrible and appalling calamity to be "always ready," for they know not at what hour the Lord would come, " whether at the second or third watch, whether at nightfall or at midnight." Mr. Henry Sawtell and his wife came to Newfane about 1774, and began the clearing of a new farm at a point midway between Newfane Hill and Williamsville. He was highly esteemed for his integrity. His wife was regarded as a pious, amiable woman, an exemplary, affectionate mother. After having undergone the hardships and vicissitudes attending the commencement of a new settlement, though not wealthy, Mr. Sawtell was in comfortable circumstances, and contemplated the erection of a more convenient and suitable dwelling for his family. But fate had decreed "that but for a little time" and they would need no earthly dwelling.

THE OLD SHIRE VILLAGE.

In the early settlement of the town, a village grew up on the summit of a hill, which rose like a cone in the center of the town, and in 1787 Newfane was constituted the shire town of Windham County, and the courts were removed from Westminster to Newfane Hill, so called. From 1790 to 1820, the village consisted of a court house, jail, meeting house, academy, three stores, two hotels, a variety of shops, such as were found in all New England villages at an early day, and about twenty private residences. The village stood upon the summit of the hill, and afforded a prospect as extensive and picturesque as any in New England. From the summit, near the meeting house, might be seen not less than fifty townships, lying in Vermont, New Hampshire and Massachusetts. On the west, Haystack in Wilmington, and Manicknung in Stratton, towered above the ridge of the Green Mountains, which formed the western boundary of the county. On the north, Ascutney was plainly visible to the naked eye, and on a clear summer day, the White Hills in New Hampshire could be distinctly seen by the aid of a telescope. The Highlands of New Hampshire and Massachusetts, extending for a distance of more than eighty miles from Sunnapee to Holyoke, were distinctly visible on the east, while Monadnock and Wachusett, with their cloud-capped summits, seemed to mingle with the heavens; and along the margin of the horizon to the southeast, little was to be seen but a broad sea of mountain tops, displaying, in wild disorder, ridge above ridge, and peak above peak, until the distant view was lost among the clouds.

VIEW FROM PUTNEY WEST HILL.

We cannot, in this connection, omit a description of the view from Putney West Hill, near the northeast corner of Newfane, and near the old road that passes from Dummerston and Putney to Newfane. From an eminence near the highway, the view in mid-summer is unsurpassed by any in New England. Looking south, you have on the right, the narrow and deep valley of the Wantastiquet, and on the left, the broader valley of the Connecticut. The whole compass of the horizon opens to the view. You can trace the line of the Green Mountains from Florida, in Massachusetts, to Mount Holly on the north. Saddleback, Haystack, Manicknung and Shatterack tower far above the Green Mountain ridge. From the Connecticut valley your eye stretches over the entire space from Ascutney to Holyoke, and you see hill and valley, clearing and forest, villages, hamlets and cottages, until you reach the summit of the majestic Monadnock ; and from thence you look north along the line of the Blue Highlands toward the White Hills. The surface of the Connecticut, for ten or fifteen miles below Brattleboro, and the cemetery on Prospect Hill, in the east village of Brattleboro, and the village of West Brattleboro are distinctly visible. The serrated, irregular and broken surface of the country, extending from the Wantastiquet to the summit of the Green Mountains on the west. is highly interesting, and reminds one of the Sierras of Spain and California.

SITE OF THE NEW SHIRE.

In 1825, the site of the public buildings were changed from Newfane Hill to what is now called Fayetteville, a village two miles east of the old center in the valley of the Wantastiquet or West River. The present site of the shire is three miles east of the geographical center of the county, and one mile south of the center of population. It is easy of access from all parts of the county. A new court house and jail were erected at an expense of $10,000. In 1853, by an Act of the General Assembly, commissioners were appointed, who altered and improved the public buildings at a cost of $13,000. After the removal of the shire from the hill to the valley below, the owners of the real estate on the hill commenced removing their buildings to Fayetteville and Williamsville, the two villages that have sprung up since the removal of the public buildings, and as late as 1860 not a building remained to mark the pleasant site of the old shire of Windham County. Fayetteville, the present site of the shire, has entirely grown up since 1825. It contains a court house, jail, two churches, two hotels, two stores, one grist and saw mill, two blacksmith shops, two carriage factories and fifty dwelling houses. It is pleasantly situated in the northeast part of the town on Smith's Brook, near its junction with the Wantastiquet or West River.

Williamsville, in the southeast part of the town, is situated on the South Branch, near the mouth of Baker's Brook, and contains about thirty dwelling houses, one hotel, one meeting house, two stores, two saw mills, one flouring mill, one tannery, two blacksmith shops, one bobbin factory, one carriage factory, one carding machine, one fulling and cloth dressing mill, and one planing mill and pail factory. This village was named after William H. Williams, an enterprising citizen, who resided many years in Newfane, and died in 1866 at a very advanced age.

Pondville, in the extreme south part of the town, contains a meeting house, one store, two saw mills, one flouring mill, one carding machine, and twenty dwelling houses.

POPULATION.

The population of this town in 1771, was 52; in 1791, 660; in 1800, 1,000; in 1810, 1,276; in 1820, 1,506; in 1830, 1,441; in 1840, 1,403; in 1850, 1,304; in 1860, 1,192, and in 1870, 1,113.

TOWN CLERKS.

The following is a list of the Town Clerks from the first organization of the town, in 1774, to the present time:

Luke Knowlton, from 1774 to 1783; Hezekiah Boyden, from 1783 to 1784; Luke Knowlton, 1784 to 1789; Calvin Knowlton, from 1789 to 1792; Nathan Stone, from 1792 to 1834; Joseph Ellis, from 1834 to 1836; William H. Hodges, from 1836 to 1839; Otis Warren, from 1839 to 1867; Marshall Newton, from 1867 to 1868; Dennis A. Dickenson, from 1868 to 1874.

REPRESENTATIVES TO THE GENERAL ASSEMBLY.

Ebenezer Myrick, 1779; William Ward, 1780; Ebenezer Myrick, 1781; Daniel Taylor, 1782; William Ward, 1783; Luke Knowlton, 1784-5; William Ward, 1786-7; Luke Knowlton, 1788-9; Calvin Knowlton, 1790-1; Luke Knowlton, 1792; Moses Kenny, 1793; Ebenezer Allen, 1794 to 1804; Luke Knowlton, 1805-6; Elijah Elmer, 1807; Joseph Ellis, 1808-9; Martin Field, 1810; Sylvanus Sherwin, 1811; Luke Knowlton, 1812-13; John Brooks, 1814; Luke Knowlton, 1815; Sylvanus Sherwin, 1816; Horace Dunham, 1817; Luke Knowlton, 1818; Martin Field, 1819; Sylvanus Sherwin, 1820; Martin Field, 1821; Sylvanus Sherwin, 1822; Jason Duncan, 1823-4; Sylvanus Sherwin, 1825; William H. Williams, 1826; D. W. Sanborn, 1827; Sylvanus Sherwin, 1828; Joseph Ellis, 1829-30; Henry

Wheelock, 1831-2; George Williams, 1833-4; Roswell M. Field, 1835-6; James Elliott, 1837-8; Walter Eager, 1839; Nahum Eager, 1840-1; Walter Eager, 1842; Otis Warren, 1843-4; Oliver P. Morse, 1845; no representative in 1846; Marshall Newton, 1847; George Arnold, 1848; Sir Isaac Newton, 1849-50; F. O. Burditt, 1851-2; Chas. K. Field, 1853-4-5; Marshall Newton, 1856; Otis Warren, 1857; Emory Wheelock, 1858; Otis Warren, 1859; Charles K. Field, 1860; O. L. Sherman, 1861-2; A. J. Morse, 1863-4; H. T. Robinson, 1865-6; John Rice, 1867; Holland Plimpton, 1868; E. P. Wheeler, 1869; Dana D. Dickinson, 1870-72.

PERVERSION OF LEGAL MAXIMS.

By a strange perversion of legal principles, which prevailed among the early settlers of Windham County, it was supposed that whoever married a widow who was administratrix upon the estate of her deceased husband represented insolvent, and should thereby possess himself of any property or thing which had been purchased by the deceased husband, would become an *executor de son tort*, and would thereby make himself liable to answer for the goods and estate of his predecessor. To avoid this difficulty, Major Moses Joy, of Putney, who became enamored of Mrs. Hannah Ward, of Newfane, the widow of William Ward, who died about 1788 leaving an insolvent estate, of which Mrs. Ward was administratrix, and married her within three months after taking out letters of administration. The marriage took place in the old Field Mansion on Newfane Hill, February 22d, A. D., 1789, and was solemnized by Rev. Hezekiah Taylor. Mrs. Ward placed herself in a closet, with a tire-woman, who stripped her of all her clothing, and while in a perfectly nude state, she thrust her fair, round arm through a diamond hole in the door of the closet, and the gallant major clasped the hand of the nude and buxom widow, and was married in due form by the jolliest parson in Vermont. At the close of the ceremony, the tire-woman dressed the bride in a complete wardrobe which the major had provided and caused to be deposited in the closet at the commencement of the ceremony. She came out elegantly dressed in silk, satin and lace, and there was kissing all round. A similar marriage took place in Westminster, in this county. See Hall's History of Eastern Vermont, page 585.

An instance, illustrating the strange perversion of legal maxims which prevailed among our ancestors at an early day, fell under the observation of the writer of this sketch. The Hon. Luke Knowlton, Sen., died December 12, 1810, and, at the time of his decease, there were many unsatisfied judgments existing against him. The morning after his decease, a creditor who had obtained a judgment of about forty dollars, applied to the late General Field, his attorney, for an execution with which he could seize the body and commit it to prison, hoping thereby to wring the amount thereof from the relatives and friends of the debtor. But the attorney refused to have an execution issued, insisting that it would be regarded as an outrage to take the dead body of a debtor and commit the same to prison. The prevailing notion at that time was that inasmuch as the execution ran against the body, that the officer might take the body of the debtor, whether dead or alive, and commit the same to the common jail. The same notion prevailed in England as late as 1816. The creditors of the eloquent Richard Brinsley Sheridan, just before his decease, in July, 1816, became so clamorous that they caused a Sheriff's officer to arrest the dying man in his bed and was about to carry him off in his blankets to a sponging house, when the attending physician interfered, and by representing to the officer the responsibility he must incur, if, as was too probable, his prisoner should expire on the way, succeeded in averting the outrage.

In the Vermont Republican, printed at Brattleboro, in July, 1855, a story is told of a custom which prevailed in this County at an early day, of holding even the dead body of a debtor liable to arrest, and that a case occurred in the town of Dummerston, when a dead body was arrested on its way to the grave and detained until some of the friends "backed the writ," and thus became bail for the debtor's appearance at court. As the return day of the writ was put far ahead the defendant was in no condition to appear and consequently "lurched his bail." In 1820 Dr. John Campbell, of Putney, had obtained a judgement against Anthony Jones and Joel Lee, upon a jail bond executed by Jones and Lee. By virtue of an execution issued upon said judgment, Lee was arrested and confined in the common jail, on Newfane Hill, and under the law which prevailed in this State at that time he was not entitled to the privilege of the jail yard, but was subjected to close confinement. He died within the prison, in the summer of 1820, and his son requested the privilege of taking his body away for the purpose of burying it in the cemetery at Brookline, with his relatives and friends, but the jailer refused to permit the body to be taken away, insisting if he permitted the body to be removed it would be regarded as an escape, and he and his bail would be made liable to satisfy the original judgment, and not until the creditors had consented, would the jailor permit the body to be removed.

THE WHIPPING POST.

At an early day corporal punishments were inflicted at every term of the Court on Newfane Hill. The writer of this sketch, when a mere boy, well remembers witnessing the whipping of old Mother White, of Wardsboro, in August, 1807. She was convicted of passing counterfeit money, and sentenced to recive thirty-nine lashes upon her bare back. A great crowd of men and women collected to witness the whipping. The Post was in the form of a cross, with a transverse strip near the top, to which her bare arms were bound, and her body was stripped to the waist. The High Sheriff applied a certain number of stripes, and the balance were allotted to his Deputies, some seven in number, and some of whom applied the blows with great vigor. Near the close of the whipping her back became raw, and she suffered excessive pain and she shrieked and screamed terribly in her agony. The writer of this sketch, although very young, remembers the scene distinctly. The Meeting House and Academy stood a few rods above the site of the Whipping Post, and their windows were filled with women, gazing intently upon the revolting scene. This was probably the last woman publicly whipped in Vermont, for the Legislature abolished the Whipping Post that fall and provided for the building of a States Prison at Windsor.

NUMBER OF SOLDIERS IN THE REBELLION.

The town of Newfane readily and promptly furnished her quota of soldiers, on the call of the President, for the suppression of the Slave-holder's Rebellion. She stands credited by the War Department with having furnished the following number of soldiers for the several Vermont regiments and other army organizations:

Second Reg't, 7; Third Reg't, 1; Fourth Reg't, 6; Sixth Reg't, 1; Seventh Reg't, 1; Eighth Reg't, 38; Ninth Reg't, 3; Eleventh Reg't, 10; Twelfth Reg't, 1; Sixteenth Reg't, 17; Seventeenth Reg't, 6; Vermont Cavalry, 5; Sharpshooters, 3; United States Navy, 6; soldiers not credited by name, 6; substitutes furnished, 6; commutation money paid by 7 men. Grand total of men furnished, 124; of whom 17 were killed or died in the service.

BIOGRAPHICAL SKETCHES.

HON. LUKE KNOWLTON.

Born in Shrewsbury, Mass., November 4, 1738. He served as a soldier in the old French War, and in 1759 was stationed at Crown Point awhile, and suffered great hardships during his march from Crown Point to Charlestown, No. 4. From a journal he kept during his service as a soldier, we learn that his company, in marching through the wilderness, exhausted their stock of provisions and were obliged to kill a pack-horse to save themselves from starvation. He married Sarah, daughter of Ephraim Holland, of Shrewsbury, Mass., January 5, 1760, and with his family moved to Newfane in February, 1773, which was the fourteenth family that settled in town. He continued to reside in this town until his death, which occurred December 12, 1810, at the age of 73 years. His wife died September 1, 1797. He was chosen first Town Clerk, at the organization of the town in 1774, and continued to hold that position for fourteen years. He was Town Representative in the General Assembly of the State of Vermont during the years 1784, 1785, 1788, 1789, 1792, 1803, and 1806, and a member of the old Council from 1790 to 1800; Judge of the Supreme Court in 1786 and a Judge of the Windham County Court from 1787 to 1793. John A. Graham, in a series of rambling letters descriptive of Vermont scenery, written and published about the close of the last century, thus speaks of Judge Knowlton. "Newfane owes its consequence in a great measure to Mr. Luke Knowlton, a leading character and a

man of great ambition and enterprise, of few words, but possessed of great quickness of perception and an almost intuitive knowledge of human nature, of which he is a perfect judge."

He was a Loyalist, and in consequence of the great sacrifices he made in behalf of the British Government, in the early part of the Revolutionary War, he received a large and valuable grant of land in Lower Canada, upon a part of which the present town of Sherbrooke is built.

Previous to the year 1784 Judge Knowlton gave in his adherance to the government of Vermont, and voluntarily became a citizen of the State. In the division of the $30,000 which New York received from Vermont, on the accession of the latter State to the Union he received $249.53, on account of the losses he had sustained by being obliged to give up lands which he held under a New York title. He was liberal and generous to the poor, entered heartily and zealously into all the public enterprises of the day, gave to the County of Windham the land for a common on Newfane hill, at the time of the removal of the shire from Westminster to Newfane, and contributed largely towards the erection of the first Court House and Jail in Newfane. He was remarkable for his great suavity of manner, and exceedingly decorous in his deportment. By reason of his great gravity and exceeding humility he acquired the appellation of "Saint Luke." His family consisted of seven children, three sons and four daughters, five of whom survived him. Six were born in Massachusetts and one in Vermont, as follows:

Calvin, born in 1761, died January 20, 1800: a graduate of Dartmouth College, class of 1783; married Sophia Willard, of Petersham. Mass., in 1793; studied law and practised his profession in Newfane until he died. Patty, born in 1762, died in Ohio in 1814. She married Daniel Warner, and was the grandmother of Hon. Willard Warner, late United States Senator from Alabama, and during the civil war was a member of General Sherman's staff in his celebrated "March to the Sea." Silas, born 1764, married Lucinda Holbrook at Newfane, November 30, 1786, died in Canada aged eighty. Sarah, born May 2, 1767, married John Holbrook at Newfane,

November 30, 1786. She died March 22, 1851, aged eighty-four. Alice married Nathan Stone, April 24, 1788. She died November 14, 1865, aged ninety-six. Lucinda, born August 8, 1771, married Samuel Willard. They lived awhile in Sheldon, Vt.; from thence they removed to Canada where she died, May 4, 1800.

The foregoing children were all born in Shrewsbury, Mass. Luke Knowlton, Jr., was born in Newfane, March 24, 1775; died at Broome township, Canada East, September 17, 1855, aged eighty. Of the children two, Calvin and Lucinda, died before their father; all the others survived him. His grandsons are men of marked ability, among whom are Paul Holland Knowlton, Broome township, Lower Canada, son of Silas Knowlton, who has occupied distinguished political positions in the province, and was for many years a member of the Canadian Parliament; Rev. John C. Holbrook, of Syracuse, N. Y., an eloquent divine, highly esteemed for his piety and learning; Hon. Willard Warner, of Alabama; Hon. George W. Knowlton, of Watertown, N. Y., a courteous old gentleman of more than four-score years of age, who exemplifies, in his virtue, simplicity and happiness, the powerful influence of the intelligence, industry and self-denial of his puritan ancestry; Hon. Frederick Holbrook, of Brattleboro, who for two years during the War of the Rebellion, was Governor of the State of Vermont, and in the discharge of his official duties he exercised the prudence and discretion, united with the energy and ability which characterized his worthy ancestor, the subject of this notice.

REV. HEZEKIAH TAYLOR.

The first pastor of the Congregational Church in Newfane was born in Grafton, Mass., in 1748; graduated at Harvard College in 1770, and was settled as pastor of the Congregational Church in Newfane the 30th day of June, 1774. The church was organized the same day of his settlement, and at that time there were but fourteen families in the town, and the church consisted of only nine members. He died August 23, 1814. He was possessed of a firm and vigorous constitution, of great endurance, an indomitable will, and a resolution unshaken by the care of his flock and the labor and hardship incident to the early settlement of the town. Possessing habits of great industry, with a liberal education, and a disposition of great kindness and benevolence toward all with whom he was connected, he faithfully ministered to the spiritual and temporal wants of his people. Of an exceedingly genial temperament, overflowing with wit and humor, he was the delight and ornament of the social circle. His efforts and example contributed eminently to the happiness and prosperity of the early inhabitants of the town.

Parson Taylor was a very social, genial man, and fond of a joke when the occasion offered, like Parson Byles of Boston, and Bunker Gay of Hinsdale. It is related of him that at one time he met the Rev. Aaron Crosby at the grist-mill. Each had brought his grain in a wheel-barrow, and while waiting to have it ground, they amused themselves by wheeling each other about. Mr. Crosby was seated upon the wheel-barrow, when Mr. Taylor wheeled him to the mill-pond and tipped him in, then said to him, "Now run home and change your clothes, and I will wheel your grist home for you."

Mr. Taylor was sometimes pretty sharp in his replies, as the following anecdote will show. A certain member of his church removed from Newfane to the neighboring town of Jamaica. While there, under the influence of the Baptists, he changed his views, and applied to Mr. Taylor for a letter of dismission to the Baptist church. Parson Taylor, upon receiving the application, drew him out at some length in defense of his new views. Among other things, and as a perfectly satisfactory reason for his course, the man said. "I do not think there is any true church in the world, but the Baptist church." "Well, well." said Mr. Taylor, "what about that letter, how shall I write it? Shall I say from the devil's church in Newfane to the church of Christ in Jamaica?"

The jolly parson was accustomed on his way to Brattleboro to call at the old tavern of Luke Taylor, in West Dummerston. Joseph Gleason occupied a blacksmith shop near by. The parson called one day at the tavern on his return from Brattleboro, and while sipping his toddy Gleason entered the bar-room. The parson enquired of him what success in his business? Gleason answered he had but little work, the times were hard and he was discouraged. The parson told him to be of good cheer, to exercise his wits as well as his hands, and jocosely said to him "whenever he saw a traveller ride up to the shed whom he supposed was going to Brattleboro, to slip over with his pincers and strip off a shoe from the horse. The traveller would find his horse limped, and would stop on his return and have the lost shoe replaced." A few weeks after, Uncle Joe saw the parson ride under the shed and hitch his horse. He slipped out of his shop on the sly, and pulled off a shoe. On his return, the parson rode up to the shop and told Gleason to put on a shoe, for his horse had lost one in going to Brattleboro. Uncle Joe set the shoe, led the horse to the shed, and walked into the bar-room where he saw the parson sipping his glass of toddy. The parson enquired of him how much to pay. Nothing, Uncle Joe said, for he had been exercising his wits as well as his hands; he had been trying the experiment that was suggested to him a few weeks before, and had reset the same old shoe he had pulled off. Whereupon the parson laughed heartily at the joke, treated Uncle Joe with a glass of toddy, and acknowledged himself the victim of his own joke.

HON. EBENEZER ALLEN

Was born in Medway, Mass., in 1758; removed to Newfane in 1785. He represented the town in the General Assembly for ten consecutive years, from 1794 to 1804. He was for a time a Judge of the County Court, also, a Judge of Probate for the District of Marlboro, and was actively engaged in public business until his death, December 16, 1805. He was an enterprising, active and eminently practical man, and highly esteemed for his patriotism and public spirit.

REV. AARON CROSBY.

Born in Shrewsbury, Mass., November 27, 1744; graduated at Harvard in 1770. married Mary Taylor, sister of Rev. Hezekiah Taylor, August 22, 1774. His family resided in Newfane from 1774 until his death, in 1824, with the exception of the term of his pastorate over the church in Dummerston, Vt., from 1784 to 1804. He died January 13, 1824. He was for many years a missionary among the Indians on the head waters of the Susquehanna. He acted under the patronage of a society in Scotland. The war of the Revolution interrupted his labors and compelled him to return to New England.

WARD EAGER.

BY HIS GRANDDAUGHTER.
Mrs. FANNY A. BAKER, of Putney, Vermont.

The subject of our sketch, son of Bezaleel and Persis Eager, was born in Northboro, Mass., April, 1750. His mother's maiden name was Ward, and she was related to the Wards of Worcester County, Mass., who distinguished themselves in the war of the Revolution by their patriotism and loyalty. He came to Newfane about the time of the commencement of the war, in which he served awhile as a soldier. He was engaged in the battle of Bennington and Saratoga, but the perils he encountered and the hardships he endured he never communicated to his family in after years, for he was excessively modest and taciturn, and never talked of himself. The musket and cartridge box he bore at the battle of Bennington and the taking of Burgoyne at Saratoga, he retained with scrupulous care until his decease. He came to Newfane when it was little more than a wilderness, and when the land he purchased was a dense forest. He married a Mrs. Abigail Pike, a widow lady, whose maiden name was Holland. During the early years in which his forest home was in course of clearing he toiled assiduously, but when, in later years, he found himself in comparatively affluent circumstances, and his sons could relieve him from the care and labor of the farm, he gave himself up almost exclusively to literary pursuits.

He cherished a passionate fondness for mathematical studies; particularly geometry, and for many years was the only practical surveyor in the town and vicinity. He took a lively interest in the study of astronomy, and prepared the astronomical calculations for two or three almanacs. He was excessively modest and unobtrusive in his deportment, and declined public office although he was repeatedly urged to accept of municipal appointments. The only office he was ever known to accept was that of Town Treasurer, which he held for many years. He was reticent, taciturn and generally regarded as unsocial, for he loved seclusion and quiet, and much preferred his books to a free social intercourse with his neighbors, or the society of the many cultivated men for which the town was distinguished at an early day. He was a member of the Congregational Church, although he differed with his brethren upon the subject of baptism. It is said of him that without consulting his family or friends he quietly rode away one Sabbath morning into a neighboring town and received the ordinance of baptism by immersion, and the fact was studiously concealed from his family for a long time. No notice was ever taken of this departure from the peculiar faith of the church of his adoption, and he lived and died in full communion with the Congregational Church, although during the last years of his life he was suspected by his brethren of a strong leaning to Unitarianism. Quietly and serenely, in the retirement he so much loved and coveted, his days passed away until his life had reached almost four score years, when he died, March 24, 1824. He left at his death three sons and three daughters.

His sons, Benjamin, Nahum, and Walter, were prominent men in town, distinguished for their enterprise, probity and practical good sense. Nahum and Walter Eager represented the town two years, respectively, in the General Assembly of this State, and for more than thirty years they filled many of the most responsible offices in town.

GEN. MARTIN FIELD.

Born in Leverett, Mass., February 12, 1773; graduated at Williams College in 1798, and received the honorary degree of A. M. from Dartmouth College in 1805. He studied law with his uncle, Lucius Hubbard, Esq., of Chester, Vt., and upon the decease of Calvin Knowlton, in 1800, and at the special instance and request of Hon. Luke Knowlton, he came to Newfane in January, 1800, and entered upon the practice of the law. He married Esther Smith Kellogg, daughter of Daniel Kellogg, of Amherst, Mass., February 21, 1802, an accomplished lady of fine personal appearance, of great goodness and exemplary piety. He was indebted, in a great measure, for his success in life to her great industry, prudence and discretion. She died June 6, 1867, aged 88 years, surviving her husband thirty-four years. He was full of anecdotes, and could tell a story with inimitable grace. His forensic efforts abounded with flashes of wit and occasional bursts of caustic sarcasm and biting ridicule, which he could use with great skill and effect. These peculiar powers rendered him a popular and distinguished jury advocate. His varied accomplishments and genial temper, with a heart overflowing with an irrepressible spirit of humor and mirthfulness, joined to a strong passion for music, of which he was extravagantly fond, rendered him an ornament to the social circle. A skilful player upon the violin, he never abandoned its use until he became so deaf that he could not distinctly hear its tones. He was eminently successful in his profession, and for nearly thirty years enjoyed a large and lucrative practice, which he was compelled to abandon by reason of his excessive deafness. On relinquishing his practice he commenced the study of Geology and Mineralogy, and by great perseverance and industry he collected what, at that time, was regarded as the rarest and most extensive cabinet of minerals in the State. A few years since it was generously given to Middlebury College by his widow, Mrs. E. S. Field. He was, for ten years, State's Attorney for Windham County,

and repeatedly represented the town of Newfane in the General Assembly and Constitutional Conventions. In 1819 he was elected Major General of the first division of the Vermont Militia.

We have copied from the 26th volume of the American Journal of Arts and Sciences, the following extract from an obituary notice of the subject of this sketch, written by a distinguished lady of Baltimore, Md., who was formerly a resident of this county:

"On account of his incurable deafness several years before his death, he declined the active duties of his profession, and, as a resource to an energetic mind, and as a solace in hours that might have been tedious for want of some interesting object of pursuit, he turned his attention to scientific investigation. When he was educated the natural sciences were scarcely studied in the schools and colleges of this country. He began with the elements, commencing with Mineralogy, and for a time was zealously engaged in collecting a beautiful cabinet; but he found that, in order to become a skilful Mineralogist, there was a kindred science to be grasped, and one without which he could not penetrate beyond the surface. He saw that it was beautiful and curious, and felt a desire to know those mysterious laws of combination by which, from a few elements, the wonderful variety of material things is produced. This desire led him to the study of Chemistry. He purchased books and an apparatus, and for a time he directed his inquiries to the elements of matter and the laws by which they are governed."

"He was not satisfied with studying nature in his cabinet, and with reading the observations of others. He became an outdoor worker in science. Few points of interest were there among the romantic scenery around him that were not familiar to him; and many a precipice, glen and lofty summit of the Green Mountains can bear witness to his persevering research into the nature and arrangement of the rocky strata of which they are formed. His minute observations of philosophical and scientific facts were in various ways manifested in the pages of the scientific journals of this country, and particularly in the American Journal of Science, a work in which he ever delighted, and to which he felt himself indebted for much of that love of science and those acquirements which enabled him to endure with cheerfulness a misfortune by which he was, in a measure, cut off from the social enjoyments of life. It is a great thing for a man who has been active in business to withdraw from those scenes in which his mind was stimulated to constant effort, to see the place he has filled occupied by others, and to feel that the world can move on without him; but this condition is incident to human nature. Fortunate are those who, at such a period, can, like him who is the subject of this sketch, find, in the contemplation of the works and operations of nature, a resource against *ennui*, and a security against bitter and unavailing regrets."

He died at his residence in Fayetteville, October 3d, A. D. 1833, aged 60 years.

ESTHER S. FIELD,

[WIFE OF MARTIN FIELD.]

Whose maiden name was Esther Smith Kellogg, was a grand-daughter of Daniel Kellogg, Sr., of Amherst, Mass., who married Esther Smith, daughter of John Smith, of Hadley, Mass., a lineal descendant of that grim old Puritan, Lieut. Samuel Smith, who came from Ipswich, England, to Boston in 1634, and removed from thence in 1638, with a large company, and settled on the banks of the Connecticut in the vicinity of Hartford, the "new Hesperia of Puritanism." In 1659, with sixty "Withdrawers or Separatists" as they were then called, who were opposed to the liberal and latitudinarian doctrines and practices of Drs. Hooker and Stone in relation to "baptism, church membership, and the rights of the brotherhood," he removed to Hadley, Mass., whose rich and fertile meadows were regarded as a paradise by the early Puritan settlers of the valley of the Connecticut. While residing in Hadley he occupied important positions both in

church and state. This stern old Puritan possessed great energy, an indomitable will, and was by profession and practice a strict Congregationalist, persistently adhering to all the formulas, austerities, and self-denying ordinances of the Calvanistic faith. He impressed upon his descendants to the latest generation his peculiar and marked characteristics.

The subject of this sketch was thoroughly trained in her childhood in the discipline and religious faith of her Puritan ancestors. She early made a profession of her faith, and at the age of fifteen she was admitted a member of the First Congregational Church in Amherst, Mass. Thrift, industry and economy were among the peculiar and prominent characteristics of her ancestors, and for their constant exercise she was proverbial. Possessing a vigorous constitution, she was untiring in her labors and faithful in the discharge of her domestic duties. Distinguished for her prudence and discretion, she carefully avoided all allusions or suggestions which would tend to excite suspicion or grieve an erring or wayward neighbor. Her strong sense and excellent judgment gave her great prominence and influence in the church of which she was a member, and the social circle in which she moved. She was a keen and close observer of the human face, and an accurate judge of human character, and when she fixed her dark penetrating eyes upon the face of a stranger she rarely failed to stamp his character at once, and that, too, with marked precision. She exercised the most perfect self-control, was familiar yet dignified in her bearing, positive in her opinions, grave and serious in her deportment, yet was never regarded as imperious or arrogant.

Her husband enjoyed an extensive professional practice and possessed a large landed estate, a great portion of which he cultivated. Her superior executive ability, united with great energy, enabled her, during his absence, successfully to control and direct the labors upon the homestead, and at the same time to fully discharge the onerous duties incident to the care of a numerous household. Her husband was genial and social, full of humor and mirth, oftentimes filling the house with his "jocund laugh." The wife, however, true to her refined womanly instincts, her sense of propriety, rarely disturbed by his merry and harmless jests, with great discretion pursued "the even tenor of her way." Patiently and with unfaltering devotion to the higher and nobler purposes of life, she always maintained her self-possession, studiously avoided all levity and frivolity, rarely relaxed the gravity of her deportment, and never failed in the end of controlling both husband and household. She always remembered, with a kind and grateful spirit, the favors conferred upon her by her friends and generously repaid them. She was withal so affable, gentle and benevolent that she won the admiration and good will of all with whom she was associated. She was a faithful and affectionate wife and mother, who exemplified, in her pure and spotless life, the influence of the severe discipline and stern religious teachings of her puritan ancestors. It affords her children great pleasure to be able to offer this slight tribute of filial affection and respect to the memory of a kind and loving mother.

ROSWELL MARTIN FIELD.

Son of Gen. Martin Field, was born in Newfane. February 22, 1807, died at St. Louis, Mo., July 12, 1869, aged 62 years. He fitted for college with Rev. Luke Whitcomb, of Townshend, Vt., and entered Middlebury College in the autumn of 1818, at eleven years of age. Graduating in 1822, he studied law with Hon. Daniel Kellogg, of Rockingham, Vt., and was admitted to practice in September, 1825, at eighteen years of age. He practiced law in Windham County from 1825 to 1839, when he removed to St. Louis, where he remained until his death. He represented the town of Newfane in the General Assembly of this State during the years 1835 and 1836. He was elected State's Attorney for Windham County in 1832, 1833, 1834 and 1835. While a member of the Legislature in 1835, he wrote an able report in favor of abrogating the rule of the common law excluding atheists from giving

testimony in courts of justice. The proposition failed of adoption, but in 1851 it was renewed by Hon. Loyal C. Kellogg, of Benson, then a member of the House of Representatives, and passed into a law. Since that period, "no person is deemed incompetent as a witness in any court matter or proceeding on account of his opinions on matters of religious belief." The special pleas which he drew and filed in the libel suit of Torrey vs. Field, reported in the tenth volume of Vermont Reports, were declared by Judge Story to be masterpieces of special pleading. These contributions, with the exception of a multitude of briefs in cases reported in the Vermont and Missouri Reports, are all the memorials of his learning that are left. He was a finished scholar, and read Greek, Latin, French, German and Spanish, besides having an extensive acquaintance with English literature and general science. He could speak with great facility, not only French but German. He was frequently employed in suits by reason of his great familiarity with foreign languages, for the mere purpose of correcting any errors of interpreters in their translations of the testimony of foreigners who could not speak English, and whose evidence was necessarily communicated to a court and jury by an interpreter. It was as a lawyer that he won his greatest distinction. When he went to St. Louis, in 1839, he had to contend with such men as Benton, Gamble and Bates. To none of these was he second in legal attainments, sound judgment and keen foresight. As an advocate he was eloquent, and as a lawyer, learned. His attainments were of that solid character that they served him upon every professional emergency. His first distinction at the bar was obtained in cases involving the intricate old Spanish claims, which he mastered at an early day. His opinions always had great weight in the Superior Courts of the State, and at the time of his decease, he was esteemed as the ablest lawyer at the Missouri bar. By the junior members of the profession he was regarded as an oracle, and freely gave advice to all young lawyers who sought his counsel. He cheerfully and readily aided young men of talent and worth whom he found struggling for success and position against poverty and adversity. He gained a national reputation in the famous Dred Scott case, which he started and carried on until the appeal was entered in the United States Supreme Court, when he turned it over to Montgomery Blair, then residing at Washington. In the dark days of the rebellion, during the years 1861 and 1862, when the friends of the Union in St. Louis and Missouri felt that they were in imminent danger of being driven from their homes and their estates confiscated by rebels and traitors, Gen. Lyon, Gen. Blair, and R. M. Field were among the calm, loyal and patriotic men who influenced public action and saved the city and State. In his social relations he was a genial and entertaining companion, unsurpassed in conversational powers, delighting in witty and sarcastic observations and epigrammatic sentences. He was elegant in his manners, and bland and refined in his deportment. He was a skilful musician, and passionately fond of children, and it was his wont in early life to gather them in groups about him and beguile them by the hour with the music of the flute or violin. He was confiding and generous to a fault, but for a few years before his decease he became reserved and distrustful, had but few intimate associates, and mingled but little in general society, for his confidence had been violated, his generosity abused, and his charities wasted. He was utterly devoid of all ambition for power and place, and he uniformly declined all offers of advancement to the highest judicial honors of the State.

Judge Hamilton, of the Circuit Court of St. Louis, in his address to the bar, suggests of him that " he was always under the controlling influence of principle, faithful toward his clients, honorable and upright with his professional brethren, and in all his relations, social, political and professional, frank and sincere to a fault. His heart was warm with the sweetest charities of humanity, and his friendships were as enduring as life itself." His proficiency in other walks of learning than the law would have rendered him remarkable if he had been unacquainted with jurisprudence. It was the accuracy, no less than the extent of his knowledge, which distinguished him above those around him. He seemed to have mastered the principles, the foundation of every subject with which he claimed any familiarity, and it was part of his nature to claim nothing to which his title was not perfect. He never used words without appropriate ideas annexed to them. Nothing of the kind of knowledge which remembers the rule, but leaves forgotten or never knew the reason of the rule. His scholarship was critical and exact. He made the perusal of the Greek and Latin classics his most delightful pastime. In fact, he resorted to this and scientific research, particularly in the department of pure mathematics, for his chief mental recreation. It is greatly to be regretted that he neglected to combine, with his cessations from professional labor, some employment which would have revived and strengthened his physical frame. He was averse to active exercise, and for some years before his death he lived a life of studious seclusion, which would have been philosophical had he not violated, in the little care he took of his health, one of the most important lessons which philosophy teaches. At a comparatively early age he died of physical exhaustion, a deterioration of the bodily organs, and an incapacity, on their part, to discharge the vital functions, a wearing out of the machine before the end of the term for which its duration was designed. The defects of his character were due to a complete absence of the incentive to exertion which rivalry causes. It is obvious to all who read this slight censure, how unassailable is the man of whom it can be said that his principal defects arise from a want of one of the weaknesses of humanity. He was eminently qualified to serve, as well as to adorn society, and in all likelihood he would have found, in a greater variety of occupation, some relief from the monotonous strain under which his energies prematurely gave way. He possessed in full measure the capacity for rendering this service, but unfortunately he shrank from offering himself for its performance. It is not a paradox to say that if he had been more covetous of gain and of fame, more susceptible to the spur of emulation, and less firmly persuaded of the things ordinarily proposed as the reward of ambition, his life would have been happier and more useful to mankind. If he had possessed more ambition, his reputation would have been national, and he would have ranked among the most distinguished lawyers of the country. At a session of the Supreme Court of the State of Missouri, soon after the decease of Mr. Field, Samuel Knox, Esq., a member of the Bar, suggested to the Court that it had lost an able and faithful coun-

selor and its highest ornament in the death of Mr. Field. He
was so modest in all his greatness, said Mr. Knox, as never to
excite envy, so varied in his gifts, so extended his attainments,
so wide his range of thought, that no person in his society
could experience anything but pleasure, in his conversation
anything but profit and delight. Uniting great industry and
acquirements with the most brilliant wit and genius, well and
accurately informed on all subjects, both in science and the
arts; endowed with a memory that retained whatever it
received, with quick and clear perceptions, the choicest, most
felicitous and forcible language in which to clothe his thoughts,
no one could doubt his meaning or withhold the tribute of
wonder at his power. His statements were always terse and
clear, his arguments cogent and logical, his conclusions difficult to evade. In a long and eventful professional life, no
charge of duplicity or unfairness, no cunning trick, no suspicion of dishonor ever tarnished his fair fame, or raised the
slightest doubt of the highest professional honor and personal
integrity. One thus distinguished is no ordinary loss—a loss
to the Court, to the profession, to the community in which he
lived. Mr. Knox then offered the report of a committee,
appointed by the St. Louis Bar, at a meeting called to pay a
tribute of respect to the memory of Mr. Field, and moved
that the report be entered upon the records of the Court, " an
enduring memorial of the love and regard of the members of
the St. Louis Bar for their departed brother." Judge Wagner,
in behalf of the Court, responded as follows : " The members
of this Court have heard with the deepest regret of the death
of R. M. Field, and the warm and deserved tribute which has
just been paid to his memory receives an assenting response
from the hearts of all those who knew him. In the decease of
our lamented friend and brother, the Bar of Missouri has lost
one of its brightest ornaments. To a naturally keen, vigorous
and analytical mind, he added a thorough mastery of legal
principles combined with high scholarly attainments. Perhaps no man at the Bar of this State ever brought to the
consideration of any question a greater amount of exact legal
learning or clothed it with a more impressive and attractive
logic. When he gave the great energies and powers of his
mind to a cause, he exhausted all the learning to be had on

the subject. He studied law as a science and delighted to examine its harmonious structure and explore its philosophic principles. So deeply was he imbued with its true spirit, and so great was his reverence for its excellence, that he maintained them with the most jealous regard and would sooner have failed in success than have won a cause by trenching upon a sound legal rule. He made no parade of learning, and in his social intercourse he had a childlike simplicity. With his professional brethren he was full of courtesy and kindness and his whole conduct was marked by entire integrity and perfect truth. He adorned every circle in which he moved, and so beautiful was his life in all its relations that he won and enjoyed the esteem and regard of all who knew him. It is fit and proper that the death of such a man should be marked by all the honors which we can pay to his memory. It is just that we should pay this last tribute as an evidence of our appreciation of his great abilities and exalted virtues. It is therfore ordered that the report of the proceedings of the Bar, which have been presented, be entered of record on the minutes of this Court, and out of respect for his memory it will be further ordered that this Court do now adjourn."

WILLIAM H. WILLIAMS.

Son of Larkin and Anna Williams, and grandson of Col. Abraham Williams, was born in Chester, Mass., February 24, 1776. His father died in 1778, and soon after he was bound out to a farmer residing in Paxton, Mass., during his minority. He was treated with great severity by his master and deprived of the benefit of a common school education, and subjected to excessive labor until he was fourteen years of age, after which he returned to Chester to learn the cloth dressing business, at that time the most lucrative and prominent branch of industry in New England. While learning his trade he enjoyed the privilege of attending school six weeks in the year, and learned what he could of reading, spelling and grammar from "The Only Sure Guide," the only text book he ever possessed, and which is now in the hands of his widow. After learning his trade he worked two years in Paxton, after which he came to Newfane, in October, 1797, and took charge of the cloth dressing and oil making works of Thomas and Darius Wheeler. In 1801, he bought the mills of the Wheelers and worked them until his decease. He engaged in the mercantile business in 1814, and continued in trade for more than forty years. During the war of 1812 he was extensively engaged in the manufacture of potash and woolen cloth. He erected a large flouring mill, also a carding machine and saw mill. In 1798 he commenced a diary, which was continued by himself and family until his death. In it is jotted down every days' doings and every important event which occurred during his life.

He was a resident of Newfane about seventy years, gave a name to the village where he resided and died; contributed largely towards the erection of the village church in 1834, and was at all times liberal and generous in his donations for the support of the gospel.

He was a member of the Methodist church, represented the town in the General Assembly, filled many munici-

pal offices and faithfully discharged the duties incident to the same. He was enterprising, industrious and eminently practical in all his views and efforts. He was munificent in his contributions for the furtherance of all public enterprises which stimulated the growth and prosperity of the town, and although he suffered severely by fire and flood at different times during his life, yet by his untiring industry and perseverance he repaired all his losses and accumulated a handsome fortune, which he left to his family. He married Abigail Robinson, October 17, 1802. She was born March 25, 1781, died July 6, 1821. He married Rosanna Miller for his second wife, February 22, 1826. She was born May 19, 1794. He had nine children by his first wife and none by his second wife. Here follow the names, births and deaths of his children, only two of whom survived him:

George Williams, born September 14, 1803, died May 26, 1841.

Anna Williams, born January 24, 1805, died January 26, 1805.

Hastings Williams, born March 5, 1806, died December 26, 1808.

Mary Williams, born May 26, 1808, died May 27, 1834. She married Roswell Robertson, January 26, 1831.

Sarah R. Williams, born March 30, 1810. Married Roswell Robertson, December 10, 1835, and died October 9, 1839.

Louisa Williams, born October 26, 1811, married John A. Merrifield, January 17, 1843.

William L. Williams, born December 9, 1813, died at Dubuque, Iowa, January 11, 1864.

Abigail E. Williams, born March 3, 1816, married Charles Converse, of Ohio, September 25, 1808.

John W. Williams, born January 9, 1818, married Gertrude Brown April 22, 1841, and died May 25, 1851.

DANIEL FISHER

Was born in Newfane in February, 1776, died August 17, 1862, aged eighty-six. He married, for his first wife, Millicent Durren, of Newfane, in 1797. She died in 1813. He married, for his second wife, Miss Priscilla Ritter, of Walpole, N. H., in September, 1815. She died June 9, 1862 His children, by his first wife, were Clark Fisher; Lydia, who married Nathaniel Sampson, of Brattleboro; Orrison Fisher; Caroline, who married Richmond Dunklee, of Newfane; Millicent, who married Richard P. Pratt, of Newfane; Hannah, who married Isaac Burnett, of Dummerston, and Simon Fisher, the only surviving son. Daniel Fisher, Sr., the father of the subject of this sketch, was born in Milford, Mass., in 1752, and removed to Newfane in 1774. He purchased a large amount of real estate, situate in the eastern portion of the town, supposed to exceed one thousand acres in quantity, and embracing within its limits the fertile and productive meadows on West River. At an early day he was known and called by the name of Corn Fisher, for the reason that he raised upon his meadows great crops of Indian corn, which he sold to the early settlers on the hills and mountains west of Newfane. He was exceedingly thrifty and prudent, and at his decease he left a large estate. He died in 1820, aged sixty-eight. Daniel Fisher, the subject of this sketch, inherited a large property from his father, which he judiciously distributed among his children and grand-children before his decease. He was generous and even munificent in his donations and subscriptions for various public enterprises. He was distinguished for his integrity and benevolence, cordial and kindly in his greetings and generous in his hospitalities; liberal and kind to the poor and suffering, never closing his door or his hand to their applications for relief. He was of a tall, commanding figure, and manly and dignified in his deportment. He early united with the First Congregational Church in Newfane, and died at an advanced age, universally respected and beloved for

his integrity and benevolence. The father and son were both distinguished for their practical good sense, and were often elected to the most important municipal offices in the town, and faithfully discharged their official duties.

GEN. PARDON T. KIMBALL.

Born in Newfane, July 2, 1797, died April 5, 1873. He was nearly seventy-six years of age at the time of his decease. His death resulted from injuries received by a fall from his carriage, in the month of November, 1872. He was greatly distinguished for his energy and enterprise. He represented Windham County in the State Senate for two years, and for the last fifty years of his life he had filled the most important municipal offices in his native town. As a citizen he faithfully discharged all his duties, and greatly distinguished himself by the zeal and energy with which he entered into all the enterprises which were calculated to promote the growth and prosperity of his native town. He was munificent in his contributions for public improvements, and generous and liberal in his gifts for the relief of the suffering poor. It was oftentimes said of him, that he had a great heart and it was in the right place. His friendships were enduring, and his heart was full of the kindest charities for the poor and of sympathy for the suffering and distressed.

DEACON MOSES KENNEY

Was born in Northboro, Mass., September 11, 1747, died in Newfane, June 23, 1808, aged sixty-one years. He was supposed to have descended from a family by the name of Keayne, as there were many of that name in the vicinity of Boston and Lynn from 1630 to 1670, and none by the name of Kenney until after that period. (See Shurtliff's Records, second volume). He married Azubah Parmenter, about the year 1770. She was born in Sudbury, Mass., January 17, 1751, and died in Newfane, January 3, 1837, aged eighty-six years. They removed to Newfane during the year 1774. They had twelve children, four of whom died in infancy and early childhood. The others all lived to an age past middle life. Sally, who married Zadock Chapin, was born in Massachusetts, September 11, 1771, removed to Pennsylvania with her husband, and died in 1831. John, born in Massachusetts, April 18, 1773, died in Newfane, September 6, 1849. Lucy, wife of Capt. Chandler Carter, born in Newfane, August 27, 1777, died in Newfane in 1825. Captain Carter was a prominent citizen, a skillful mechanic, a fine military officer, highly respected for his honesty and industry. He died in Michigan about 1864. Holloway Kenney, born February 18, 1781, removed to Lower Canada, and the day and place of his death is unknown. Charlotte, born May 26, 1783, died in Lower Canada, February 22, 1843. She married Luke Knowlton, Jr., of Newfane, March 18, 1799. They had fifteen children, four of whom died in infancy. They removed with their children to Lower Canada in 1821, where he died in 1855, aged eighty years. Silas Kenney was born April 12, 1785, died May 5, 1863. In 1813 and 1814 he commanded a company of cavalry composed of citizens of Newfane and Wardsboro. While he held a subordinate position in the company, and it was under the command of Captain Barnard, of Wardsboro, they assembled at the dwelling-house of Silas Kenney, and ascending a stone wall which he had just completed, they marched and counter-marched upon its top, which

Mrs. Azubah Kenney.
WIFE OF
DEA. MOSES KENNEY.

was at least six feet across. The wall was built upon the roadside and twenty rods or more in length. After his discharge from the command of the cavalry company he organized and commanded a company of riflemen, who were the pride and boast of the town, the rank and file numbering not less than one hundred tall and stalwart men, beautifully uniformed with green frocks, and caps ornamented with black plumes. For a few years it was regarded as the best drilled and most attractive military company in the State.

Olive, wife of Jonathan Hall, was born April 25, 1787. She is now living, and the oldest person in Newfane who was a native of the town. Munnis Kenney, born December 10, 1788, died April 5, 1863. He fitted for college at the old academy on Newfane Hill, graduated at Middlebury College, studied law and practised his profession in Townshend, Vt., for a number of years, represented the town of Townshend in the State Legislature many times. In 1830 he removed to Webster, Washtenaw County, Michigan. While living in Michigan he was a prominent and influential citizen of the town and county where he resided. Sewell Kenney, born April 1, 1791, died in Chicago, Illinois, October 14, 1844.

Deacon Kenney possessed a vigorous and robust constitution, and in all his farm labors was exceedingly active and industrious. He owned at his decease more than a thousand acres of land, and at the time of its purchase it was a dense forest. He cleared off the timber and forest trees, found the surface covered with boulders and broken masses of granite, with which, by excessive labor, he constructed long lines of heavy stone wall on the division lines of his several lots. His labors were so arduous and excessive that he seriously impaired his constitution, and sickened and died at the comparatively early age of sixty-one years. He left a large estate to his children, and of the thousand acres or more of wild forest land which he originally purchased, he had cleared and fenced, with heavy stone wall, more than six hundred and fifty acres, about equally divided between tillage, grass and pasture lands. He built the first grist mill in town, at the outlet of Kenney Pond, so-called, within a hundred rods of his homestead; represented the town in the General Assembly, filled many municipal offices in the town, was a deacon in the church at the time of his decease, and in all his relations in life was distinguished for his industry, probity and public spirit.

We have copied the following sketches from a history in manuscript of the Newton family, by Rev. Ephraim Holland Newton, late of Cambridge, N. Y.

COL. EPHRAIM HOLLAND.

Son of Ephraim Holland, Senior, was born in Boylston, Mass., in the year 1755.

He married Eunice Newton, of Shrewsbury, February 17th, 1783. She was born March 13th, 1754. He was a soldier of the Revolutionary war. He had two sisters whose husbands, Luke Knowlton and Joshua Morse, were loyalists, and to escape the indignation of the Whigs, fled to Vermont, then called an " Outlaw," for it was not a State, neither did it belong to a State, and took refuge in the present township of Newfane, afterwards the county seat of Windham County and there they finally settled.

After the close of the war Ephraim Holland visited his sisters at Newfane, was induced to make a purchase of a lot of wild land of 100 acres and there settled as a farmer, a tavern keeper and a merchant; was respected, being elevated at various times to offices of trust as a town officer; was an ambitious military man and promoted from post to post until he was placed at the head of the regiment, as their Colonel, at a period when the station was held as a mark of honorable distinction. Being absent from home on a journey he reached South Hero, one of the Islands of the County of Grand Isle, in Lake Champlain, and put up at a public house for the night. After leaving the next morning, to pursue his journey, he went to his horse and fell dead by its side in the dooryard, in the presence of witnesses. February 28th, 1822. He was buried upon the Island, and grave stones were prepared and sent to be placed at the head of his grave. He went to Newfane in 1784, or 1785, made his purchase and commenced his settlement in the woods. He put up a small shed-like framed building with one roof, for a house, about one mile south easterly from the centre of the town, on the northerly side of the road leading from the site of the public buildings in Newfane to Brattleboro. In this shed-like house I was born as told me by my parents and received my name from the owner. To this house additions were afterwards made which made it a dwelling of respectable appearance and afforded good accommodations as a public house. About the year 1840 it was taken down and removed to the village of Fayetteville where it now stands.

Eunice Newton, the widow of Col. Ephraim Holland, was rather tall, straight and slim, of ladylike demeanor, a thorough housekeeper, a good cook, kind-hearted, a woman of great industry and of dignified deportment. She lived many years after the death of her husband, and received an annual pension from the government as the widow of a deceased soldier of the revolution; and after she had reached the ninety-fourth year of her age, accidentally set her clothes on fire with a bunch of matches, and was so badly burned that after a few days of great suffering she died at the house of Sir Isaac Newton, in Newfane, Vt., October 15th, 1848, and was buried in the cemetery in the northwesterly corner of Newfane. She was the last and oldest survivor in the lineal descent from her grandfather. She has left no child or descendant to represent her. This branch of her father's family is now extinct. The next oldest in descent from her father is Ephraim Holland Newton, the oldest son of Marshall and Lydia Newton.

MARSHALL NEWTON, Senior.

BY REV. EPHRAIM H. NEWTON.

Marshall Newton, the third child of Marshall Newton and Eunice Taylor Howe, his wife, was born in Shrewsbury, Mass., January 13th, 1757, and was bred a blacksmith. When at the age of eighteen years, in 1775, he entered into the service of the American army of the Revolution in what he used to say was "the first eight month's service," the same year in which Gen. Washington was elected by Congress as Commander-in-Chief of the American forces, and repaired to Cambridge, Mass., and took his station at the head of the army. As he took the command he arranged the army into three divisions, the left wing was stationed at Prospect Hill, under Gen. Lee, the right wing under Gen. Ward was stationed at Roxbury, while the central point of the division Washington took to himself at Cambridge. At this time Marshall Newton, Junior, belonged to the right wing of the army under Gen. Ward, occupying Roxbury and Dorchester. Here I would remark that Gen. Ward was from Shrewsbury and Marshall Newton, Junior, was born and brought up in the same neighborhood, in sight of each others' residence. He uniformly expressed a strong attachment to Gen. Ward and spoke of him in high terms as a military officer and a good citizen.

After the expiration of the time of his enlistment, Marshall Newton enlisted again; so also from time to time as the periods of his engagements terminated. He became attached to the service, and during the long and bloody struggle of eight years, he spent seven years of that time in the service of his country. A portion of that time he belonged to the corps of artificers, and was employed as a blacksmith, traveling with the army, with his traveling forge as a portion of the baggage of war equipage.

Although I used to sit upon the dye-tub in the chimney corner, when a child, and after his hard day's work hear my father talk with the old soldiers, who always found welcome quarters at his house, and narrate with thrilling interest the war scenes of his military career, yet at this distant period of more than half a century I am unable to give in detail the marches, stations, battles, victories, conquests and defeats in which he participated in a seven year's service.

I have heard him speak of Dorchester Heights, the night scene of fortification which so alarmed Gen. Howe that he evacuated Boston and gave the American army the possession of that city. I have also heard him speak of being in the battle of Long Island, of being at the evacuation of New York city, of being in the battle of White Plains. I have also heard him speak of being in the "Jarseys," as he used to call it, with Gen. Washington, also, of being at Saratoga at the capitulation of Gen. Burgoyne, in 1777. At this time he belonged to Col. Job Cushing's regiment, who also was from Shrewsbury. This regiment was on the left wing of the division of the army, and was not brought into close line of battle before the enemy gave up. He was in the ranks when the American army was drawn up in double columns to witness the surrender of Gen. Burgoyne. He saw his army when they stacked arms, and stood in the ranks when they passed through the American columns, unarmed, mortified and vanquished, while the bosoms of the American soldiers swelled with the joy of a rich triumphant conquest; a conquest, too, which inspired the American Colonies with the assurance of success in a final victory. I have heard him say he was not wounded in the army. In one instance a soldier at his side was shot down, but not killed; he took him upon his shoulder and carried him from the field. In one instance upon a retreat, near, or in the suburbs of New York city, the enemy were so close upon him that he lost his pack, blanket and clothes, excepting what he had on. In another instance, about the same time, he was taken with cramp in his feet and limbs, in this condition he crawled into some bushes and lay undiscovered by the enemy as they passed, and the next day was successful in joining the ranks where he belonged. At times he was placed on short allowance, on horse beef, from old horses unfit for service; at times diseased with the distempers of the camp; at times subject to great fatigue, severe hardships and much suffering, from cold, hunger and want of suitable clothing. His bed was upon the ground sheltered by his tent, and sometimes only by the canopy of heaven; yet I never heard him complain or cast the least reflection upon his officers or his country, for the remembrance of hardships was lost in the heart cheering gratification of a completed ascendancy over British oppression, and the glorious acheivement of American liberty.

After the declaration of peace he returned to Shrewsbury and engaged in some money speculations; thence he went to Shoreham, Vt., in 1784 or 1785, and there, for the first time, met with Timothy Fuller Chipman. They were both employed in carrying the chain in surveying the township into lots, which occupied their attention for several weeks in the woods. In 1785 he visited Newfane for the purpose of seeing his sister and making her a visit. He was sufficiently pleased with the location to be induced to make a purchase in view of settlement; accordingly he bought six acres of land in its wild and forest state, on which he erected a shop about fifty rods from his sister's, to whom he was always fondly attached. This was a frame building erected in 1785 or 1786, where he commenced his business as a blacksmith, which business he pursued until his death, December 15th, 1833. He put up his house in 1786, finished the outside and painted it, partly finished the inside, but did not complete the inside work for several years after. In this house all his children were born, excepting the first-born; here he lived and died. He was a man rather above the middle size, rather corpulent, weighing nearly two hundred pounds, generally in good health with the exception of rheumatism, probably the result of hardships and privations in the army. For close attention to his business, laborious and persevering toil, he was scarcely excelled. Possessing means to stock his shop and carry on his business with advantage to himself and others, also being desirous of accommodating his customers, he confined himself to his shop early and late. Kept work on hand in advance, both for the farmer and mechanic, which met a ready sale.

The country was new, the inhabitants principally new settlers after the war, and many of them from the army, having lost their all in the depreciation and final loss of

Continental money, yet struggling hard to clear up their new lands and make a living. He was indulgent, refused nothing by the way of barter for his work, trusted all who wished, and it was a very rare case where it was not sought, and waited patiently for his pay.

In 1786, he, Marshall Newton, married Lydia Newton, the eldest daughter of Solomon Newton, a farmer of Shrewsbury, Mass., and the same year she accompanied him to Newfane, a distance of about seventy miles and called in those days a three days' journey. His house not being prepared to occupy conveniently, he moved into the house with his brother-in-law, Ephraim Holland, and remained with them until after the birth of their first child, named Ephraim Holland.

In those early times he used to take in fur, and purchased the pelts of game in that and the neighboring townships; this with other produce, in the winter he would carry to Boston, and exchange for iron, steel, and such blacksmithing tools as he could purchase to a better advantage than make, together with groceries and necessaries for the family. This was his annual custom for years. Among my earliest recollections are the skins of wild game and packages and bales of fur in a course of preparation for the market. As his children advanced to a suitable age, in his annual visits to the metropolis of New England, he was mindful of means for their improvement and used to bring them school books and little picture books for their amusement and instruction. Among these small toy books was the "New England Primer," "Cock Robin," "Capt. Gulliver," "Robinson Crusoe," "Children of the Wood" and "Mother Goose's Melodies," which constituted about all the variety of books for children of that age. I also recollect the high gratification experienced on his return, and the great impatience and self-denial endured in being under the necessity of going into another room out of sight, and then to the trundle bed until morning, to give him an opportunity of bringing his wares into the kitchen and smoking them over the fire as precautionary measures against the small-pox. Boston was one hundred and ten miles from Newfane, and the journey down and back was performed in about twelve days. However trifling are these incidents in themselves considered, they serve to illustrate the contrast between that and the present age.

My father took a deep interest in the education of children. He said the want of it himself led him to see the need of it in others. Yet he was a tolerable reader, wrote a fair hand and was sufficiently versed in arithmetic to render him accurate in business and quite equal to men of his age; still, he felt the loss of a better education and was ready to give his children every desirable advantage for their improvement. His oldest son he boarded out, at the age of four years, and sent him to school. The first school in the school district to which he belonged was opened in the southeast room of his house. After a school-house was built and teachers employed, he gave them a welcome home for board at their pleasure or convenience. Although a heavy taxpayer, he warmly advocated free schools at the expense of taxpayers to give the children of the poor advantages and all the perquisites and benefits of schooling as well as the rich.

He was a ready and liberal contributor to the erection of the public buildings and other improvements of the place. Was active in the erection of the academy and bore a heavy share of the expense, became a liberal patron and gave his influence in sustaining its interests.

In business matters he had a preference to his own rather than that of others, and uniformly refused offices of official trust as they were tendered to him, so far as they could be consistently avoided unless it was to share the burden with his fellow citizens. His business was at home and not abroad, seldom leaving it, even to make a social visit or to while away an hour, so devoted was he to his employment as a mechanic, and so ready for a bargain with those who sought it, that he would buy and sell farms and other property without leaving his anvil or stopping his work to go and look at his purchases and sales. To some this may look like presumption and even hazardous, yet his bargains did not impoverish him. He was fond of good living and provided liberally for the wants of his family, was generous hearted in extending the hospitalities of his house to strangers as well as friends, to the poor as well as the affluent. He was kind to his family in anticipating their wants and in making ample provision for their comfort and happiness. His descendants for several generations will probably share in the avails of his industry and economy as reserved and bestowed for their benefit. The example of his industrious habits will prove a fortune to the possessor. May his mantle rest upon his descendants.

In politics he was a whig of the school of Washington, ardent to sustain the genuine principles of Washington's Administration, under whom he fought, and to whom he was knit as a child to a father. In religion he called himself a Presbyterian, but as no organization of that body existed to his accommodation, he cordially gave his support and attendance to the Congregational religious denomination.

In the first acts of Congress granting pensions to soldiers of the revolution who were in needy circumstances, Marshall Newton being a man of property was not included. He felt the injustice of this act. He said he was cut off because he had not spent his living in idleness and dissipation. He had spent seven years in the army and after leaving it, by hard work had made a fortune and by heavy taxes had contributed largely to the support of government and the rise of the country, and for all this was denied an equal standing with the poor and dissipated. He said it was not the need or the want of the money that he cared for, but the principle he felt to be wrong. After a course of years Congress passed additional acts, upon which he made application for a pension, which was granted but did not reach him but a few hours before his death.

His last illness was about two weeks, occasioned by the following circumstances: He went to his wood-house for a handful of wood, a small stick fell against his shin and grazed off a small piece of skin, which he considered trifling and gave him but little uneasiness, but taking cold it settled, became inflamed, the limb much swollen, and in spite of all effort to the contrary, mortification followed, which caused his death on Sabbath evening, December 15th, 1833, in the 77th year of his age, which was severely felt as a sore bereavement by his family and friends. His funeral was at his mansion, by the services of the Rev. Jonathan McGee, pastor of the Congregational church, in Brattleboro East Village, and by a large collection of friends and citizens, he was buried in the common burying ground. easterly from the public buildings in the centre of the town. and a grave stone with inscription thereon. at the head of his grave, marks the place where his body rests.

To return, as before stated Marshall Newton, born January 13th, 1757, in 1786 married Lydia Newton, born at Shrewsbury, Mass.. August 5th, 1765. daughter of Solomon Newton, a farmer, to whom at Newfane, Vt.. were born:

Ephraim Holland Newton, June 13th, 1787.
Eunice Taylor Newton, December 24th, 1788.
Sir Isaac Newton. April 12th, 1791.
Daniel Newton, February 15th, 1793, died April 6th. 1839.
Twins, sons, March 14th, 1796, died same day.
Hannah Newton, September 18th. 1799.
Louisa Newton, August 14th, 1803.
Marshall Newton, April 1st, 1805, died June 29, 1870.

REV. EPHRAIM HOLLAND NEWTON, D. D.

From the Presbyterian Historical Almanac for 1855.

He was born in Newfane. Vermont, June 13. 1787. His ancestors were from England. and settled in the eastern part of Massachusetts, about the year 1630. His father. Marshall Newton. served for seven years in the Revolutionary army, and his grandfather, Marshall Newton. of Shrewsbury. Mass., was a Lieutenant in Colonel Williams' Regiment in the " Old French War." Young Newton spent the early part of his life in labor with his father in the blacksmith shop. He had a special fondness for books, and determined to acquire something more than a common education. While at work with his father making axes he mastered English grammar, and laying his book upon the forge near the bellows-pole committed it to memory page after page until the whole was familiar.

When in his nineteenth year he taught a district school in Marlboro', Vt., with very marked success. He fitted for college with Alvan Tobey, of Wilmington, and at the Windham County Grammar School, in Newfane, and entered the Freshman class at Middlebury College, October 6, 1806, under Rev. Jeremiah Atwater, President, and graduated, August 16, 1810, under Rev. Henry Davis, President. In the autumn of 1809, during a powerful revival of religion in the vicinity of Middlebury, which extended to the college, he was hopefully converted, and in April, 1810, he, with about one hundred others, made a public profession of religion, and united with the Congregational church in Middlebury under the pastoral care of Rev. Dr. Merrll.

He entered the Theological Seminary, in Andover, Mass., in November, 1810, and completed his theological course there in September, 1813. He was licensed to preach the gospel by the Haverhill Massachusetts Association of Congregational Ministers, April 14, 1813. His first field of labor was in Marlboro', Vt. He commenced his labors here in October, 1813, and was ordained and installed March 16, 1814.

Dr. Newton's ministry in Marlboro' continued until January 1, 1833, and it was a successful ministry—one hundred and thirty-three persons were received to the church. A new church edifice was erected and the cause of education and morality received a valuable impulse through the whole community. Dr. Newton was installed pastor of the Presbyterian church in Glens Falls, N. Y., February 28, 1833, and during his pastorate of about three and a half years in this place one hundred and seventy-two members were added to the church.

In November, 1836, he commenced his labors with the Presbyterian church, in Cambridge, of New York, where he served as pastor until August, 1843. During his pastorate here eighty-three were added to the church, besides others who came into the church soon after his resignation, the fruits of special religious interest that prevailed during the last months of his ministry here. In July, 1843, he was elected Principal of Cambridge Washington Academy, which post he occupied with great efficiency and success until August, 1848.

During this time he supplied the Reformed Dutch church. in Easton, N. Y., for one year; also, the Reformed Dutch church, in Buskirk's Bridge for two years.

Having a fondness for the natural sciences. Dr. Newton gave his attention early in life to mineralogy and geology, and availing himself of the opportunities he enjoyed to collect specimens in these departments, he had gathered one of the largest and most valuable private cabinets in the land. This cabinet of about ten thousand specimens attracted the attention of connoisseurs and elicited proposals for purchase from several quarters. All these he refused, and in August, 1857, presented it to the Theological Seminary in Andover, Mass., and there gave the summer months of several successive seasons in arranging these specimens and preparing a catalogue. He afterwards gave his library of about one thousand volumes to Middlebury College.

In 1860 he returned for the first time, after an absence of twenty-seven years, to Marlboro', Vt., and finding his former parish destitute of the preached word, he consented to occupy the pulpit for a time, preaching as he had strength, while at the same time he was engaged in gathering materials for a history of that township. He found here a most discouraging state of things, but he addressed himself with zeal to the work of restoring that wasted heritage of the Lord. He spent the most of his time here until the fall of 1862, when he was elected to represent that people in the Legislature of Vermont, and while in the discharge of his duties as a member of that Legislature he was attacked with a severe fit of sickness from which he never fully recovered. In the fall and winter of 1863 and the spring of 1864 he was the acting pastor at Wilmington, Vt., and there sustained his last labors in the pulpit. At the time of his death he had made arrangements to supply that people for the winter.

In August and September Dr. Newton made his first visit to the West. He went to visit two sons and their families in Cincinnati, Ohio, to visit other kindred and to secure a suit of fossils and shells from the Ohio river, and his last contribution to the cabinet in Andover.

He returned, October 15th, to the house of his son-in-law, John M. Stevenson, Esq., in Cambridge, N. Y., where he had made his home for the last eight years, and while engaged in labors at the academy for a few days took a severe cold, failed rapidly, and died October 26, 1864. Dr. Newton was tall in person, dignified in appearance, and genial in his manner. The prevailing expression of his countenance was that of benevolence, and he never failed to command the respect and to win the affection of those with whom he was associated.

As a preacher he was plain, earnest and Scriptural, seeking to present the great truths of the Bible in their simplicity rather than exhibit ornament in style or oratory. His ambition was to acquire knowledge, and make himself a learned man, that he might be more useful among his people and become qualified to instruct the pupils committed to his care.

He was especially active in all that concerned the welfare of his people, in things both religious and secular, and a zealous and successful worker in the town and country benevolent associations of the day. For his attainments in Theological and general knowledge his Alma Mater conferred on him the honorary degree of D. D. From early life he manifested a great interest in the cause of education, and his first effort after being settled as a pastor in Marlboro' and Glens Falls was to establish schools, which were successful and proved a lasting benefit.

At Cambridge he found a good academy already established, and immediately gave it the benefit of his energies and counsels. After resigning his pastorate he was its principal for five years. Subsequently he became its president, and his interest in this institution continued during his life, and his last public act was in performing an official duty in that academy.

Dr. Newton took a great interest in agricultural matters, and by his advice and example among the people of his first charge, introduced many beneficial changes in their mode of farming, especially in sheep husbandry. After giving up the academy at Cambridge he retired to a small farm where he remained for several years. During this period he devoted much time to the cultivation of varieties of seeds and vegetables, with a view of learning what were the best, and by this means gave much valuable information to the neighboring farmers. He contributed many articles for publication in the agricultural journals, and at the time of his death was president of the Washington County Agricultural Society.

Rev. I. O. Fillmore, who followed Dr. Newton in the pastoral office in Cambridge, writes as follows: "My acquaintance with Dr. Newton began with my ministry in Cambridge. He was one of my parishioners there. He had passed through some troubles that had grown out of the old and new school controversy, which at that time was agitating some of the churches in that part of the country. The parties in the church and congregation were about equally divided, a small majority being with those who espoused the old school side of the controversy. With this side Dr. Newton had identified himself. Of course, he encountered the opposition of the other party. This item of history is given, not to revive feeling, now happily passed away, but to show that what Dr. Newton encountered arose from the state of things in the church and not from anything chargeable upon him personally as a man or a minister. Any other minister, at that particular juncture of affairs, would have experienced equal or greater troubles.

"If this state of things, and the delicate position he occupied, put some restraints upon our intercourse, it was not long before all reserve and restraints were thrown off, and I think I may say our friendship was mutual and cordial. I learned to love him and to seek his counsels and aid, and I may as well state here that the bitter feelings which controversy and party spirit had engendered in the minds of some, all passed away, and the whole church and congregation loved and honored him as an honest, upright man, a devoted, faithful minister of Christ, and as a Father in Israel.

"In summing up his characteristics and virtues I am at a loss where to begin or where to end. He must have been well on to three score years when I first saw him, perhaps in the fifty-sixth or seventh year of his age. He was spare in person, rather tall. His countenance was grave, sometimes wearing a shade of sadness. My first impression of him was that he was a severe and gloomy man. But I found him to be the reverse. He was usually cheerful and pleasant in conversation and intercourse. There was in him a vein of humor and wit, which would now and then reveal itself, but not so as to compromise his dignity or seriousness.

" He was a man of great industry, never allowing himself to be idle. When he retired from the more active duties of a regular ministerial charge he was engaged at first as principal of Cambridge Academy, which was never more flourishing than under his supervision; afterward he devoted himself to agriculture, in which he excelled.

" In matters of business he was proverbially accurate and honest, and was one of the best accountants I ever knew. He used to say that the manner and accuracy of keeping accounts determined a man's success in business. Respecting his attainments in scholarship, I am not able to speak, except that in the natural sciences, he is said to have excelled. There was a time when in mineralogy and geology he was equal to any in the land. Had he given his undivided attention to these sciences, he would have been the peer of any of our eminent geologists.

" During my ministry in Cambridge he gave a course of sermons on the first chapter of Genesis, in which he displayed high attainments in geology and great ability in reconciling that science with revelation.

" As a preacher Dr. Newton was sound and scriptural rather than imaginative, ornamental, and oratorical. His sermons were models of system and Scripture illustration. He was a great friend to all the benevolent operations of the church, and was especially interested in the cause of Foreign Missions. Acquainted with the early efforts of the American Board and with many of the first missionaries, he never lost sight of the operations of that noble institution. He was also a warm friend and patron of the Board of Missions in that church with which he was so long identified.

He was always ready to assist at missionary meetings and concerts. His extensive knowledge, and his accurate presentation of statistics, were of great advantage, and always interested his hearers. He was a man of prayer and a lover of the doctrine and order of the church with which he was connected.

"In every sense he was a good and faithful man and minister, and I was not surprised to learn that death found him ready to go and join the church triumphant and engage in the higher service in the temple not made with hands. He came to his grave in a good old age, like a shock of corn fully ripe. The memory of the just is blessed. May the example of his fidelity to the cause of Christ and of his many virtues excite to imitation, and may the mellow rays of his sunset linger long in the memories of his children and other friends."

Rev. A. B. Bullions, of Troy, N. Y., writes thus: "Dr. Newton was a man of great industry, perseverance, enthusiasm, and fidelity to his trusts. His life was filled up with usefulness, and wherever he was placed he labored conscientiously and successfully for the well-being of the community. As a preacher, he was orthodox, discriminating, and faithful to the souls of men. As a Christian, he was humble and trustful, always living near his Saviour. As a friend, he was genial and warm-hearted. Apart from the duties of his sacred calling, he devoted much of his time to the cause of education, and to every interest designed to benefit the community in which he lived. Having a sure and safe judgment, he knew how to devise well; and possessed of a remarkably methodical mind, combined with great perseverance, he could accomplish well all he undertook. He was never in a hurry, and yet his influence was powerfully felt in every good work. He labored all his life, and almost up to the day of his death; and his record is not only on high, but also among a grateful people, who will now sadly miss his presence, and his unselfish devotion to their welfare. But 'blessed are the dead which die in the Lord, for they rest from their labors, and their works do follow them.'"

He was married, January 29, 1815, to Huldah, eldest

daughter of Gen. Timothy F. Chipman, of Shoreham, Vt., who was a lineal descendant from John Howland, one of the Pilgrim fathers who came to this country in the Mayflower, in December, 1620. She was an excellent and devout woman, who entered into rest in Jackson, N. Y., November 26, 1853. By her he had five sons, and one daughter, as follows:

A son, born July 8, 1817, died same day.

Silas Chipman Newton, born December 29, 1818, died, at Cincinnati, Ohio, February 11, 1871.

Ephraim Holland Newton, Jr., born February 17, 1821, died April 13, 1822.

Seraph Huldah Newton, born August 6, 1823, married John W. Stevenson, Esq., September 20, 1843, who was born October 22, 1818, died September 8, 1872.

Ephraim Holland Newton, Jr., born January 7, 1825, died in Byram, Miss., September 27, 1874.

John Marshall Newton, born July 16, 1827.

Three sons and one daughter survive, to cherish, with many other friends, the memory and mourn the loss of a good father and a good man.

HON. MARSHALL NEWTON,

[SON OF MARSHALL NEWTON SENIOR,]

Was born in Newfane, April 1, 1805, and died June 29, 1870, aged sixty-five years. The subject of this sketch was possessed of more than ordinary intelligence and good sense. He was modest and unobtrusive in his deportment, and exceedingly practical in all his views and observations. Respected for his judgment, and popular and unaffected in his manners, he was, for forty years, honored with the most important municipal offices in the gift of his townsmen. And he discharged his official duties with great fidelity. He represented the town in the General Assembly two years, was high sheriff of the county one year, and for six consecutive years was elected and served as first assistant judge of the Windham County Court. At the time of his decease he was county treasurer and deputy county clerk. His neighbors and townsmen reposed great confidence in his integrity and good judgment, and he was largely engaged in the execution of responsible trusts, during the last years of his life, growing out of the settlement of estates, and the discharge of various important commissions that were entrusted to his care. He was greatly beloved by a large circle of friends for his genial social qualities and his simple, childlike, modest and unobtrusive deportment. He possessed a heart full of kindness, and, in the enjoyment of ample means, he dispensed his charities to the poor and suffering with a liberal and open hand. He was greatly respected while living and sincerely mourned at his decease.

JONATHAN ROBINSON, Senior.

Born in Milford, Mass., July 12th. 1754, married Sarah Taylor, sister of Rev. Hezekiah Taylor, and removed to Newfane in the early part of 1775. He bought of John Wheeler, November 13th, 1775, a farm in the parish, so called, which he occupied until September, 1796, when he exchanged farms with Lieut. James Lamb. The Lamb farm which he received in exchange embraced an extensive meadow a hundred rods or more below Williamsville, where Sackett's men who were killed in the fight with Hobbs, June 27th, 1748, were buried. In 1796, when Jonathan Robinson took possession of the farm, a large number of graves were distinctly visible near a clump of chestnut trees standing on the lower portion of the meadow, and they were said to be the graves of those who were killed in the fight with Melvin at the mouth of the South Branch, formerly called the lower fork of the Wantastiquet.

But by an examination of the journal of Capt. Melvin, which has been published in the papers of the New Hampshire Historical Society, and the journals of Stevens and Taylor, it is conclusively settled that the fight of Capt. Melvin with the Indians occurred at Jamaica. about four miles below the upper fork of the Wantastiquet, and seventeen miles north of Newfane; the most reasonable theory is, that those who were killed in the fight which occurred between Sackett and Hobbs were buried here. The fight is fully described in the address which precedes these biographical sketches. It is worthy of notice that the chestnut trees growing on this meadow are the only trees of the kind found in this county outside of the valley of the Connecticut river. This meadow is some ten or twelve miles west of the Connecticut river.

Jonathan Robinson died April 14th, 1819.

Sarah Robinson. his wife. died March 9th, 1809.

They had ten children, as follows:

Simon T. Robinson, born April 19th, 1779. died in Townshend, May 11th, 1813.

Abigail Robinson, born March 25th, 1781, married Wm. H. Williams, died July 26th, 1821.

John H. Robinson, born August 3rd, 1783, died September 17th, 1843.

Aaron C. Robinson. born October 3rd, 1785, killed by a fall from his wagon June 4th, 1864.

Jonathan Robinson, born November 5th, 1787. died July 23rd, 1829 at Wardsboro.

Hezekiah Robinson, born March 31st. 1791, died February 7th, 1851, at Waterloo, Canada.

Sally Robinson, born January 12th, 1795, died April 16th, 1871.

Hannah C. Robinson, born July 5th, 1798, married Arad Taylor, January 11th, 1821, died September 1st, 1853.

Mary C. Robinson, born July 29th, 1800, died in infancy.

Hollis T. Robinson, born August 25th, 1803.

AARON C. ROBINSON,

The third son of Jonathan Robinson, Senior, succeeded his father in the possession of the farm and occupied the same until his decease, in 1864, and during his possession added to it largely by the purchase of adjoining lands. He possessed more than ordinary ability. His strong sense and excellent judgment gave him great prominence among his townsmen. For thirty years or more before his death, he was uniformly selected and appointed Road Commissioner, at almost every term of the Windham County Court, upon petitions to lay roads and bridges in the several towns in the county.

It is creditable to his superior judgment that there are more or less highways in every town in the county, that were surveyed and laid out under his especial direction and supervision, and since they were built they have greatly subserved the interest and convenience of the public.

He married Betsey Crosby, of Brewster, Mass., June 18th, 1816. She was born July 12th, 1791, died October 20th, 1867.

They had four children, as follows:

Mary C. Robinson, born July 18th, 1817, married Dennis A. Dickinson February 25th, 1845.

Eliza A. Robinson, born August 10th, 1831.

Aaron W. and Betsey C. Robinson, twins, born August 9th, 1833; Aaron W. died December 13th, 1838. Betsey C. married O. L. Sherman, of Newfane, September 10th, 1856.

JONATHAN ROBINSON, Junior,

The fourth son of Jonathan Robinson, Senior, was educated for a merchant and was largely engaged in mercantile business in Wardsboro, where he resided at the time of his decease. He was highly respected and honored by his townsmen; represented the town in the General Assembly, was for a few years a Judge of the Windham County Court, and was highly esteemed for his ability and enterprize.

HEZEKIAH ROBINSON.

[BY REV. FREDERICK ROBINSON.]

Son of Jonathan Robinson Sr., was born at Newfane, Vt., March 31st, 1791. He received a good elementary English education at the Academy of his native town, where his close application and abilities gave sure promise of the success which he achieved in after life. From the age of eighteen he was for several years engaged in wool-carding, and the manufacture of woollen goods in the summer, employing the winter in school teaching, in which he was eminently successful.

In 1817 he married Seleucia Knowlton, oldest daughter of Assistant Judge Luke Knowlton, of Windham County.

His father-in-law, whom he always held in great respect and friendship, having removed to Canada, Mr. Robinson followed him in 1821, and settled in Stukely, Shefford County, where he built a carding mill. The following year he purchased a valuable mill site in the adjoining township of Shefford, with small grist and saw mills, and to which he removed his carding mill. A few years later he rebuilt the mills and opened a store. At Judge Knowlton's suggestion he called his new purchase Waterloo.

Here, in a new country, with small capital, and by no means robust health, and with a young family dependent on him, his energy and perseverance were called into full exercise. But by prudence, foresight, and untiring industry, he, with God's blessing, acquired a considerable fortune.

His unswerving integrity commanded the respect and confidence of the community. He was repeatedly chosen to municipal and other offices, which he filled with ability and credit. By the Governor of the Province he was, in 1831, appointed Justice of the Peace for the District of Montreal, and in 1836 the first post master of Waterloo. From the time of his appointment to the date of his death, in 1851, he was the leading magistrate in the neighborhood.

In 1815 he became a member of the Congregational Society in his native town, then under the pastorate of the Rev. Jonathan Nye. Shortly after his removal to Canada he became a member of the Church of England (Episcopal) and was ever after warmly attached to her Scriptural Liturgy, a constant attendant upon her worship, and a devout and regular communicant. He contributed liberally towards building the first church (Episcopal) in Waterloo, and gave seventeen acres of valuable land, now comprised within the village limits, towards the endowment of the parish.

The village which he practically founded, is now, in 1876, a thriving town of nearly three thousand inhabitants, the seat of public business of the county, and the commercial centre of a wealthy and enterprising district.

Mr. Robinson's family consisted of five sons and four daughters, all of whom, with the exception of one daughter, who died in childhood, married and settled in Waterloo, or its vicinity.

Children of Hezekiah Robinson:

Charlotte Knowlton Robinson, born at Newfane, November 28th, 1818, married in 1839 to Roswell Albert Ellis, Esq., J. P. Merchant.

Jonathan Robinson, born at Newfane, November 4th, 1820, died at Waterloo, Canada, October 26th, 1866. For several years warden of the county of Shefford. Merchant.

Frederick Robinson, born February 20th, 1823. Clergyman of the Church of England, parish of Abbotsford, Diocese of Montreal.

Seleucia Robinson, born November 2nd, 1824, died May 3rd, 1835.

Hezekiah Luke Robinson, born January 1st, 1827. Merchant.

Sarah Melinda Robinson. born December 5th, 1828, died November 23rd, 1873. Married in 1852 to Dr. J. C. Butler, physician and surgeon.

George Canning Robinson, born August 25th, 1831. Clergyman of the Church of England, parish of Aylmer, Diocese of Montreal.

Abigail Knowlton Robinson. born April 1st, 1834, died November 17th, 1860. Married in 1854 to J. D. Parsonage, merchant.

Edward Robinson. born September 6th, 1837, died November 4th, 1864. Merchant.

HOLLIS T. ROBINSON,

The youngest son, was bred a merchant in the store of his brother Jonathan, and for several years was engaged in mercantile business. He represented the town of Newfane in the General Assembly, and for many years he has officiated as trial justice in Newfane. He resided seventeen years in Canada, and for fourteen years was a Sheriff's Bailiff in one of the eastern counties.

He married Eliza Tufts, daughter of Rev. James Tufts, of Wardsboro, and they had four children, all of whom are now living.

HON. LUKE KNOWLTON, Junior.

BY REV. FREDERICK ROBINSON.

Luke Knowlton, Jr., son of the Hon. Judge Luke Knowlton, of the Supreme Court of Vt., and of Sarah Holland, his wife, was born in Newfane, March 24, 1775, and educated first at the elementary school, at Westminster, Vt., then at Chesterfield academy, N. H., and finally as a private pupil and law student of his brother Calvin, a graduate of Dartmouth College, N. H., at Newfane, where he was admitted to the bar about 1796. He was a successful practitioner although he had no special fondness for the profession, and became assistant judge of Windham county, and also represented Newfane for several years in the General Assembly of Vermont.

In 1799 he married Charlotte, daughter of Deacon Moses Kenney, of Newfane, who was then under sixteen years of age. Her father opposed the match on three grounds, viz.:

First—" She is too young." Second—" I cannot spare her." Third—" I can give her no dower."

To this *demurrer* the young advocate replied:

First—" She will grow older every day, and as fast in my hands as in yours." Second—" You have a wife and other daughters, and can better do without her than I can." Third —" It is your daughter that I want and not a dower."

The man of law was successful in his suit—the *demurrer* of the Deacon being withdrawn.

This union proved to be fruitful, the issue being ten daughters and five sons, nine of whom still survive. Eight daughters and four sons grew up to man's estate, and all married, except one daughter, whose union with an estimable young man was prevented by her death. All became highly respected members of the community in which they lived.

Previous to his father's death, in 1810, Mr. Knowlton became interested with him in wild lands in the Province of Lower Canada; this led to repeated journeys, on horseback,

to that district, involving journeys of four hundred to five hundred miles each trip, and eventually resulted in his settling, in 1821, in Stukeley, Shefford county, Lower Canada, on the farm on which his brother Silas settled, in 1798. Here his three youngest children were born, and his youngest child was buried, in 1824, by the side of his brother's wife, who died in 1801. In 1825 Judge Knowlton removed to Brome, then in Shefford county, and settled upon a farm, where he remained thirty years, till his death, aged eighty, in 1855, having survived his wife twelve years.

Impaired health prevented Judge Knowlton from taking an active part in public affairs after his removal to Canada, but his intelligence and integrity of character made him a valued citizen of the country of his adoption, as they had done in his native country. He was a man of fine personal appearance, of which his portrait, taken when upwards of seventy years of age, and in feeble health, gives an inadequate idea. He died, as he lived, esteemed by all who knew him.

THE HON. COL. P. H. KNOWLTON, M. L. C.

BY REV. FREDERICK ROBINSON.

Paul Holland Knowlton was the son of Silas Knowlton and of Sarah Holbrook, his wife, and grandson of the Hon. Judge Luke Knowlton of the Supreme Court of Vt., and one of the first settlers in Newfane. He was born in Newfane in 1787. In March, 1798, his parents moved into Shefford county, Lower Canada, with their two children, Holland, aged eleven and Luke, aged three. Capt. John Whitney and wife, with one child accompanied them. The party stopped at West Shefford till May, when the women and children were placed upon horseback and moved on to Stukeley, some twelve miles distant, by a bridle path through the forest. Here they were left in a rude log cabin, covered and floored with split basswood planks, with no door to close the entrance, while the two men returned to West Shefford for further supplies and fodder for the horses. Mrs. Knowlton and Mrs. Whitney closed the entrance to the cabin with a blanket, and kept up a brisk fire all night for fear of wild beasts, but sleep they had none.

Thus early was Holland Knowlton subjected to the privations familiar to the first settlers of an unbroken forest. His only sister, Samantha, was the first child born in Stukely, in June, 1799. Two years later he suffered an irreparable loss in the death of his mother, at the birth of his youngest brother, Samuel. The same year Holland was sent back to Newfane to attend the academy where he received his education. During this period he boarded in the family of his uncle, Luke Knowlton, then a prominent lawyer, in Windham county, and a valuable friend of a young man. He also had intimate intercourse with his grandfather, Judge Luke Knowlton, Sen. Such companionship was invaluable to Holland, and no doubt had much to do with the success which he achieved in after life.

In 1807 he returned to Stukeley, and two years later married Miss Laura Moss, of Bridport, Vt., then engaged in teaching in Stukeley, and settled upon a farm where he remained six years.

In 1815 Holland Knowlton settled upon a large farm, in Brome township, then forming a part of Shefford county. Here he entered into mercantile business on such a scale as suited the requirements of a new settlement. Some years later he left the farm and moved a short distance to an eligible site, and built mills, store, etc., and procured the erection of a church, and the settlement of a clergyman of the Church of England. Various mechanics and others were induced to establish themselves at the same place, which soon became a thriving village and was called Knowlton.

Holland Knowlton's political life begun in 1827, when he was elected member of the Provincial Parliament of Lower Canada, for Shefford county. In 1837 Mr. Knowlton, who had previously been appointed a Justice of the Peace, took an active part in the support of the government against

the Papineau rebellion, and was appointed Lieut. Colonel of the militia.

In 1839 Col. Knowlton was appointed a member of the special council for the government of Lower Canada, after the abolition of the Parliament, consequent upon the rebellion, and in 1841 a member of the Legislative Council of United Canada, which position he held till his death, in 1863.

In 1855 the Hon. Col. Knowlton procured the erection of Brome county, of which Knowlton became the county seat, and is now, 1876, an important village of about fifteen hundred inhabitants, and is a railway station.

He was a man of great public spirit, foremost in procuring the opening up of new roads, in encouraging education, municipal institutions and increased facilities for the administration of justice. The county of Brome is especially indebted to his sagacity and influence, personal and political, for a large share of its progress and prosperity.

Having no children of his own, Col. Knowlton adopted the eldest daughter and youngest son of his brother Luke, to whom he was a kind father, and who inherited his estate. The former succeeded to the homestead and is married to H. S. Foster, Esq., registrar of Brome county; and the latter is married to a daughter of the Hon. Col. Foster, ex-senator of Canada; also, a native of Newfane, and a prominent railway contractor and manager.

It may be added that Dr. S. S. Foster, the father of H. S. and the Hon. Col. Foster, was a former resident of Newfane, and an early settler of Shefford county, of which he was twice elected member of Parliament. He was a leading local physician and surgeon, and, for several years previous to his death, a member of the Provincial Board for granting licenses to practice medicine and surgery.

HON. AUSTIN BIRCHARD,

Born at Wilmington, Vt., December 5, 1793. In June, 1805, he went to Saratoga Springs with his father, who died there the twenty-second of August following. After the death of his father he lived at Wilmington with his mother, employed on the farm and in the tavern, until her death, which occurred March 3, 1813, with the exception of a few months, when absent at school or attending store.

About the first of May, 1813, he left Wilmington for Paris, Oneida county, N. Y., where he resided about fifteen months engaged mostly at farm work. In the winter of 1813-14 he took a journey to Canandaigua, then considered almost the far west by Vermonters, with his uncle, Mr. Amasa Birchard.

In the fall of 1814 he returned to Vermont, attended the academy at West Brattleboro three months, and taught a district school three months the winter following. In April, 1815, he engaged himself to the late Hon. Samuel Clarke, of Brattleboro, for two years, as clerk in his store. In April, 1817, he entered into partnership for two years with the late Hon. John Noyes in a store in Dummerston as active partner, under the firm of Noyes & Birchard. At the end of two years the firm was dissolved, and his brother Roger was received as his partner in trade, under the firm of A. & R. Birchard, and business continued at the same place.

In April, 1819, he married Roxana, eldest daughter of the late John Plummer, Jr., of Brattleboro. Soon after their marriage they visited Saratoga for her health, but she continued to decline and died July 9, 1820.

In April, 1822, he removed to Newfane Hill, the county seat, and continued trade under the firm of A. & R. Birchard.

In September, 1824, he married Mary A., daughter of the late John Putnam of Chesterfield, N. H., by whom he had four children, two sons and two daughters. Sardis,

Austin Birchard

his youngest son, gave his life for his country in the war of the Rebellion, and died a prisoner at Andersonville, Ga., August 20, 1864.

On the shire being located at Park's flat, now Fayetteville, in 1825, he immediately commenced building a small store at that place and had it finished about the first of May, 1825. and filled with goods. In the fall of 1825 the new county building, having been completed, he was appointed deputy jailor, and was charged with the duty of removing the prisoners and property from the old jail to the new. He served as jailor two years, and in the meantime built his large store and dwelling house.

The subject of this sketch was an early advocate of railroads and other public improvements; cheerfully labored on the building committee and other committees of the society formed for building the first meeting-house in Fayetteville; also, on the prudential and other important committees of the Congregational society for many years. He served twenty consecutive years, 1828 to 1848, on the board of auditors of the town of Newfane. He was elected a member of the old council in 1833, at that time a co-ordinate branch of the State Government, and re-elected in 1834. He was elected one of the board of the Council of Censors, in 1841, and proposed an amendment to the constitution, abolishing said board and providing a different mode of amending the organic law of the State, which failed of adoption, but the proposition was renewed in 1870, and adopted by the Constitutional Convention of that year. In 1846 he was elected State Senator. In April, 1850, he retired from trade, his constant occupation for thirty-five years. In January, 1854, he was appointed treasurer of the Windham County Savings Bank, and held the office twenty years.

He was a strenuous opponent of slavery and secret societies, from early manhood. A cheerful contributor to the Missionary and Bible societies, and other public and private charities. In 1864 he united with the Congregational church.

REV. LEWIS GROUT.

Rev. Lewis Grout was born in Newfane, Vt., January 28, 1815, attended Brattleboro Academy in 1834, '5, '6 and '7, and Burr Seminary in Manchester, Vt., in 1838; graduated at Yale College in 1842; taught in a military, classical and mathematical school, at West Point, N. Y., for nearly two years; studied theology at Yale Divinity College two years, 1844 and 1845, and graduated from Andover Theological Seminary in 1846. He was ordained as a missionary and married to Miss Lydia Bates, in Springfield, Vt., October 8, 1846; set sail from Boston for South Africa October 10; stopped for a few weeks in Cape Town, and reached Port Natal, Africa, February 15, 1847. Here, among the Zulus, in the District of Natal, he labored as a missionary in the service of the American Board, for fifteen years, and at the end of that time, with health impaired, he returned to America, and landed in Boston June 7, 1862. Health somewhat restored, he preached a year for the Congregational Church in Saxton's River, and then accepted a call to the church in Feeding Hills, Mass., where he was installed and labored till the first of October, 1865. He then received an appointment from the American Missionary Association as Secretary and Agent of that Society for New Hampshire and Vermont, and in their employ has continued till the present time, now, September 1876, about eleven years, having his home in West Brattleboro.

He has had two children, one a son, who died in Natal; the other a daughter, Annie L. Grout, who graduated at Abbott Female Academy, Andover, Mass., in 1870; had charge of Belair Institute, in West Brattleboro, for four years; taught in a Ladies' Seminary in Philadelphia a year, and is now teaching in Atlanta University, Atlanta, Ga.

WILLIAM L. WILLIAMS,

The third son, was a clerk in his father's store during his early youth, and when he attained to his majority he entered into a copartnership with his father in the mercantile business, which he prosecuted successfully for many years. He removed to Dubuque about 1860, and was extensively engaged in business as a Produce Broker at the time of his decease. He was exceedingly popular in his manners and highly esteemed for his intelligence and sound practical judgment. While residing in Newfane he manifested a lively interest in the growth and prosperity of his native town, was munificent in his donations in aid of all the enterprises that would contribute to its progress and advancement. He gave generously to the poor, was kind to the sick and suffering; he was courteous and affable in his bearing, proverbially honest and upright in all his business relations, modest and familiar in his deportment. His whole life was without reproach and his death at the comparatively early age of fifty, was a source of great regret to all his friends and associates. He accumulated a handsome property which he bequeathed to the two sons of his deceased brother, John W. Williams.

CHARLES K. FIELD.

Charles Kellogg Field, oldest son of Martin Field, was born in Newfane April 24, 1803, fitted for college at Amherst, Mass.; entered Middlebury College in 1818, at the age of fifteen, graduated in 1822. After studying law three years in the office of his father, was admitted to the Bar and commenced the practice of his profession in Newfane; remained in that town until 1828, when he removed to Wilmington, Vt.; returned to Newfane in December, 1838, removed to Brattleboro in 1861. Married Julia Ann Kellogg, of Cooperstown, N. Y., June 29, 1828. Represented the town of Wilmington in the State Legislature during the years 1835, '36, '37 and '38. Was elected Delegate to the State Constitutional Convention in 1836. Represented the town of Newfane in the State Legislature during the years 1853, '54, '55, and '60, and represented the town in the Constitutional Convention for 1843, '50 and '57. He was elected a member of the Council of Censors in 1869, and chosen President thereof at its first session in 1869, and in 1870 was chosen a member of the Constitutional Convention for 1870 from the town of Brattleboro.

JOHN WHEELER.

John Wheeler, one of the early settlers of Newfane, was a descendant of the fourth generation, from Thomas Wheeler, of Concord, Mass., who was living there in 1640. Capt. Thomas Wheeler and Shadrach Hapgood, with twenty others, went to Brookfield to treat with the Indians in 1675. They were drawn into ambush, where Capt. Thomas Wheeler was wounded and Hapgood was killed.

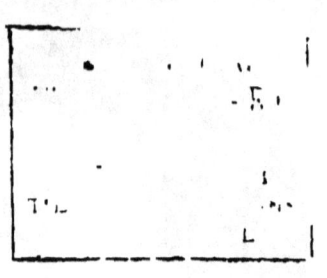

A descendant of the one married a descendant of the other in 1717, and were the parents of John Wheeler, born 1735. Ward, in his " Register of Shrewsbury Families," says: "He was at Fort William Henry at the time of the memorable and unparalleled massacre of the English and Provincial troops, by the Indians, in 1757, after its surrender to Montcalm, the French commander."

John Wheeler's wife was Jedidah Bigelow, of Marlboro, Mass., and a descendant of John Bigelow, who came from Suffolk, England, and settled in Watertown, Mass., where he died in 1703, aged 86. She was also supposed to be a descendant of Nathaniel Hathorn of Lynn, Mass., who was living there in 1683, and whose children, or a part of them settled in Marlboro, where Jedidah Hathorn was married to Samuel Bigelow, the father of Mrs. Wheeler, in 1729. John Wheeler and wife were dismissed from the church in Shrewsbury, Mass., to the church in Newfane, in 1774.

Their children were,

Darius Wheeler, born in 1761, married Frances Balcom and went to Alleghany county, N. Y., about the year 1815.

Susanna Wheeler, born in 1762, married Jonas Stockwell, of Dummerston Hill.

Thomas Wheeler, born in 1765, married Amy Wood of Dummerston, settled in Newfane, where he died about the year 1813, and his widow afterwards became the second wife of Elijah Elmer, Esq., of Newfane.

Mary Wheeler, born in 1767, married Joel Stockwell, of Dummerston Hill.

Elizabeth Wheeler, born in 1769, married Daniel Taylor, Jr., of Newfane.

Catherine Wheeler, born in 1771, married Gamaliel Arnold, of Dummerston Hill.

The children of Thomas and Amy Wheeler were,

Austin Wheeler, born in 1797, went to Waterloo with Hezekiah Robinson, in 1821. Married first, Charlotte Sophia, daughter of Luke and Charlotte Kenney Knowlton. His second wife was Charlotte, daughter of Samuel and Sylvia Keep Miller, of Dummerston. His third wife was Melona Ann, daughter of George and Orilla Pease Williams, of Newfane. He settled in Brome, Quebec, where he died in 1866.

George Wheeler, born in 1799, married Ferona, daughter of George and Orilla Pease Williams. He lives in Newfane.

Thomas Wheeler, born in 1801, married Julia Lucy, daughter of Jason Duncan, of Newfane, now living in Muskegon, Mich.

Franklin Wheeler, born in 1803, died unmarried in Newfane, in 1843.

Julianna Maria Wheeler, born in 1807, married Asa Blunt, of Bolton, Quebec.

Laura Ann Wheeler, born in 1809, married Luke Morgan Knowlton, of Brome, Quebec, died in 1845.

John Elhanan Wheeler, born in 1812, married Mary Ann Roylance, of New York city, died in Kewanee, Ill., in 1867.

REV. OTIS WARREN.

BY REV. HOSEA F. BALLOU.

Died, at his residence, in Fayetteville, (Newfane,) Vt., May 17, 1867, Rev. Otis Warren, in his fifty-ninth year.

The character of Rev. Mr. Warren was such as deserves a biographical sketch.

He was born in Pomfret, Vt., November 23, 1807. His father, Oliver Warren, died when Otis was but seven years old, leaving him and three younger sisters in the care of an affectionate and faithful mother, who is still living in Pomfret. At nine years of age Otis was placed in the care of strangers, to earn his daily bread. His widow says: "He often spoke of this as the bitterest cup of his life." At the age of fourteen he was apprenticed to learn the cabinet-makers' trade, in Barnard, which he pursued faithfully six years, enjoying only the advantages of a common school education, but, as it was his natural inclination to do well whatever he did, he became an exact and efficient mechanic. Feeling, as he did, a determined purpose to improve in knowledge, doubtless with a view to prepare himself for greater usefulness, and in a field more congenial with his tastes, he purchased the last year of his minority and devoted himself assiduously to labor only as a means to enable him to pursue his favorite study.

Having become intensely interested in the doctrine of a universal Father and an all-efficient Saviour, he procured the works of Ballou, Balfour, Hudson and others. These with a pocket Bible were his constant companions, generally having a well-worn book upon his bench or in his hand, and midnight and often the gray light of morning would find him with unclosed eyes and book.

The sacred Scriptures became as familiar to him as "household words," and a determination to become a teacher in our spiritual Israel was fixed in his mind. He encountered many difficulties. The facilities at that time afforded the student of God's Theology were nothing in comparison with those enjoyed at the present day, as the elder portion of our ministers can but too well remember. But his failing health, never firm, was his greatest trial. Still, nothing daunted, he would say : " Be life longer or shorter, I must devote it to the one object of opening the eyes of the blind."

In October 30, 1832, he married Miss Emily, second daughter of Isaiah Tinkham, Esq., of Pomfret, a lady of many accomplishments, and every virtue, his constant companion and able coadjutor in his public labors and domestic life, known only to be respected as an industrious, faithful and prudent companion, who survives him, with their three children, two sons and one daughter, all married and enjoying an enviable reputation for intelligence, virtue, probity and usefulness.

After studying awhile with the lamented Rev. A. Bugbee, he preached his first sermon in West Brattleboro, in the summer of 1833. In the autumn he returned to his native town and preached there and in the vicinity, until he received an invitation to become pastor of the Union Society, in Newfane, Vt., to which place he with his family removed in August, 1836, where he was ordained the September following, and where he lived in happiness and peace with the society and acquaintances, in a ministry of more than twenty years.

In 1858 he journeyed to western Iowa for a change of scenery and the benefit of his waning health. He preached at Onawa through the summer and returned during the winter with little or no improvement in health or strength. After this he preached but occasionally, but continued in answer to numerous calls to attend funerals, often, no doubt, when prudence would have prevented, until about a year before his death, when his friends became somewhat alarmed at an increasing cough, which, however, it was hoped would be better in the milder season, but he grew weaker and his cough increased until autumn, when he sought medical advice. All was done that skill and affection could do, but it could not stay the insidious consumption. Death had no terrors for him. " I shall live my appointed time, I have nothing to fear as long as I believe in a father at the helm. God is good to us in this life, and I think he will be in the next, at any rate I am willing to trust him," was his reply to the solicitude of his friends.

He was wholly confined to his bed only about one week, but was not able to walk or move about the house much for two months. A week previous to his death, his physician kindly told him that there was no prospect of his getting more strength or being any better. "Then," said he, pleasantly. " I will make my preparations as I would to go a journey." He conversed with his family and friends, and gave them advice with as much composure as when in health; gave directions with regard to his funeral, wishing his friends not to mourn, but to manifest the quietude which he felt.

He suffered greatly during the last few days, but when the final summons came his countenance became placid, and with a smile, he passed to the better land. Thus lived and died a righteous man. A man of integrity, an unassuming minister, not a sensation preacher, but a good minister of the New Testament—beloved by all his brethren and friends, and respected by all his acquaintances. His standing may be known from the fact that for four years he represented the town of Newfane in the Legislature of Vermont, and was twenty-nine consecutive years elected Town Clerk, and held the office at the time of his death. A great concourse of citizens, of all denominations, attended his funeral. Too much cannot be said of him, nor can we cherish too deeply his memory. He had no enemies.

May God be with the widow and fatherless and enable us to sympathize with them in their affliction.

JOHN ELHANAN WHEELER,

Son of Thomas Wheeler, born in Newfane, in 1812, was from a child, thoughtful, reticent and studious, simple in his manners and modest in his deportment. He entered the office of the "Greenfield (Mass.) Gazette," as an apprentice when he was fifteen years of age. After serving his apprenticeship there, he worked for some time in the office of the "Windham County Democrat," in Brattleboro. Afterwards was many years employed, by Mr. Greeley, as foreman in the office of the "New York Tribune," and still later was one of the editors of the "Chicago Tribune." He died of consumption, in Kewanee, Ill., in 1867. The following lines written by him, are descriptive of the writer, as he seemed to those who knew him well. They are all that remains of his genius and literary taste, although he wrote many New Year Carrier's Addresses for the New York and Chicago Tribunes:

THE TRUE OF SOUL.

The solemn stars in their far shining, quiver
   As if unstable on their thrones of blue,
But there they shine in fadeless glory ever,
   And night to night their sleepless watch renew.
The needle trembles as with doubtful motion,
   Yet, wav'ring. points to the unchanging pole ;
A guide, unerring, on the trackless ocean,
   When storm-clouds gather, and when billows roll.

Though turned aside by all things in their flowing,
   Reflecting all things in their liquid pages,
Seaward the streams perpetually are going,
   Throughout the cycles of the endless ages;
Or sealed by frost, or in the spring-time sparkling,
   Or lashed to foam, or placid as the lake,
Or bright in noontide, or at midnight darkling,
   One course they hold—their channels ne'er forsake.

Like these, the True of Soul may seem to falter,
   By passion tossed like sere leaves in the wind,
Yet bends he ever at the one High Altar,
   For but one law his will at last can bind;
Motives, a mingled crowd, are round him thronging,
   Whispered suggestions come from heaven and hell,
But upward borne by an immortal longing,
   Blest angels greet him, and the demons quell.

And ever strives he for the pure and holy,
   The constant foe of falsehood and of wrong,
Sworn champion he of all the poor and lowly,
   Against the cunning and against the strong;
His heart their home, upon his features glowing,
   The gentlest thoughts obey the souls behest,
And outward sent, or guests from heaven inflowing,
   Hover like doves around their wonted nest.

Sad on his ear fall sorrow's wailing voices,
   And quick the hand obeys the generous will;
Diffusing joy, he like a God rejoices,
   For love, in widening circles, seeks to fill
All desert hearts with sun-bright hopes,—reviving
   The flowers, long withered on their arid waste,
And to the latest seeds of goodness giving
   Reflected growth, with heavenly fruitage graced.

No compromise he makes with evil doing,
   Though he would gladly bless all evil-doers,
And win them from the way they are pursuing,
   With words persuasive as a maiden's-wooers;

With bright example, which is far more winning,
   Than the best homilies which men may preach,
For who would turn the sinner from his sinning,
   As taught the greatest Teacher, he must teach.

In Nature's book, that rare and wondrous volume,
   He sees but types of things more true and real ;
Its varied aspects, beautiful and solemn,
   Suggest a deeply hid, sublime Ideal—
A Fount of Beauty whence all beauty floweth—
   Exhaustless Love, free, infinitely tender—
Eternal Wisdom, which all knowledge knoweth—
   A complex One, whose smile rays forth all splendor!

ERRATA.

On page 35, third line from bottom, substitute "Sarah Holbrook" for "Lucinda Holbrook."

On page 73, fourteenth line from top substitute, "John McAllister Stevenson," for John W. Stevenson.

On page 73, sixteenth line from top, substitute June, for January.

ADDENDA.

The following was furnished to us after the preceding pages had been printed. It should have been added to the biographical sketch of the Hon. Luke Knowlton Sr. It is copied in an abstract form from the records of the Supreme Court, which were deposited at an early day in the Clerk's Office for Rutland County. "Freeman vs. Francis Prouty."

Indictment for burglary; respondent was tried at Westminster, February Term, 1784.

The Jury returned a verdict literally as follows:

"The Jury in this case find that the prisoner did break and enter the house of Luke Knowlton Esq., in the night season and did take and carry away the said Luke Knowlton, and if that breaking a house and taking and carrying away a person as afoersaid amounts to burglary we say he is guilty, if not, we say he is not guilty." The judgment of the court on the verdict was that he was not guilty.

Luke Knowlton and Col. Samuel Wells were regarded as friends of the American cause and supported zealously the claims of New York to the New Hampshire grants, but in 1782 they were suspected of being in the service and pay of the British Government in Canada. Consequently on the twenty-seventh day of November, 1782, Congress in secret session ordered their arrest. They received notice of the order and escaped to Canada before the officers could arrest them. Luke Knowlton returned home within a year and was residing at his house in Newfane in November, 1783. The Yorkers in Windham County supposed him still negotiating with the British, and resolved to arrest and remove him to some other State. Francis Prouty, Thomas Whipple and Jonathan Dunkley, of Brattleboro, John Wheeler and Darius Wheeler of Newfane, with others, being armed with "clubs, guns, swords, pistols and bayonets," forcibly broke and entered his house at Newfane, on the morning of November 16, 1783, took him prisoner and carried him across the boundary line into Massachusetts and left him. As soon as the seizure and abduction of Luke Knowlton was known, Gen. Fletcher, of Townshend, ordered the military to assemble. A portion of the regiment commanded by Col. Stephen R. Bradley, rallied immediately and reported themselves ready to act, but Knowlton's return and the sudden dispersion of the Yorkers terminated all further action on the part of the Vermonters.

On the eighteenth of November, Edward Smith, a constable of Newfane, entered a complaint against the rioters. Thomas Whipple, charged with an assault, plead guilty and gave bonds in £100, for his appearance before the Superior

Court at its next session at Westminster. Jonathan Dunkley was arrested and gave bonds in the same amount for his appearance before the Supreme Court. Francis Prouty, the ringleader, was afterwards found at his own house in Brattleboro by Barzillai Rice, a deputy sheriff; he was in company with his neighbors and friends armed with muskets and pitchforks. Prouty confronted the sheriff and threatened to "let out his guts" if he entered his house or touched his person. Prouty was never arrested until the 8th day of January, 1784, his house was surrounded by a party of Vermonters and he was captured and committed to Westminster Jail. On the third of February, 1784. the Superior Court commenced its session at Westminster, Moses Robinson chief justice presiding. Francis Prouty was arraigned and tried upon three several indictments, one for burglary, upon which he was acquitted, as the foregoing record shows. On one for resisting sheriff Barzillai Rice, to which he pleaded not guilty and was acquitted; and one for seizing and carrying away forcibly Luke Knowlton out of the state of Vermont. To the last indictment he pleaded guilty and was fined £30 with costs of prosecution, and to be imprisoned in close confinement for forty days.

Darius Wheeler of Newfane was arrested and John Wheeler became bail for his appearance before justice Fletcher. No record can be found of the examinations of John and Darius Wheeler; it is presumed that they were discharged and suffered to go at large.

In Walton's "Governor and Council," Vol. 2, page 116, it is suggested in a foot note that Newfane was sometimes called "New Patmos."

On page 95, last line, read "Freemen" for "Freeman."

TOASTS AND RESPONSES.

1. *The President of the day.* One of the stalwart, solid men of Newfane, though nothing but moss (Morse).

This was happily responded to by Mr. Morse, but the speech was not reported.

2. *The Judiciary of this State.* Adorned as much by the modesty as by the learning and sound judgment of those who wear the ermine.

To this the Hon. H. H. Wheeler replied as follows, viz.:

It has given me great pleasure to be present on this occasion, to show in some measure the respect and regard that I have for the past and present inhabitants of this town. I have personally known it during the last quarter of its century. During the first ten years of that time it was, mostly, the home of my parents and myself, and since then it has been their home and that of others of my near relatives. And since then, too, I have spent some time in every year, and in some years considerable time in attendance at court here. These things have given me an extensive acquaintance with its people which has created and continued much respect and esteem on my part for them. From the manner in which I have been called upon now, however, I suppose that I am expected to say at least something about the relations of this town to the courts. In 1786-7 Luke Knowlton, a man prominent among the early inhabitants, and some of whose descendants still reside here, was a Judge of the Supreme Court. In an act of the Legislature of the State, passed March 8, 1787, which provided for the organization of courts and for their sessions, it was enacted that the time and place for the annual sitting of the Supreme Court should be "At Westminster in the county of Windham on the first

Tuesday next following the fourth Tuesday of August next, and thereafter at Newfane in said county of Windham on the first Tuesday next following the fourth Tuesday in August, if the inhabitants of said Newfane shall, before that time, build a court house according to the condition of a bond executed by Luke Knowlton, Esq., and others, to the treasurer of Windham county." I suppose that the inhabitants of the town built a court house, according to the condition of the bond, for at the October session of the legislature in the same year an act was passed that provided, "That after the session of Windham County Court in November next all writs and processes to be issued returnable to the said court in June term, 1788, shall be returnable at Newfane in said county." This court house was set in the middle of the common on the hill, which was given by Luke Knowlton for that purpose. The session of the county court at that June term, 1788, would appear to be the first session of any court of general jurisdiction in the town. In the latter part of August, or the fore part of September following, the Supreme Court of the State must have sat there. At that session Moses Robinson, who was the first chief justice of the State, and who had been a judge of the court every year but one, and chief justice every year but two after the organization of the State. Paul Spooner, who had been a judge of the court every year but two, from the organization of the State, and chief justice one of the years that Robinson was not, and Stephen R. Bradley, the first person ever admitted to practice as an attorney, by the courts of Vermont, were the judges.

I have been thus particular in speaking of the session of that court, for it must have attracted a good deal of attention from the people at the time and have been quite an event in the history of the town. The court house built by the people of the town was consumed by fire, probably in the year 1790 or 1791. An act of the legislature was passed, October 18, 1791, laying "a tax of a half penny on the pound on the list of the polls and rateable estates in the county of Windham as taken the present year for the purpose of rebuilding a court house in Newfane in the county of

Windham, on the ground where the court house lately stood." The court house was rebuilt on the same ground, and the courts, at times Nathaniel Chipman, Noah Smith, Royal Tyler, Theophilus Harrington, Richard Skinner, Cornelius P. Van Ness and Asa Aiken were members of which, continued to hold their sessions at the old court house on the hill, until the court house was built at Fayetteville, where it now stands. After that at times Chas. K. Williams, Stephen Royce, Samuel S. Phelps and Jacob Collamer, of the judges not now living, attended the courts here, and became known to, and more or less familiar with the people of the town.

But the efficiency and usefulness of the courts do not depend upon the judges alone, but are largely dependent upon the members of the bar. When the courts were first established at Newfane, Luke Knowlton then lately a judge of the Supreme Court, probably practised before them. I have never learned that any other attorney then resided in the town. Perhaps among those who came from other towns was Charles Phelps, of Marlboro, who was the first lawyer that ever resided in the State. Afterwards Gen. Martin Field became an attorney and a prominent inhabitant of the town; and William C. Bradley of Westminster, Jonathan Hunt of Brattleboro, John Phelps of Guilford, and Charles Phelps of Townshend, became, among others, prominent practitioners. After them came Jonathan D. Bradley, Roswell M. Field, a native of Newfane, and one of the brightest and ablest of the lawyers in the State and in the nation; and later still, Edward Kirkland, John E. Butler, Henry E. Stoughton, Oscar L. Shafter, Stephen P. Flagg and many others, not now living. I cannot mention them all, nor say but a few words about any of them. All of these must have been often in this town, and have been more or less familiar with the people of the town. Some of them wielded an important influence in the nation, some of them in the State, all of them some influence in the county, and upon this town, the shire town of the county.

3. *Our Historian.* A Field well tilled and rich in the fruits of learned lore.

Response not reported.

4. *The Band.* May they ever play Yankee Doodle close to the heels of a retreating foe.

The Band responded by playing Yankee Doodle, with the " Doodle " well put in.

5. *Our Public Schools.* The pride and glory of the town.

6. *Our Ancestors.* Embalm their memory and practice their virtues.

7. *The Soldiers of Newfane.* As in the past, so in the future they will stand by their country in the hour of her peril.

8. *The greetings of Newfane's first Centennial to its second in* 1974. We will take care that you shall not be ashamed of us.

Posterity will bear the greetings, and make the responses.

9. We often enough extol the deeds and virtues of our fore-fathers, and tell how much we owe to them, but we hear little of what we owe to our fore-mothers.

Our Fore-mothers. But for them we should not be here.

Responded to by M. O. Howe.

10. The people of Newfane hating everything dry but dry wit, are diligently cultivating something which is ever-Green.

This sentiment was happily and humorously responded to by J. J. Green, as follows:

Ladies and Gentlemen:—I acknowledge the corn. Green I am, and Green I always expect to be. But we read in the Good Book that Solomon in all his glory was not arrayed like a lily of the field, and yet, the lilies are clothed in Green. I look about me, and I behold all nature clothed in her most beautiful garb. There's nothing in it but Green. And as I behold this vast assembly, these professional men and learned judges on the stage, I ask myself for what have they come here to-day? and the closing century answers: It is to hear Fane's Field,

> Green with historic lore,
> The crop of an age that's gone before.

11.   *The ladies of Fane,*
      May they ever sustain
      Their mothers' good name,
      And, as of yore,
      Of children have a score.

Response by C. K. Field.

12. *Our Ancestral Mothers.*

Responded to by Rev. Lewis Grout, as follows:

Our Ancestral Mothers—Rich in health, good sense, grace and culture, with spinning wheels for pianos, cradles for melodeons, and wide-awake boys and girls for pupils and performers, they made their homes happy, and their memory to be revered.

Mr. President, Ladies and Gentlemen:—There are some occasions when it is not easy to give expression to the thoughts and feelings that go flitting through the mind and heart; and, to some of us, such is this day. To have been born and reared on these hills or in some of these valleys, and then at the age of fifteen or twenty years to have gone away and have been absent some thirty or forty years, and now return, look around, see the present and recall the past, is to have remembrances and sentiments too many and too deep to be brought to the surface and put in words at the moment. Crossing the Green Mountains, a day or two since, when I had climbed up to the highest ridge, I turned and took a look at the regions left in the rear; and what a glorious outlook was that—hills and valleys, forests and farms, gardens and villas, nature and art, the works of God and the works of man, all mingled and lying at my feet in the perfection of beauty and variety. So, climbing up to this day of a hundred years, we turn for a moment and take a look at the past; and what a grand review is this. Right here, at our feet, and around us, we see the fruitage of three generations of trials and joys, endeavors and achievements, in the richest of variety.

In this court house, under the shadow of whose walls and the shade of these trees, we are assembled; in that home of the traveler, there on the left; in yonder bank, where the surplus gains of industry and economy are treasured for a rainy day; in those walls across the way, where the lawless are kept out of mischief; in those neat and beautiful dwellings, the school house and the church, on the right and in the rear; in these pillars and walls, on which hang the portraits and mementos of ancestors, whose disembodied spirits are, perchance, looking down upon us and upon the events of the day, with an interest surpassing even that which we feel; in these lawyers and judges and ministers of the gospel, and in all this gathering of intelligent and enterprising men and women, we have embodied before us the memorials and results of a hundred years of life, labor and success, in all of which our ancestral mothers bore a large and steady part. In all that privation, industry and enterprise, out of which have come these blessed legacies, our mothers and the mothers that went before them, were never found wanting.

Much has been said of our ancestral fathers. We love to speak of them as living in times that tried the souls of men. Historians, poets, orators have recited and sung their praises. Records of their deeds are often written in statues and pillars of bronze, marble and granite. Nor can we speak or think of their worth too often or too highly. But to us, of what particular account had our fathers been, without our mothers? Even now the early days and noble deeds of those heroic women come up to my mind, as I heard and saw them in my boyhood, fifty years ago; and it seems but yesterday that I listened to their story or looked upon their labor. How they left the society and comforts of their kindred and homes in Massachusetts, or other neighboring States, and came up into the wilds of Vermont, into the forests that then covered all these hills and valleys, on horseback, on the ox-sled, or cart, without roads, and only a blazed tree, here and there, for a guide; what dangers they met with by the way; what difficulties they had to encounter in this new field; what treasures of health, good sense, counsel, sympathy, grace and culture they brought to the aid of those they had taken "for better, for worse, while life should last" —all this and a thousand other things come thronging upon the memory, as we stand here to-day.

Nor can we keep their many home virtues out of mind. How they began their new wilderness and domestic life, many of them in log huts of only one or two small rooms, and lived there contented and happy, till industry and economy could furnish something better; how they were never slow or afraid to milk the cow, feed the pig, harness and drive the horse, or rake after the hay-cart; could bring the water from the brook, the spring, or the well in the field; could hatchel the flax and card the wool, spin and weave, cut and make, bake and brew, make butter and cheese; and yet manage somehow to keep the cradle almost always a rocking, and have a troop of light infantry always well equipped and in best of tune and training. Such were the ancestral mothers whose names we honor to-day. We do well to rise up and call them blessed. If there is any name that is sacred and dear to me, after that of my God and Saviour, it is that of *mother*. And so it is. I doubt not, with you all. I look upon that picture (of Mrs. Newton), as it hangs before me on that pillar, and call to mind her character; I see and hear some of her grand-children here to-day; I remember what children she gave the world—especially that one, the Rev. E. H. Newton, to whose instructions I listened with deepest interest every Sabbath for some ten or twelve years, in early life; and upon whom I always looked as the perfect gentleman, the cultured scholar, and the eloquent preacher, and I get, in this way, some good idea of what we all owe to our ancestral mothers.

I have said this day finds us on the dividing ridge of two centuries; or, if you will allow me to change the figure, I will say we are standing upon the bridge that links the two together and carries us over from the one to the other. As we pass, let us carry with us the treasures of good our ancestors wrought out and handed down to us. Let us be grateful for the institutions they planted for us, cherish the virtues they practiced, remember the good instructions they gave us, heed the pure and noble examples they left us; and so be ready to hand all these blessings over, untarnished and improved, to those who shall come after us.

This has been a good day, a day of rejoicing, of happy meeting and greeting. But these festive hours must soon come to a close. Soon we separate, and go, some to our birth-place homes here in this good old town of Newfane, and some to the homes we have made in other towns and States,—never to return and meet all here again, as to-day. But if we are true to our mission here below, we may yet meet in that yonder world above, and have a reunion there, more lasting and glorious than earth can give.

HISTORICAL NOTES.

BY J. J. GREEN.

To me, it seems, that in order to understand and fully appreciate the history even of our own town, we must take it to a certain extent in connection with the contemporary history of the surrounding towns. Our several charters were all originally obtained from one governor, and the difficulties met and overcome in one town were common to all the towns; so that in celebrating the centennial of Newfane and making that the central theme, around which all things else cluster, we find the subject thoroughly permeated with interests whose ramifications extend throughout the county of Windham, and, we may say, the state and the nation. Else why do we find this multitude assembled, as by common consent, on this, the ninety-eighth birthday of John Bull's most noble daughter, that child, Miss Columbia, who, as you all know, was born into the family of nations a 13-pounder.

and has lived and grown as none other child ever did, until to-day her eagles cover the seas, her strong arm buoys up the young and steadies the aged to their final rest. Now from figures of speech, go with me to the recorded facts and figures of history ; and know ye that the English began the first permanent settlement, within the present limits of Vermont, one hundred and fifty years ago, by the erection of Fort Dummer, in 1724, in the southeast corner of the present town of Brattleboro. Settlers established themselves across the river in Hinsdale at the same time. These people came from the province of Massachusetts, and for sixteen years there was a contest between the authorities of Massachusetts and New Hampshire in regard to the control of this territory. Finally, on the fifth of March, 1740, George the II decreed that the line between New Hampshire and Massachusetts should be surveyed in accordance with certain special instructions, and in 1741 the line was run by Richard Hazen, and found to leave Hinsdale and Fort Dummer to the north; whereupon the King recommended the assembly of New Hampshire to care for and protect the settlers about Fort Dummer. From this royal recommend, Gov. Wentworth naturally supposed that the King recognized the jurisdiction of New Hampshire as extending to the same point west as that of Massachusetts ; namely, a point twenty miles east of the Hudson river ; and accordingly on the application of Williams and sixty-one others, January 3, 1749, he chartered a township six miles square, in what he conceived to be the southwestern corner of New Hampshire. The town was named Bennington, in honor of Gov. Benning Wentworth. Bennington then is the first town in the State that ever received a royal charter. There is nothing in history to show that the original proprietors ever attempted to settle the town; but on the close of the French War in 1760, Capt. Samuel Robinson, while on his return from Lake George to Hoosac, lost his route and went down the Walloomscoik river instead of the Hoosac valley. He was so well pleased with the country that he went to Portsmouth the following winter and bought out the old proprietor, and began the settlement of the town June 18, 1761. Here, then, we find that Brattleboro is the first town that was settled in Vermont, and Bennington the first one to hold a royal charter.

In following up this chain of historical facts, we find that Halifax is the first town within the limits of the present county of Windham that ever received a charter from the King. This charter is dated May 11, 1750. The town was first settled by Abner Rice, from Worcester County, Mass., in the summer of 1761. Wilmington is the second town in the county, chartered April 25, 1751; Marlboro, the third, chartered April 29, 1751; Westminster, the fourth, chartered November 9, 1752; Rockingham, the fifth, chartered December 28, 1752; Newfane the sixth. An application was made to Gov. Wentworth, by Abner Sawyer and others, on the eleventh day of April, 1753, for a charter of a township six miles square in that portion of the province of New Hampshire lying west of the Connecticut river. On the nineteenth day of June following, the town was chartered, to be known as the town of Fane. Townshend was chartered the next day after Newfane, June 20, 1753; Vernon, September 5, 1753. Dummerston was first chartered to Josiah Willard, December 23, 1753, and re-chartered by Gov. Tryon, in 1766. Brattleboro and Putney were both chartered December 23, 1753; Guilford, April 2, 1754; Grafton, April 6, 1754. Londonderry was chartered February 20, 1770. Athens was chartered May 2, 1780. Wardsboro was chartered to William Ward and others of Newfane, November 7, 1780, and divided into two sections, north and south Wardsboro; and in 1810 the south part was incorporated as the town of Dover. Jamaica was chartered November 27, 1780. Brookline was set off from Newfane and Putney in 1794, and was organized March 5, 1795, and was first represented in the legislature by Benj. Ormsbee, in 1823. We have not been able to find the exact date of the first charter of Whitingham.

The French and English war broke out about this time and the Connecticut river valley and Lake Champlain were the two great natural highways for the marauding parties of both armies, so that to the usual dangers and hardships of pioneer life were added the terrors of Indian massacre and captivity. The result was that the original proprietors of many of these towns never complied with the terms of their charter, and on the close of the war in 1760, new charters were issued to new proprietors. This town was re-chartered to Luke Brown and others, in 1761, and such was the demand for the unappropriated lands at this time, that Gov. Wentworth chartered more than sixty towns west of the Connecticut in 1761. The date of the settlement of Halifax has already been noted as began in 1761; and here let us add that Joseph Tyler and John Hazleton passed, as they supposed, through Fane in '61, and took up their lots in Townsend; but we learn from a descendant of Ebenezer Dyer that Hazleton actually settled within the limits of Fane, on the farm now owned and occupied by Mrs. Polly Franklin and her sons. In 1763, Stockwell and Whitamore penetrated the wilderness of Marlboro each by himself. Whitamore, coming from Connecticut, entered the town on the south side; Stockwell, coming from Springfield, Mass., entered the town on the east side. For nearly a year these two families lived in entire ignorance of each other's presence, each supposing that their's was the only white family in town.

In the spring of 1766 Jonathan Park, then a young unmarried man, twenty-three years old, and Nathaniel Stedman, twenty-one (also a single man), started forth from Worcester County with axe, tinder box and kettle slung on their shoulders, to seek a home in the forests on the Hampshire grants. They made their halt in the township of Fane, selecting their lots on or near the top of the highest hill in the centre of the town. Stedman took up and cleared the farm that is to-day known as Nathan Merrifield's old farm. Park cleared what is known as old Newfane hill common. During this summer they occupied a cabin together on Stedman's lot,—and it would seem that sometime during this season, Ebenezer Dyer, a lawyer from Worcester County, who was out prospecting for a home, came to their camp and enquired the route to Hazleton's clearing. Dyer was a full blooded rebel, or anti-king's man. He came here a refugee from Worcester county, where he had lain in jail seven years for refusing to pay a royal fine of nine shillings. When an opportunity offered itself the three men started out together to look for Hazleton's cabin. They came out on to the round top of the high hill just west of the present village of Fayetteville, and pointed out the course in a northeast line to the river. Stedman returned to their camp, and Park and Dyer descended into the valley and found the flats on which Fayetteville stands. Once in the valley, surrounded by the dense forest, their only course was to make the best of their route to the river; and this they reached on what is to-day best known as the Windham County fair ground farm. Dyer was so well pleased with the land that he marked the trees and selected this for his lot; and now being satisfied that they must be below Hazleton's, they followed up the river and found his clearing on what we know as the Franklin farm. It seems to be evident that these three men returned to Worcester County in the fall and spent the winter. In the spring of 1767, Park and Stedman returned, driving with them a pair of steers and a heifer for live stock. With reference to the exact time that Dyer moved his family into town, we have only been able to learn that Mrs. Dyer was the first white woman that ever spent the winter in town.

We may here relate an incident illustrating the hardships that these men endured. In order to winter their steers and heifer, they went out into the north part of the town, some five miles from their camp, to a natural meadow, now known as the Knowlton meadow, and cut and stacked swamp hay and built a shelter for their stock; and every day throughout that long, dreary winter, 1767-8, one or the other of these men plodded his way through the lone, dreary forest to feed their stock, and back to camp at night; and during the winter Park returned to Massachusetts, leaving Stedman alone in the forest with his stock to feed, for twenty-six days. In the summer of 1768 Park commenced his clearing in Fayetteville, and built the first framed house in town, covering the frame with hemlock bark. Stedman left the hill either then or soon after, and settled on the farm now owned and occupied by his grandson, W. A. Stedman. Stedman died in 1812, October 16, aged 67. Park lived to be 84, dying July 18, 1827. The remains of both these men are buried in our village cemetery; while

Mr. Dyer's dust lies sleeping on the bank, just outside the southeast corner of the fair ground, with no monument to mark the spot; consequently we are unable to ascertain his age or the date of his death.

There are twenty-two descendants of Jonathan Park now living in town; eight of Ebenezer Dyer's, and two of Nathaniel Stedman's; and it is to the oldest descendants of all these men that we are indebted for the above, and many more interesting facts that must of necessity be left out of this article.

Now, although Fane is our central point, it becomes necessary, in order to clearly understand the whole chain of historical facts connected with its settlement and organization, to leave for a time the town itself, with its various personal reminiscences, and consider the contest between Gov. Tryon, of New York, and Wentworth, of New Hampshire, for the control of the territory between the Connecticut river and Lake Champlain. As early as 1763, Wentworth had chartered one hundred and thirty-eight towns west of the Connecticut, reserving unto himself five hundred acres of land in each town. He was thus fast becoming the wealthiest and largest land owner in the colonies. Gov. Tryon was much moved, and felt deeply aggrieved over Wentworth's financial success, and sought to claim this territory under an old patent granted by Charles II., to the Duke of York, in 1664, in which the Duke was to hold all of His Majesty's domain west of the Connecticut river and east of Delaware bay. The title was held to have become obsolete; whereupon Tryon forwarded a petition to the King, purporting to be signed by a large number of the settlers of the grants, in which they prayed the King to transfer the control of these grants to Gov. Tryon. The King and his council granted what they supposed was the request of His Majesty's loving and faithful subjects, and directed Wentworth to stop issuing charters west of the Connecticut river. The settlers on the grants were surprised to learn of the decree, but in no wise alarmed; for they supposed that inasmuch as they had received their charters from a royal governor and paid a royal price for their lands, that a change of governors would in no way affect the validity of their titles. Gov. Tryon and his council, upon the confirmation of their title to the territory, held that he had always been the royal governor, and consequently, that all of Wentworth's charters were illegal and void. He demanded of the settlers that they should give up their original charters and re-purchase their lands under new charters given by his authority. On the third day of July, 1776, the colonial assembly of New York passed an act incorporating the county of Cumberland, with the county seat at Chester, which was afterwards changed to Westminster, where a court house and jail were built. The county of Cumberland embraced all of Windham and the greater part of the present county of Windsor, and one tier of towns on the east of Bennington County. It was twenty-six miles wide on the Massachusetts State Line, and seventy-five miles in length on the Connecticut river. Bennington was in Albany County, New York. Gov. Tryon set all the machinery of law and courts to work and backed the whole by the militia of New York, to carry out his demands and make the settlers pay for their lands under his charters. Against such proceedings in most of the towns they openly rebelled, and many were the scenes of personal violence, and the kidnapping and carrying to Albany jail of many a farmer, there to lie in durance vile a year or more, and have their property confiscated; all for the crime of defending the farms they had bought and paid for. Finally, driven to desperation, the settlers appointed Capt. Samuel Robinson to go to England, and lay a true statement of the case before the King; and on the twenty-sixth of June, 1767, he obtained an order from the King annulling the act incorporating the county of Cumberland; and on the twenty-seventh of July the King issued a special order, forbidding Tryon from chartering any more towns in this disputed territory. Tryon and his assembly paid no regard to the King's orders, but treated him as Congress sometimes treats our Presidents. They re-passed the act over his veto, February 20, 1778, and chartered Cumberland a second time, March 17, 1778.

Such was Tryon's determination to make the settlers acknowledge his authority and pay for their lands a second time, that the only course left for them was open defiance or base servility—and that was not in the blood of the Green

Mountain boys. They were a band of nature's noblemen, determined to do and die for each other. They resolved to submit no longer to any foreign governor, but to become an independent people from the Connecticut to Lake Champlain. Out of this fiery furnace, moulded by such heads and hands as Allen's and Baker's, came our glorious young Vermont. Bennington, Brattleboro, Guilford and Westminster were the theatres of warfare in Albany and Cumberland Counties; for you must bear in mind that the Westminster massacre was a fight with a sheriff's posse of Yorkers. Newfane, too, witnessed a personal battle between the surveyors and Ebenezer Dyer, who, when they came to run the line for the town lots, drove them off of his farm, and so effectually kept them off that they simply marked his place on the town plan " The Dyer lot." They were acting under the Tryon charter, granted May 11, 1772, to Walter Franklin and twenty others of New York city. May 12 he sold this charter to Luke Knowlton and John Taylor of Worcester County, Mass. May 17, 1774, the town was organized and held their first town meeting; and to-day we have met to commemorate their final organization. And inasmuch as Mr. Dyer's name has just come up, let me say in this connection, that in this year, 1874, Elihu Park, of Fayetteville, a grandson of Jonathan Park, has in his possession, and is to-day using for his books and papers, the original and identical desk that was on duty in lawyer Dyer's office more than one hundred years ago, in Worcester County, Mass.

"THE VERMONT FREE PRESS."

EXTRACT OF A LETTER FROM THE EDITOR, HON. Z. EASTMAN.

Chicago, Ill., June 30, 1874.

To the Chairman of the Committe of Arrangements:—

It is now a little more than forty years ago that I first set my foot in Fayetteville. I remember the day well; and my weary drive and walk, and the anxious looking for the place where I was to find rest for the sole of my foot, and occupation for body and mind, as I wended my way up the valley of the West River, with a team and wagon loaded with the press and type with which I was to commence the vocation of my life as a printer and editor. Yours to me was then an unexplored region. James A. Tenny had preceded me and arranged for my coming as his partner. In the woods below Mr. Kidder's shop, I thought the place very distant, as the sun had then gone down behind the hill, but I soon emerged from the dark wood to Kidder's factory, and soon other buildings came in sight, the Merrifield farm house, and there were signs of coming to light; and soon I came to the bridge across your little river, below what was then Green's saw mill, and at the end of the straight road leading up through the heart of the village, I had the whole glory of Fayetteville directly before me, sleeping so quietly amid the hills that surrounded it. And it was to me a pleasant sight. I felt as if I had got to the end of a toilsome journey. I was most cordially received by the citizens. I had come there to establish a newspaper. I was then but a boy, less than eighteen years of age. My arrival must have been about the middle of May, 1834, for I think the first number of my paper was dated June 7, 1834. Looking upon it now, after a period of forty years, I can say it is a creditable looking sheet, so far as the printing is concerned. Your town ought to have had a continuous paper from that day to the present. The competing newspapers were the Brattleboro Messenger, by the then venerable Mr. Nichols, the Enquirer at Brattleboro, by E. G. Ryther, and the Bellows Falls Intelligencer. I suppose these newspapers have been swamped in the deluge of time, as the Vermont Free Press was, although my little sheet was the first to go under.

Of the citizens of Fayetteville who first hailed me I would remember to mention the Hon. Austin Birchard, Dr. Olds, Mr. Dunklee, the jolly landlord, Anthony Jones, who used to wake the morn with his shrill whistle, and meant to make the whole village happy with ready fun, broad jokes and broad laugh, and a peculiar kind of innocent oath, he would occasionally let off, which I now have in mind. Such a person could not help but be a smiling picture, and prominent mark in my recollection. Dr. Perry, who used to drive over almost daily from Brookline, in his gig, is a prominent figure yet. I remember with great profit my friends and distant relatives, the Fields, especially Charles K. and Roswell M. The former, I presume, still resides with you. R. M. went to St. Louis, having a western passion like myself, where, obtaining distinction in his profession, he died. I used to be very intimate with him, and I think his splendid genius and intellect had much influence over me in those early days. In his office was the then young Oscar L. Shafter, studying law, and with him I became quite intimate; and I always highly respected him. He, as you remember, went to California, became prominent and died about a year ago, one of the associate justices of the State. It was in the office of R. M. Field, while Shafter was there a student, that I first heard of the murder of Lovejoy, at Alton, in defence of the freedom of the Press. I then said I would go to Illinois and print an abolition paper, or something like it, if I died for it. That proved in the end a prophetic utterance in part, for I did come to Illinois and edited the leading Anti-Slavery paper here, for fifteen years, and I am yet alive. Oscar L. Shafter was at that early day an abolitionist. He wrote a series of articles in my Vermont Free Press, as you will see (as I understand it is to have a place in the procession) on the question, which he answered, " Is the African Negro a man ?"

I went to Fayetteville to make there my first start in business and in the calling and mission of my life. I started out to be a professional journalist. The Vermont Free Press, which you have in your midst, was my first venture. I cannot say that it was a pecuniary success. I lost in it some portion of my patrimony saved for me through my orphanage. But I believe it was a profitable loss. It gave me early experience in business and in human nature and in my profession. My would-be partner abandoned me, a boy, to take care of himself. With a little pluck and a little money I staid on to see the end, I might say the ruin of my hopes. I found at any rate, as many a New England boy has found, that the place in which Providence planted him was either too small or too large. I found Fayetteville not wholly the place suited to my aspirations. In 1836 I turned my face to the westward. That country, at least, is large enough for any person, or small enough, and a free choice can be made. I found in the West many people who had emigrated from Vermont. I became partially acquainted with S. A. Douglas who was a Vermonter, and Abraham Lincoln who was not a Vermonter. Of the two I found Mr. Lincoln's the most profitable as a partial acquaintance. But as I live with a Vermont wife, I have proved that the Vermonters are the most agreeable for intimate acquaintance. I have seen your Vermont people and Windham County people in all parts of the West, and I have ever found those I would gladly acknowledge as friends. Vermont has helped largely to make the greatness of the West. You may be proud of Vermont transplanted to the prairies.

My life since I left your peaceful village has not been wholly a failure. I early took a forward movement in that great question in saving the country, by the eradication of the curse of slavery. I helped doctor the patient—but my friend Lincoln cut that cancer out with his sword. I have had an adventurous life. Providence has been my guiding star. Six times I have crossed the Atlantic. I have lived eight years in a foreign land. I have looked princes in the face, and I have found them no more worthy than men who keep sheep in your mountain pastures, or make sugar from the maples on your hills. I have lived in a great city which had only 8,000 people in it when I first saw it. I now see it with 400,000 inhabitants. I have seen the larger part of it consumed in a day to ashes, carrying away a small fortune of my own. I have seen it come again like Jonah's gourd, but as substantial as stone and brick can make it. In all this experience I have thought of the town you celebrate as the great starting point of all. While tossed upon the ocean waves I have thought of the quiet of your homes. While reposing in foreign lands, in the beautiful country we call our mother England, or in the whirl of giddy Paris, or 'mid the ice mountains of Switzerland, I have dreamed of your village as Alexander Selkirk dreamed of his native land, and at once I seemed to be there. One of the great expectations of my future has been my return visit. I have ever meant to drop down suddenly among you. This would have been a favorable opportunity if I were not previously engaged. But I still hope to fulfill my expectations. When I do I would like to meet the children of the fathers and mothers I knew and tell you the story of my life.

Z. EASTMAN.

THE SLEEPING BEAUTY.

A NEW VERSION.

BY ANNA O. STEDMAN.

Alas! I am so very tired,
  This glorious summer's day;
It seems to me a long, long time
  Since last I came this way.
You say you don't remember me?
  Well, that is not so strange,
For in the last one hundred years
  Of course must be some change.

Nor is it strange that, having lain
  So long upon the shelf,
In making an appearance
  I must introduce myself.
Alas! how sad that none remain
  Of all I used to know
And love, and rest my heart upon,
  One hundred years ago.

And while the recollections sad
  Are crowding on my brain,
As in the busy life around
  My youth returns again;—
I hear some graceless youngster say,
  From out the crowd below:
"What's the old woman driving at?
  I wish she'd let us know."

Shades of my ancestors! Not thus,
  As you too fully know,
Spake we unto *our* grandmothers,
  One hundred years ago.
Still, yielding to the high demands
  Of the present "high-toned" day,
I'll strive to answer his commands
  As briefly as I may.

My children, you have doubtless heard,
  To your juvenile delight,
The story of the Sleeping Maid,
  The gallant rescuing Knight?
Ah, yes, you all remember well,
  But did you know until
This moment that that castle grand
  Once stood on New Fane hill?

But yes, this maid of high renown,
  (A maid no longer, she.)
Upon the heights of this old town
  Reared a large family;
And feeling weary with her work,
  She donned her big night-cap,
And quietly she settled down
  To take another nap.

It was in seventeen seventy-four
  The sleepy fit came on,
And as nothing very special
  To disturb her has been done,
She very calmly snoozed away,
  Just as she did before,
Till she was wakened by the noise
  Of eighteen seventy-four.

'Tis true she had some curious dreams,
  As happens to the best.
And once or twice came very near
  Being broken of her rest.
But they did quite well without her,
  And built, and bought and sold,
Until her children, like herself,
  Were growing gray and old;

And then the fancy came to them
  That 'twould be finer still
To place their habitations
  In the valley 'neath the hill.
Now, you must know, it could not be
  So many girls and boys
Could move their goods and chattels down
  Without a little noise—

But on they came, and reared the homes
  That shelter them to-day,

But that the old hill held most grand
 They could not bring away.
Its air, its streams, its proud old mounds
 With verdure covered o'er,—
These be its heaven-born heritage
 Till time shall be no more!

The years rolled on, a greater thrill
 Shook mightily the land.
When the voice of God doth speak to men,
 Where shall His children stand?
Not in the ranks of cowards!
 Not in the bonds of slaves!
Sooner shall heaven's dews nightly fall
 Upon their martyr graves!

So, with whitening lip and sinking heart,
 The mother said "good-bye,"
And tried to smile upon the boy
 She was sending forth to die.
And wives grew pale, and closer clasped
 Their babies to their breasts,
And prayed—but, ah! you know it all;
 Why need I tell the rest—

How many of that honored band
 Who proudly marched away,
Have fallen by a traitor's hand,
 How many stand to-day
The victors in as brave a host
 As e'er to battle led?
Then let us give them equal praise,
 The living and the dead.

But the God of battles spake again,
 The tide of blood was stayed,
And His sunshine blessed once more the land
 Laid waste by treason's raid;
And the ancient dame, but half aroused
 By the mutterings of her foes,
Just quietly fell back again
 To finish her repose.

'Tis true that in the vale below,
 So peaceful though it seem,
The waters did not always flow
 Smoothly as one might deem;

But tell me, what can you expect
   In this dull world of ours,
Where women talk, and men but loaf,
   To while away the hours?
Surely, the proverb learned in youth
   Will never be less true,
That "Satan finds some mischief still
   For idle folks to do."

Nathless, altho' some trifling wave
   Would sometimes swell the tide,
Yet, mainly, with this quiet life
   All seemed quite satisfied—
Until a certain year when Spring
   Came in with gentle breath,
Wafting away the memories
   Of cold, and sleep, and death—

With her some magic influence came,
   Some subtle, mystic spell,
That warmed the blood and thrilled the veins
   Of all o'er whom it fell :—
Not that which spring-time always brings—
   Sometimes, alas! too late,—
When leaflets burst, and lovers woo,
   And robins seek their mates—

Yet none could read the spell, till one,
   More brilliant than the rest,
Remarked in Yankee fashion
   To his neighbor, that he "guessed"
If they'd wake up their ideas,
   'Twas very plain to show
That this old town first drew its breath
   One hundred years ago.

Then his brother Yankee answered him:
   "Wa-al, what are you goin' to do?
You just shell out your notions, man,
   I'll be bound we'll put you thro'."
"Do!" quoth his patriotic friend,
   In tones that pierced him thro',
"We'll have a celebration grand,
   That's what we're going to do!

"We'll have some grand orations, fit
   For Independence Day,

And the finest band of music
    That ever came this way.
We'll get up a rousing dinner
    Of the best that can be found,
And ask our friends and neighbors in
    From all the country round.

"We'll tell them all the wondrous deeds
    Our forefathers begun,
And *try* to think of something smart
    That we ourselves have done.
We'll call our sires and grandmothers
    From out their place of rest,
And, though you youngsters of to-day
    May do your prettiest,
You'll see them march about the town
    As lively as the best.

"Talk of your expositions,
    World's fair, or fancy ball;
Beside our great Centennial
    They'll be nowhere at all!
I tell you, we'll get up a show
    Will knock these others flat;
If we don't make the thing a go.
    You're welcome to my hat!"

Well, they have, doubtless, done their best,
    But whether they've complied
With these amazing promises,
    Our Guests can best decide.

Now she who armies could not rouse,
    Nor civic feuds surprise,
On hearing all these murmurings
    Began to rub her eyes;
And, rousing up her weary limbs,
    She said, in accents slow,
"If they have a grand Centennial,
    I surely ought to go."

'Tis therefore I have come to greet
    My numerous family,—
Although it seems incredible
    That all belong to me.
Whate'er the virtues of Newfane,
    Or her renown may be,
In latter years she is *not* famed
    For her fecundity.

But tho' we may not all have shared
   The same baptismal font,
You all are welcome, just the same,
   As sons of old Vermont;
And as justice has been fully done
   To what has gone before,
Let us attempt, with hopeful gaze,
   The future to explore.

First, by your leave, I beg it may
   Be fully understood
That, having slumbered long and well,
   I've now waked up for good;
And, borrowing our starting point
   From apostolic lore—
To leave the things that are behind
   And press to those before—
What shall we hope for as we look
   Through the long mist of years?
What shall we pray for, bending low
   To him who ever hears?

Shall we hope our beauteous valley
   Ne'er may cease to bud and bloom?
That our streams may join their music
   With the spindle and the loom?
That the iron horse may find his way
   Among these hills of ours,
Helping us coin the quiet day
   Into busy, golden hours?
And may we ask for better things;
   That knowledge grow and love increase,
And learn of all good gifts below,
   The best of all to dwell in peace.

God knoweth best; these issues all
   To Him we humbly leave,
While with most earnest hearts we strive
   His promise to believe,
That whoso seeketh, he shall find,
   Who asketh shall receive.
And, tho' 'tis sad to own, our lives
   Are not perennial,
So 'twould be vain to ask you to
   Our next Centennial;
Yet, blessed be God that nobler aims,
   More glorious hopes have we,
That, by His grace, we all may stand
   Beside the crystal sea.

A CENTENNIAL DISCOURSE,

DELIVERED AT

FAYETTEVILLE, VT.

JULY 5, 1874.

BY

REV. CHARLES BURNHAM,

ACTING PASTOR OF THE

CONGREGATIONAL CHURCH.

———◆———

"Tell ye your children of it, and let your children tell their children, and their children another generation."—JOEL I: 3.

SERMON.

"Your fathers, where are they? and the prophets, do they live forever?"—
ZECHARIAH I: 5.

To-day we stand in the entrance and upon the threshold of the second century of our history as a church. Through the good providence of God, we are permitted to see this epoch in our history, and to stand upon this post of observation, where we are compelled to look back over the past century, which is mapped out distinctly before us, and where we may see and learn the hardships, toils and conflicts that the pioneers in town and church were obliged to encounter; where we may see how they met their responsibilities, how they removed or overcame the obstacles in their path.

We look over this congregation, and call upon those pioneers to come forward in their own persons and tell us of the conflicts through which they passed;—but there is no response. "Your fathers, where are they?" Gone, all gone. The grave covers their mortal remains. Where is Hezekiah Taylor, the first pastor of this church, who served it from the day of its organization, June 30, 1774, till September, 1811, more than thirty-seven years? He, too, is gone. "And the prophets, do they live forever?" No; by reason of death there must be a succession in the ministry, but the great Head of the church, the Lord Jesus Christ, "because he ever liveth, hath an unchangeable priesthood."

The church lives, though its individual members die; the church is built upon the "Rock of Ages," and like its Divine head, it will ever live. If, as we stand upon this post of observation, we turn our minds to the century before us, who can tell what its successive years will reveal? Little very little dare we predict. Of one thing, however, we may be confident; as the successive years of the century pass away, they will bear, one after another to the grave, all here present to-day. Probably not one of us, probably not one now in town, will see the end of the century upon which we have entered. Those who will celebrate the second centennial of the town and church will say of us, as we are compelled to say of those who were here one hundred years ago, all, all are gone.

All that pertains to our well-being in time and eternity, is essentially included between two fixed and definite hours, the hour of birth, and the hour of death. Our present life involves the future; the future will be colored, stamped and fixed by the present.

Says Scott, in one of his beautiful hymns:

> "This season of your being, know,
> Is given to you your seeds to sow;
> Wisdom's and folly's differing grain,
> In future worlds, is bliss and pain.
> Then let me every day review,
> Idle or busy, search it through;
> And while probation's minutes last,
> Let every day amend the past."

We are now called upon especially to review the past, and gather up its lessons of instruction for our future guidance.

The history of this church the past century has lessons, important lessons, for us to consider, and it is my purpose now to set forth these lessons, as well as I may.

1. The first thing to be noted is the settlement of the town and the establishment of the institutions of religion.

The town was organized May 17, 1774. The church was organized and the first pastor, the Rev. Hezekiah Taylor, was settled about six weeks later, on June 30, 1774.

The Gazetteer of Vermont, published at Montpelier, in 1824, gives the date of Mr. Taylor's settlement as August, 1774. This is a mistake, as the records of the church clearly show. The same authority also says: "There were but six families when the church was organized." This is a mistake. Luke Knowlton, Esq., moved into town in 1772, and his family was the fourteenth in town. It is currently reported by some of the elderly people here, that they have often heard from their ancestors there were fourteen families in town when the church was organized. This is without doubt correct.

Are there now fourteen families in town, who would willingly and cheerfully make provision to sustain the ordinances of religion? It may well be doubted. These pioneers manifestly loved the gospel, and were willing to make sacrifices, many and great, if, thereby, they could sit beneath the droppings of the sanctuary. They were poor in worldly goods, but rich in faith; rich, too, in works, the fruits of faith. This was the eleventh Congregational church organized in the State. It was organized at a time which, emphatically, tried men's souls. It was only two years before the Declaration of Independence, when the whole country was agitated by those events which resulted in the Revolutionary war. Here there were neither roads nor bridges; neither horses, oxen, nor wagons, and the traveler must guess his way along, or find it by marked trees. All supplies must be brought on foot from Hinsdale, twenty miles distant. Yet poor as were the people, they were quite too poor to live without the gospel. What they invested in the gospel of Christ was doubtless the best investment they made. It blessed them, it has blessed their descendants till this day, and it will continue to bless those who shall come after for years to come. We, who are here to-day, inherit the fruits of the toil, the hardship, and the self-denial of those godly men and women, who lived and labored here one hundred years ago.

This fact imposes upon us solemn and weighty responsibilities. We ought not merely to do as much to bless those who shall come after us, as those who have gone before have done to bless us. We ought to do far more. Our abilities, opportunities and facilities are far greater. If they did not do more than could reasonably be expected of them, we may well ask ourselves if we are doing that which could be reasonably expected of us. Who were those heroic, self-denying people? Their names and deeds should be embalmed in the memory of us all.

The church, at its organization, consisted of the following persons: Luke Knowlton and wife, Thomas Green and wife, John Wheeler and wife, Jonathan Park and wife, and the wife of Mr. Henry Balcom. On the fourteenth of December, 1774, the church made choice of Luke

Knowlton, Esq., as Deacon. Moses Kenney was chosen the second Deacon, March 11, 1783. Brother Knowlton was appointed to wait on the communion table and read the psalm. To the younger portion of this audience this statement may need some explanation. One hundred years ago books were scarce, and there might have been but one hymn book in the whole congregation, and that in the hands of the minister. He would select the psalm, and hand the book to the deacon, who would read two lines. Then the chorister, pitchpipe in hand, would pitch the tune, and the singers would sing them. The deacon would then read two more, which would be sung, and so on to the end of the psalm.* To be sure, this was not very pleasant, but it was the best they could do.

2. Consider the method adopted to raise the salary of the minister.

Whether Mr. Taylor was settled by the town at the time of his ordination the records do not show. It would appear, however, that he was not, for we find upon the nineteenth of November, 1781, a town meeting was called " To see if the inhabitants of Newfane will vote the Rev. Mr. Taylor to be their minister." Also, " To see what means they would choose in regard to having the salary of the Rev. Mr. Taylor assessed upon the inhabitants." At this meeting it was " Voted unanimously that the town approve of and accept the Rev. Mr. Taylor to be minister of the gospel for said town." Also, " Voted to raise two hundred HARD DOLLARS to pay the salary due to the Rev. Mr. Taylor on the thirtieth day of December next." Also, " Voted a salary of sixty pounds, meaning two hundred Spanish milled dollars, per annum, to be assessed annually so long as the Rev. Mr. Taylor, remains a minister of the gospel in said town."

Thus it appears the minister's salary was raised by assessment, the same as other taxes, on all the inhabitants. This course assumed the fact that all the people were under as much obligation to sustain the gospel, as to sustain the government. The gospel benefits all the people, and so all

*At the conclusion of the centennial service a psalm was read and sung, according to the old fashion.

should pay for its support. At that time this was well enough, as the people were of one way of thinking, or were all Congregationalists. It was not felt to be any more improper to tax the people to sustain the institutions of religion, than to tax them to sustain the civil government. It may well be doubted whether our present views of religious freedom are, so far as a support of the gospel is concerned, in any degree in advance of our fathers of a hundred years ago. Now we let every man do, in this regard, what is right in his own eyes, and he may pay as he pleases, little or much. Formerly each paid according to his ability. This made the burden upon each as nearly equal as possible, and no one could claim that he was doing more than he ought—no one could complain that his neighbor was not doing his share.

We pride ourselves somewhat upon our liberal, democratic views, and our religious freedom. We pass around a subscription paper, and let every man pay for the support of the gospel whatever he pleases. We regard taxing as a kind of despotism, which gives no play to benevolence. We flatter ourselves that our present system has this advantage: It gives every man the opportunity to show of what material he is made; in short, the subscription paper is an index of character, where every man puts his own estimate upon himself.

We see by the record that the minister's salary was paid in *hard dollars*. Those dollars were hard in more senses than one. They were hard because they were in coin, and they were hard because they were so scarce, and so difficult to obtain. Our forefathers, the pioneers of the town and church, prized the gospel; they believed it lay at the very foundation of all good and permanent government, and so they suffered privations, toils and hardships, to enjoy its privileges, and to transmit them to their posterity. We do not now realize under what difficulties they labored, or how hard and long they struggled ere they could "go up to the House of the Lord."

3. Let us consider their efforts to build a meeting-house.

September 17, 1792, at a town meeting, the following action was taken: "Voted to build a meeting-house, forty feet by fifty. Voted to set said house betwixt the court house and Mr. Taylor's lane. Voted the sum of fifty pounds for the purpose of setting up a frame for a meeting-house. Voted to appoint Lieut. Ward Eager, Capt. Ephraim Holland, Deacon Moses Kenney and Mr. Ebenezer Morse a building committee."

After many delays, embarrassments and changes, on the eighth of January, 1798, arrangements were made, by which the materials for the house were to be delivered at the place of building. One man agreed to furnish four sills of specified dimensions, for a certain price; another undertook to furnish the plates, rafters, or braces, and so on. In this way the materials for the house were furnished by some twenty or thirty persons. On the seventeenth of July, 1799, the house was raised. The raising of a meeting-house, in those days, was an affair of great importance and the master workman must have picked men, trusty and true. Accordingly the men were selected from all the neighboring towns, and to distinguish them from all others, each wore a handkerchief around his head. Col. Tyler, of Townshend, fell from the frame and was taken up for dead; but he revived at length, and in due time recovered. On the twelfth of November, 1799, a contract was made by the building committee with Mr. Joseph Pond, of Warwick, Mass., to finish the house. The materials were all to be furnished for him, except the sash and pews, which were to be made at Warwick and brought to this place. The workmen were to be furnished with board while here, and twenty-five gallons of West India rum was to be supplied for their use. Mr. Pond was to do the work " in a workman-like manner," and to receive therefor $1146; $50 in cash within one year from date, and $1096 was to be paid in beef at cash price in the month of October next ensuing after date. Mr. Pond's receipt for his pay on the contract bears date November 19, 1800.

What a struggle! what toils, anxieties and vexations in securing a house in which to worship God! Do you not think the dollars paid for that house were " HARD DOLLARS?"

The whole cost of the house, as shown by the bill, was $3731.32. The pews were sold at public auction, to raise the money to pay for finishing the house. The first pew sold in the lower part of the house was to Deacon Moses Kenney for $95; this was the highest price paid. The lowest price paid for any of the pews on the floor of the house was $34; this was given by Ebenezer Morse. The pews in the gallery were sold October 1, 1800. The highest price paid was $36, and Silvanus Sherwin was the purchaser; the lowest price was $16, and Joseph Ellis was the purchaser.

These pews were paid for in the following manner: One-fifth part in cash at ninety days, or in beef at twenty days; the other four-fifths in cash at the end of one year.

4. Let us now look at some of the spiritual results from the means of grace thus enjoyed.

During the pastorate of the Rev. Mr. Taylor, of something more than thirty-seven years, there were received into the church, not including the nine at its organization, one hundred and twenty-six members, forty-eight males, and seventy-eight females.

The Rev. Jonathan Nye, the second pastor of this church, was installed November 6, 1811, and was dismissed December 29, 1819. During his pastorate of eight years and more, there were received into the church eighty-eight members, twenty-seven males and sixty-one females.

The Rev. Chandler Bates, the third pastor, was settled July 4, 1821, and was dismissed January 12, 1831. During his pastorate of nearly ten years, eighty-five were received into the church, eighteen males and sixty-seven females.

In 1832-3 the Rev. C. M. Brown supplied the pulpit and received six into church fellowship, one male and five females. Mr. Brown preached the first *temperance* sermon in the place. It produced some sensation, as such sermons were apt to do, at that early period in the temperance reformation. He apologized for preaching such a sermon upon the Sabbath, saying he " could not catch 'em (the people) at any other time." One man present, not over much pleased with the discourse, was heard to say, when the meeting was out, " The minister says he preached this sermon upon the Sabbath because he could not catch 'em at any other time, but, *by the laws*," (a favorite expression of the man), " he won't catch me here again." It appears, however, that upon reflection, he thought better of the discourse, and taking off his hat and holding it out in his hand, he said, "I do not doubt I have paid out my hat full of four-pences for flip and toddy."

The world has moved a long way in its temperance orbit since then. God speed the day when the circuit shall be complete, the battle fought, and the victory won for temperance.

In 1833 the Rev. Rodger C. Hatch labored here eight weeks. The Rev. John F. Griswold was installed pastor of this church April 1, 1834, and was dismissed July 30, 1839. Rev. L. S. Coburn was settled here October 2, 1839, and this present house was dedicated to the worship of God, at the same time. Because of continued ill health Mr. Coburn was dismissed June 14, 1842.

May 18, 1843, the Rev. Dana B. Bradford was installed pastor of this church, and was dismissed June 10, 1845. The Rev. Darwin Adams was installed pastor of the church January 28, 1846, and was dismissed February 21, 1850. The Rev. Mr. Plimpton supplied about ten months, in 1850, and was followed by Rev. Charles Whiting, who continued here till his death, in May, 1855. The Rev. Mr. Estey supplied about six months, in 1855, and was followed by the Rev. Mr. Eastman in 1856. The Rev. Mr. Bixby came in 1857, and remained five or six years. He was dismissed from the church in May, 1863, and was succeeded by the Rev. Benjamin Ober, who continued about five years, and was followed by the Rev. Messrs. Parkinson, Chase, Shurtleff and Dow, who averaged about one year each.

During the past hundred years this church has had twenty pastors and acting pastors, beside those who have supplied for a few weeks only. The average pastorate has been less than five years. Such frequent changes in the pastoral office is disastrous to the best interests of the church, since it cultivates an unsteady, fickle disposition in both church and people.

Your experience, in this respect, has been remarkable, and one by no means desirable to continue or repeat. Sometimes, often perhaps, ministers are in fault, in the matter of frequent changes, and sometimes the people. We gain knowledge by experience, and experience ought to lead us to do better in the future than we have in the past. You are called to-day to review your past history, and gather up its lessons of instruction.

In a serious review of the past you may see where you have made mistakes. It should be your purpose to avoid these mistakes in the future. You have just entered upon the second century of your history as a church. Improve upon the past. Be more active and enterprising as a Christian church. Do more for Christ.

One thing is greatly to your credit. You have uniformly felt that you must have the regular ministrations of the gospel. This has been a right feeling, and as a result of it, this people for the past century have enjoyed a stated ministry, with very small or inconsiderable interruptions.

The whole number of members in this church from its organization until this time has been four hundred and seventy-one; one hundred and eighty-eight males, and two hundred and eighty-three females. The present number of members is ninety-five; twenty-four males, and seventy-one females. The present number is more than ten times the original one. God has not forgotten this church, nor left it to die. While many have finished their course, and have gone to their reward; while many more have removed to other places, God has raised up others to fill their places. Your losses in numbers have been made more than good by additions. You commence this century of your history with nearly one hundred members; one hundred years ago, and nine, all told, constituted Christ's flock in this place. How much better your position in this respect, than it was one hundred years ago!

Your ability to sustain religion at home, and to send it to the destitute has increased even more rapidly than your numbers. Your facilities and opportunities for doing good are vastly greater than they were a century ago. If so, then a corresponding degree of responsibility rests upon you. Let it be your aim to meet fully and manfully these responsibilities. To this providence now calls you. Do not prove recreant to the high trust committed to you. Who can estimate the amount of moral influence this church has exerted during the past century? What would this place have been had no Christian church ever existed in the town? Here from Sabbath to Sabbath the people have assembled to worship God, and seek his protection and guidance. For nearly three quarters of the past century, the people here emphatically " went up to the house of the Lord," when they assembled upon the top of Newfane hill. Then the great mass of the people assembled upon the Sabbath, nor thought of absenting themselves from the sanctuary, if health permitted them to be present. They went through the storms and cold of winter,—yes, and remained all day. and sat in a cold house, in a house that never smelt fire. The summer's heat did not wilt them. They met to worship God, and clasp hands in friendship and sympathy. On this point. we ought to learn a lesson from the past. We, too, should hold fast to the worship of God, and cultivate a stronger sympathy with each other. Let there be more hand-shaking and kindly greeting, and we shall see more in God's house upon the Sabbath. If we would see fewer vacant seats in the sanctuary, we must greet all those around us with greater cordiality, and with a deeper and more heart-felt sympathy.

5. Revivals.

Revivals of religion are the crowning glory of our churches, and a very marked characteristic in the history of Christianity in our land. This church has repeatedly been visited by rich effusions of the Holy Spirit, and as the fruits of these revivals many have been added to the membership of the church. Under the pastorate of the Rev. Chandler Bates there was a revival of much power. Hollis Read, a native of Newfane, and at this time a member of Williams College, spent a vacation here, and took a deep interest in the spiritual condition of the people, and was greatly instrumental in promoting and helping forward this work of grace. His labors of love and his fidelity are held in grateful remembrance by many now living in this community. In 1843-4, under the pastorate of Rev. D. B. Bradford, there was a season of deep religious interest, and numbers connected themselves with the church. There was special interest also under the labors of Messrs. Bixby,

Shurtleff and Dow. These seasons of refreshing are to be desired and sought for; then Christians grow in grace, and "Zion lengthens her cords, and strengthens her stakes." God grant that the century upon which you have now entered may be far more fruitful in revivals than the past has been.

6. Sabbath Schools.

The first Sabbath School was opened here in the summer of 1818, by Miss Lucy Burnap, sister of Dea. Asa Burnap. Some still remember that school with gratitude and love; and some of the little cards, given as rewards for attendance, or good behavior, are still preserved. They had no superintendent then, no question books, or beautiful books for the library, as we now have. Miss Burnap was accustomed to open the school with prayer. The exercises consisted almost wholly in repeating passages of scripture, or some little hymn. It would be very interesting, could we tell who, and how many have been connected with the school from its origin, and trace their subsequent history. This cannot now be done. How much progress has been made in Sabbath School instruction, during the fifty-six years since 1818! How many facilities we have for understanding the Bible, above those who started and attended this school in its small and feeble beginnings! Honored and revered be the name and memory of Miss Lucy Burnap! We are reaping a glorious harvest from her sowing.

Another influence for good this church has exerted must not be overlooked. Seven Congregational ministers have here been nurtured, trained and sent forth into the world to do their work.

The Rev. Bliss Burnap was brought up in the family of the Rev. Aaron Crosby; he was a good man, and still lives to bless the world by his example, faith and prayers. He has preached in Malone and Bangor, N. Y., and in other places of which I am not informed.

The Rev. Luke Whitcomb was born in this town in 1789. He possessed a strong mind, and was fond of books, and ardently desired an education. After many struggles he fitted for college, and was admitted to the Junior Class, at Middlebury, where he graduated in due course. "He left college," says his biographer, the Rev. H. Beckley, of Dummerston, "with an excellent character as a man, as a scholar and as a Christian." He became pious during a revival in college, in 1811. His convictions of sin were deep and pungent, and his conversion thorough. He commenced the study of theology immediately after he graduated, but under private instruction. He preached in several places while a licentiate, but soon received a call to settle in Townshend, Vt., which he accepted. The church at Townshend had been much distracted by divisions, but by his wise and judicious labors, it became united and prosperous. This was his only settlement, which continued about five years, until his death. Without being dismissed, he sought restoration to health by going south to spend the winter, and died in Savannah, Ga., Jan. 2, 1821, about two weeks after his arrival there. He was a good man, "full of faith and the Holy Ghost." He died loved, respected, and greatly lamented by the people of his charge.

The Rev. Hollis Read graduated at Williams College, and was sent by the A. B. C. F. M., as a missionary to the Mahratta mission, in India. Here he continued till the failure of his health led him to return to his native land, where he still lives. He is the author of a number of works of great value: "God in History," "India and her People," "The Palace of the Great King," "The Footprints of Satan in History," a counterpart to "God in History," and a Prize Essay, "Commerce and Christianity." This last is a work of rare merit, and does honor to the head and heart of its author.

Rev. Ephraim H. Newton, D. D., was born in Newfane, June 13, 1787. In his younger days he assisted his father in the blacksmith's shop, but having an ardent desire for knowledge, and after many hard struggles he fitted for college and entered at Middlebury, in 1866, graduating in 1810. He then entered the Theological Seminary, at Andover, and graduated there in 1813. His first settlement was at Marlboro, Vt., March 16, 1814. His ministry there continued nearly twenty years and was very successful. 133 additions were made to the church under his ministry. He was afterwards settled at Glen's Falls, N. Y., where he continued more than three and a half years. In 1837 he was settled at Cambridge, Washington county, N. Y. In each of these places he was greatly blessed in his labors. He was a great lover of the natural sciences, and collected a very fine cabinet of minerals. These specimens attracted much attention from learned and scientific men; he was often solicited to sell them, but declined to do so. He finally gave them to the Theological Seminary, at Andover, Mass., and spent weeks in arranging and putting them in order. He valued this cabinet at $3000. The seminary puts a much higher value upon it. Mr. Newton died October 26, 1864. It is not a little credit to a church to have raised up and sent out into the world such a man. His influence yet lives and will continue to live for years to come; and through his works, like Abel, " Though dead, he yet speaketh."

The Rev. Lewis Grout was born in the southwestern part of Newfane, January 28, 1815, the eldest of nine children, of whom eight were sons. His father, John Grout,* was for some years one of the deacons of the Congregational church in Marlboro, where he and his family were accustomed to attend church. In 1836 they removed from Newfane to West Brattleboro. Lewis graduated at Yale College, in 1842, after which he was engaged for a time in teaching at West Point, N. Y. He spent two years in the study of theology at New Haven, and one at Andover, where he graduated in 1846. In the autumn of this year he was

*The genealogy of the Grout family is briefly as follows: Deacon John Grout, of Newfane, was son of John Grout, of Westminster, Vt., who was the son of Thomas, of Spencer, Mass., who was the son of John, of Sudbury, Mass., who was the son of John, of the same town, who was the son of Capt. John, of Watertown and Dudley, who came over from England to America, about 1634, at the age of eighteen, who is supposed to be the son of Richard Grout, or Groutte, of Walton, in the county of Derby, England, whose family is supposed to have settled in Cornwall, in the west part of England during the reign of Henry I., 1154-89, and to have originated in Germany, where they bore the name of Grotius or Groot, *alias* Grote, Gross, Gros, or Graus, who are believed to be the descendants of the Grudii, or the Great, of whom Cæsar speaks as among the daring tribes of Belgic Gaul, upwards of fifty years previous to the Christian era.—*See Genealogy of the Descendants of Capt. John Grout, by Rev. Abner Morse, A M., member of the New England His. and Geneal. Soc.* [L. G.].

ordained as a missionary and married in Springfield, Vt., and went out under the American Board to the Zulus, in South Africa. Here he spent fifteen years. In 1862 he returned to this country, and preached for a year at Saxton's River, Vt., after which he was settled for two years as pastor of the Congregational church, at Feeding Hills, Mass. In 1865 he entered the service of the American Missionary Association, as their agent for New Hampshire and Vermont. in behalf of the freedmen, in which he is still engaged, having his residence at West Brattleboro.

Among the fruits of Mr. Grout's literary labors are the following:

"An Essay on the Zulu and other Dialects in South Africa;" Journal of the American Oriental Society, 1849. "A Plan for Effecting a Uniform Orthography of the South African Dialects;" Journal American Oriental Society, 1851. "An Essay on the Phonology and Orthography of the Zulu and Kindred Dialects of South Africa;" Journal American Oriental Society, 1853. "Observations on the Prepositions, etc., of the Isizulu and its Cognate Languages;" Journal American Oriental Society, 1859. "History of the Zulu and other tribes in and around Natal;" printed by the Colonial Government. Natal, 1853. "Reply to Bishop Colenso on Polygamy;" pp. 56, 8vo. Natal, 1855. "Answer to Dr. Colenso's Letter." etc.: pp. 103, Natal, 1856. "The Lord Loveth the Gates of Zion: a Sermon at the Dedication of the Congregational Church in Durban;" Natal, pp. 24. 1857. "The Religion of Faith and that of Form;" two discourses, pp. 48, Natal. 1857. "The Christian Ministry." etc.: two discourses, pp. 48, Natal, 1858. "The Primitive Polity of Christian Churches;" an Installation sermon, pp. 39, Natal, 1857. "The Isizulu: A Grammar of the Zulu Language, with Historical Introduction and Appendix;" pp. 474, 8vo, Natal, 1859. "Zulu-Land, or Life among the Zulu-Kafirs of Natal and Zulu-Land, South Africa;" pp. 351, Philadelphia, 1864. "Translations of Psalms, Acts and other portions of the Bible into the Zulu Language;" printed and published in Natal. "Reminiscences of Life among the Zulu-Kafirs;" Boston Review, November, 1865. "Colenso on the

Doctrines; A Review of his Notes on Romans;" Congregational Review, September, 1869. "The Church-Membership of Baptized Children;" Bib. Sacra., April, 1871. "The Early History of the Congregational Church in West Brattleboro;" a discourse preached December 31, 1876.

Rev. Admatha Grout was born in Newfane, February 19, 1817, fitted for college at Brattleboro Academy, graduated at Dartmouth College 1845, and at Union Theological Seminary, in 1851. But failing health did not allow of his being settled in the ministry. He died in Kansas, in 1855.

Rev. Henry Martyn Grout, brother of Lewis and Admatha, was born May 14, 1831. Graduated at Williams College, in 1854, after which he taught for a time as Principal of the Brattleboro Academy, and subsequently as Principal of Monson Academy. He was licensed to preach in 1856, and labored for a time in Marlboro. He was ordained and installed over the church in Putney, September 1, 1858. Subsequent to this he was called to the church in West Rutland, where he was installed, August 26, 1862. His next pastorate, a term of four years, was over the church in West Springfield, Mass. He is now settled in Concord, Mass. He was, for several years, associate editor in the literary department of the Congregationalist of Boston. Among the fruits of his pen aside from the above, are the following:

"A Sermon, commemorative of the Hon. Edward Southworth," West Springfield. Mass., 1869. "Trinitarian Congregationalism in Concord: An Historical Discourse," etc.; 1876. Among the "Sermons by the Monday Club," of Boston, the following were written by Mr. Grout: In the first series, "David and Jonathan," "Honest Industry," "The Early Christian Church," "Philip and the Ethiopian;" in the second series, "Elijah on Carmel," "The Famine in Samaria," "Paul at Athens," and "Paul at Jerusalem."

Another name here deserves mention, though it cannot be numbered with the ministers. Willard Keyes was born and brought up in this town; while quite a young man he went to the then far west, and settled in Quincy, Adams county, Ill. There he purchased land at government price, and became wealthy by its increase in value. He was a pillar in the Congregational church at Quincy. He was a stanch, unwavering anti-slavery man. One branch of the underground railroad passed through Quincy, and I suspect the cars often stopped at his door, to let out passengers. He gave $10,000 to the Congregational Theological Seminary at Chicago, and one of its halls is named " Keyes Hall," in honor of his memory and his noble benefaction. I am persuaded, he also gave a large sum to Knox College, Galesburg, Ill., but the amount I am not able to state.

Thus have the sons of the town and the church, as they have gone out from the old homestead, from the school-house and from the sanctuary, gone to bless the places where they have lived, build up society upon that only sure and permanent foundation, the Bible. Would you willingly have the influence, which this church has exerted during the past century all blotted out? " No, no!" you all will say with united voice, " let the church live, and let her influence, during the present century upon which she has just entered, be increased ten fold." " God bless the church for what it has done, and preserve it for generations yet to come!"

The church has had a goodly array of deacons in its past history. There have been two deacon Knowltons, Luke and Nathan; two Holdens, Josiah and Forbes; two Pratts, Putnam and Morton. The other deacons were Moses Kenney, Jonathan Park, Caleb Mayo, John Wilder, Jonathan Hall, Asa Burnap, Lyman Gould, Jacob Allen, John Kimball, W. A. Stedman, Asa Kidder and Ephraim C. Walker, eighteen in all. Those who have occupied this position need not be ashamed of it, or of the service they have been called to render. It is an important and responsible office, and like the ministry, it does not always receive an adequate reward in this world. Patience will sometimes be tried, and benevolence taxed beyond measure. Let it be remembered that the Bible says: " For they that have used the office of a deacon well, purchase to themselves a good degree, and great boldness in the faith which is in Christ Jesus." The success and prosperity of a church are greatly dependent upon the piety, ability and efficiency of its deacons. These ministers, deacons, and church-members, who have been here in the past, where are they? Very many of them have passed from earth, and have, as we trust, " entered into the saint's everlasting rest."

" Your fathers, where are they? and the prophets, do they live forever?" " One generation passeth away, and another cometh," and " instead of the fathers shall be the children." It is so to-day, the fathers of the town and church are not here; some of their descendants are; so it will be in the future. When the second centennial shall come round, we shall none of us be here, though some of our descendants may be. The memory or history of what we say and do on this occasion, will perhaps pass down to that second centennial. Let it be a memorial worthy of us. These exercises and this occasion are our memorial, the stone we set up; and like Israel of old let us inscribe upon it " Ebenezer," for " hitherto hath the Lord helped us."

You can not only gather wisdom from your past history, but strength also, and encouragement for the future. You have experienced trials, toils and discouragements; there have been dark days in your history, but in the good providence of God, the trials and the toils have been courageously borne, the discouragements are things of the past, and the dark days are no more. Prosperity now smiles upon you. Let your motto be " Onward and upward," and hand in hand, and shoulder to shoulder, unitedly let us march along the king's highway, to do and dare more for the Master in the future than in the past. Let us strive together " To keep the unity of the Spirit in the bond of peace," and " God's banner over us shall be love." " Forgetting those things which are behind, and reaching forth unto those things which are before, *we* will press toward the mark for the prize of the high calling of God in Christ Jesus." Amen and amen.

A SKETCH OF THE PROCEEDINGS

AT THE

CENTENNIAL ANNIVERSARY

OF THE

CHURCH AND TOWN OF NEWFANE,

JULY 4, 1874.

The morning broke with a slight fog, which soon gathered into light, fleecy clouds, leaving the day bright and beautiful with a clear, bracing air. The committee who had the matter in charge, met early at the court house, in front of which an ample stage had previously been erected for the occasion, and completed its final arrangements and decorations. Within the portico, upon the walls of the house, were hung several portraits of the early settlers and their direct descendants; that of Mrs. Moses Kenney being the most ancient. The Newton and Kimball family were among the number represented.

Suspended over the center of the back of the stage, between the two central pillars of the portico, was the following motto in large letters, covered and beautifully trimmed with evergreen: "One generation passeth away and another cometh." On the stage was a table covered with ancient relics. The speaker's table and chair were in the front center, while the officers of the day and invited guests were to occupy the seats back and to the right of the speaker, those on the left being reserved for the choir. In front of the stage was the following motto: "Our fathers, where are they?"

Having thus briefly sketched the arrangements of the platform, we will now proceed to note the various signs of joy and glad tidings in the street. Coming from the south, the eye of the visitor met with mottoes and signs of a public welcome in front of the residence of A. J. Morse, president of the day; this is the first house on the left as you enter the village, and was originally built by Gen. Leavitt. Again were signs of public rejoicing displayed in front of the residence of the late Gen. Field, now occupied by S. P. Morse. The emblem presented by these gentlemen was the coat of arms of the ancient Morse family, and their motto : " I trust in God, not in arms." Suspended across Main street, just north of the center of the common, between the two tallest elms, was the American flag, with the following motto in large letters across its lower edge : " Welcome."

Suspended between A. Birchard's house and store was a motto in these words : " Welcome, we greet you." In front of the residence of the Rev. Chas. Burnham, Parson Taylor's present successor, the building that once served as Windham County jail on Fane hill, the eye of the visitor met with all the signs of a generous public welcome, and the following motto ; " Our country, our state, our home." This house having a public and historic character, it is proper that we should note explicitly its present location. It stands upon the south side of the common, the first house west of what was once the Union church, now remodeled and called Union Hall.

Having thus noted the various arrangements for the reception and welcome of the public, it becomes our duty to narrate the several transactions of the day, in the order in which they occurred. Between nine and ten o'clock, the singers from the several parts of the town, who were to form the choir for the occasion, in accordance with their previous arrangements, began to assemble at the residence of Mrs. Sarah Cook and her son-in-law, Mr. O. T. Ware, near the bridge south of the village, and opposite the mill yard, for the purpose of donning their ancient costumes. The necessary changes were completed without delay, and by ten o'clock all were in readiness to proceed to the school house, the point where the procession was to form. Here they met the various other ancient and modern members of the procession, some on foot and some on horseback; the whole fully and completely representing the beginning and end of the century. After encountering the delays always incident to such large public gatherings, the procession was finally formed in the order named in the programme, with a single exception, as follows: R. M. Gould, and J. Cutler, with the Fisher brothers of Worcester, Mass., and their wives returned upon this memorable day to their native town, with coach and four, and brought with them their Hon. friends the Ex-Mayor Clark Jilson, of Worcester, a native of Whitingham, Vt., and Mr. Earle, one of the city sheriffs. They came with flags, and banners, and horses gaily decked and caparisoned for the occasion. They, in company with the Hon. C. K. Field, were given a position next to the band.

At a quarter before eleven the order, " Forward march," was given by Col. A. B. Franklin, and the procession, closely pressed on all sides by the crowd, moved up the street to the foot of the common; thence to the right, past the residence of H. Rice to the front of the jail; thence to the left, past the residence of A. Birchard, the Fayetteville hotel, and the residence of S. F. Whitney, to the dwelling house of the late Gen. P. T. Kimball; thence down past the Congregational church, to the residence of the Rev. Mr. Burnham; thence to the left again, past Union Hall, to a point near the center of the common; thence direct to the stand in front of the court house, where the Rev. Mr. Burnham opened the exercises with a solemn and impressive prayer. The president of the day followed with a short address of welcome; then arose ye ancient choir and rendered, " Auld Lang Syne," in a manner that showed that time had shorn that grand old tune of none of its harmony, power or pathos. The choir was composed of the following named persons: Dea. John Goodnow, Capt. Joshua Morse, both men past three score and ten, O. E. Franklin, S. P. Miller, William T. Bruce, Geo. W. Redfield, F. O. Burditt, D. A. Dickinson, Mrs. D. A. Dickinson, Mrs. D. D. Dickinson, Mrs. Samuel Morse, Miss Fanny Morse, Mrs. S. F. Whitney, Mrs. W. J. Tuthill, Mrs. F. O. Burditt, Mrs. H. H. Smith.

The Brattleboro cornet band, one of the leading musical

organizations of its kind in the state, in which Newfane was represented by the Higgins brothers, occupying a position upon the ground, just at the left of the choir, immediately upon the close of "Auld Lang Syne," struck up one of their soul-stirring airs in a manner that touched the musical chord in the soul of all the vast audience, which was composed of people not only from all parts of the town, county, and state, but the union, many a son and daughter of Fane having returned from various states in the Union to enjoy this occasion. It was one of the largest public gatherings ever held in town, estimated by many to be at least three thousand people.

Mr. Field's address occupied about an hour in its delivery. Long before its close his voice failed him and he was obliged to hand over his MS. to his friend Col. K. Haskins, who finished its reading in a round, full voice, and a highly acceptable manner; upon its close the choir sang "Ode to Science," and the band followed with a stirring air; thus closed the exercises of the forenoon.

EXERCISES OF THE AFTERNOON.

Re-assembling at a little past two o'clock the choir and band opened the exercises as per order of the programme. The president then announced that voluntary remarks from any one were in order, but as no one seemed disposed to accept the invitation, the toast master, Rev. Mr. Burnham, came forward with his sentiments, which soon met with hearty and cheery responses, from those to whom they were directed. Not having a short hand reporter present, we have been able to give in the foregoing pages only the few answers prepared for the occasion. Eldest among the venerable ones present upon this memorable day was Mrs. Reba Holland, hale and healthy in body and mind, at the advanced age of fourscore and ten. Eighty years of her life having been spent in this town and its immediate vicinity. Her father coming from Massachusetts when she was ten years old, moved his family into an open log pen, without either floor, roof, or door, built upon the hill, to the west and opposite of the then Hazleton meadows, now owned and occupied by the Franklin brothers and their mother.

Among the others of this patriarchal circle, was Mr. Artemas Eddy, aged eighty-seven, and Mrs. Brown, and the Hon. Austin Birchard, both octogenarian residents of the town. The venerable Judge Keyes, of Brattleboro, who laid the foundation in his early practice on Fane hill for that legal lore that in his palmy days gave him the reputation of being the best read lawyer in Windham County, was to be seen with his long silver locks, bleached by eighty-seven summers, moving about with that short, shuffling step that all men knew was Judge Keyes'.

Prominent among the active men of political and judicial fame was the Hon. Ex-Judge Aldis of the Supreme Court of Vermont, now U. S. Consul to Nice, Italy.

Present upon the stage were the Hon. Judges, James Barrett and H. H. Wheeler, of our State Supreme Court; the Hon. Ex-Mayor C. Jilson and sheriffs Gould and Earle of Worcester, Mass; the Hon. C. N. Davenport, Col. K. Haskins, Col. S. M. Waite and the Rev. Mr. Grout, of Brattleboro; the venerable Austin Birchard, and various members of the centennial committee, with some of the direct descendants of the three original pioneers of the town.

Very soon upon the opening of the afternoon exercises, it became evident that a portion of the matter prepared and intended for the occasion, must necessarily be omitted for the want of time. Accordingly, Mr. Green withheld the letters and facts in his possession, but in this work they occupy the position, as matters of history, that they were to have occupied in the proceedings of that day.

Upon the close of the toasts and their responses, Mrs. Wm. A. Stedman, wife of a grandson of the original pioneer, Nathaniel, came forward clad in ancient costume, and commenced the reading of an original poem, written for the occasion; but ere she began dark lowering clouds gathered overhead, and while the half had not been told, the heavy drops began to fall, and the people were compelled to seek shelter wherever it could be found. By special request the court house was opened and Mrs. Stedman invited to go in and finish the reading of her poem. The house was soon filled to its utmost capacity and Mrs. Stedman was requested to commence and re-read her article entire; which she did in a manner that would have done credit to any professional reader. Following it were speeches from various individuals, among whom were Jilson, Gould and Earle, the latter of whom, a Massachusetts man, seemed intent upon cracking sharp jokes on his friends Gould and Jilson.

The closing words of the day, from the Rev. Mr. Olmstead of Townshend, Rev. Mr. Grout of Brattleboro, and various other gentlemen, were earnest appeals to the townspeople to see to it that the history of the town and its centennial celebration should be published; and now, after a delay of two years, a committee has finally been chosen and authorized by a vote of the town to write out and publish the work.

DECORATION OF THE CHURCH, JULY 5.

The church was beautifully decorated with evergreens. Upon the end of the church, directly behind the pulpit, was placed a large evergreen cross. Upon the left side of the cross and under the transverse piece was the date 1774, and "Taylor," the name of the first pastor; on the right side was 1874, and "Burnham," the name of the present minister. Above the cross, in large letters, was the sentence: "Holiness becometh thy house, O Lord, forever." Against the front of the pulpit was another evergreen cross, beautifully ornamented with flowers. Charming vases of flowers adorned the pulpit and the table in front of the pulpit. In front of the choir was this sentence: "Praise God in his sanctuary." A large evergreen wreath and cross adorned the windows, and the chandelier was appropriately and neatly adorned. The Sabbath was a beautiful day, and the sanctuary was thronged with multitudes from abroad, who had returned on this joyful occasion to mingle their prayers and praises with the residents of the place, in the House of the Lord.

The choir opened the exercises of the day by singing " Old Denmark :"

> " Before Jehovah's awful throne."

The introductory exercises were conducted by the Rev. Lewis Grout, of West Brattleboro, who was a native of this town. The 48th Psalm was read. prayer offered, and the hymn:

> " How pleased and blessed was I,
> To hear the people cry," etc.,

was sung to " Dalston."

Sermon.

The morning service was concluded by singing the hymn:

> " I love thy church, O God," etc.

It was sung in the old fashioned way, by reading two lines, then singing them, and reading two more. and so on.

As a fitting conclusion of the services of the day, though not a memorial service, the Rev. Mr. Burnham preached from thes ewords: "Show thyself a man," 1 Kings, ii: 2.

PART II.

PART II.

In this portion of the work will be found all the various facts and historical matters of interest, that we have been able to collect and authenticate, that have not appeared in the previous pages.

ORIGINAL CHARTER.

The application for, and Charter of 1753.

At a council holden at Portsmouth, by his Excellency's orders, on Wednesday, April 11, 1753:

Present—Theodore Atkinson, Richard Wibird, Samuel Lolley, Daniel Warner, Esq's. The secretary laid before the Council the petition of Abner Sawyer and about sixty others, praying a grant of His Majesty's unappropriated lands lying to the westward of Connecticut River, for a township six miles square, upon the condition directed to in His Majesty's instructions, and asked the Council whether they would advise his Excellency to make such a grant, to which they did advise and consent.

PROVINCE OF NEW HAMPSHIRE.

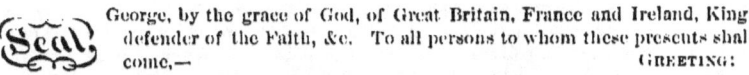

George, by the grace of God, of Great Britain, France and Ireland, King, defender of the Faith, &c. To all persons to whom these presents shall come,— GREETING:

Know ye, that we of our special grace, certain knowledge and mere motion, for the due encouragement of settling a new plantation within our said Province, by and with the advice of our trusty and well-beloved Benning Wentworth, Esqr., our Governor and Commander-in-chief of our Province of New Hampshire, in America, and of our Council of the said Province, have, upon the conditions and reservations hereafter made, given and granted, and by these presents, for us, our heirs and successors, do give and grant in equal shares, unto our loving subjects, inhabitants of our said Province of New Hampshire, and his Majesty's other governments, and to their heirs and assigns forever, whose names are entered on this grant, to be divided to and amongst them into seventy-four equal shares, all that tract or parcel of land situate, lying and being within our Province of New Hampshire, containing by admeasurement twenty-three thousand and forty acres, which tract is to contain six miles square, and no more, out of which an allowance is to be made for highways and unimprovable land by rocks, mountains, ponds and rivers, one thousand and forty acres free, according to the plan thereof made and presented by our said Governor's orders, and hereunto annexed, butted and bounded as follows, viz: Beginning at a stake and stones five hundred rods east 10° south by the needle from the northeast corner of the town of Marlborough, and from thence running six miles north 20° east by the needle to a stake and stones, from thence west 10° north by the needle six miles to a stake and stones, from thence south 20° west by the needle six miles to the north side of Marlborough aforesaid, thence by Marlborough line east 10° south to Marlborough's northeast corner, from thence continuing that course to the stake and stones first above mentioned, and that the same be and is hereby incorporated into a township by the name of *Fane*, and that the inhabitants that do ———— or shall hereafter inhabit said township, are hereby declared to be enfranchised with and entitled to all and every the privileges and immunities that other towns within our said Province by law exercise and enjoy. And further, that the said town as soon as there shall be fifty families resident and settled thereon, shall have the liberty of holding two fairs, one of which shall be held on the ————, and the other on the ———— annually, which fairs are not to continue and be held longer than the respective ———— following the said respective days, and as soon as the said town shall consist of fifty families, a market shall be opened and kept one or more days in each week, as may be most advantageous to the inhabitants. Also, that the first meeting for the choice of town officers, agreeable to the laws of our said Province, shall be held on the last Wednesday in August next, which meeting shall be ratified by Mr. Abner Sawyer, who is hereby also appointed the moderator of the said first meeting, which he is to notify and govern agreeable to the laws and customs of our said Province; and that the annual meeting forever hereafter for the choice of such officers of said town shall be on the second Wednesday in March, annually. To have and to hold the said tract of land as above expressed, together with all the privileges and appurtenances, to them and their respective heirs and assigns forever, upon the following conditions, viz: That every grantee, his heirs or assigns, shall plant or cultivate five acres of land within the term of five years, for every fifty acres contained in his or their share or proportion of land in said Township, and continue to improve and settle the same by additional cultivations, on penalty of the forfeiture of his grant or share in the said Township, and its reverting to his Majesty, his heirs and successors, to be by him or them regranted to such of his subjects as shall effectually settle and cultivate the same. That all white pine trees within the said Township fit for masting our royal navy be carefully preserved for that use, and none to be cut or felled without his Majesty's especial license for so doing first had and obtained, upon the penalty of the forfeiture of the right of such grantee, his heirs or assigns to us, our heirs and successors, as well as being subject to the penalty of any act or acts of Parliament that now are or hereafter shall be enacted. That before any division of the said land be made to and amongst the grantees, a tract of land as near the centre of the Township as the land will admit of, shall be reserved and marked out for town lots, one of which shall be allotted to each grantee of the contents of one acre, yielding and paying therefor to us, our heirs and successors, for the space of ten years, to be computed from the date hereof, the rent of one ear of Indian corn only, on the first day of January annually, if lawfully demanded, the first payment to be made on the first day of January next ensuing the date hereof. And every proprietor, settler, or inhabitant, shall yield and pay unto us, our heirs and successors, yearly, and every year forever, from and after the expiration of the ten years from the date hereof, namely: on the first day of January, which will be in the year of our Lord Christ one thousand seven hundred and sixty-four, one shilling Proclamation money for every hundred acres he so owns, settles, or possesses, and so in proportion for a greater or lesser tract of the said land, which money shall be paid by the respective persons abovesaid, their heirs or assigns, in our Council Chamber, in Portsmouth, or to such officer or officers as shall be appointed to receive the same, and this to be in lieu of all other rents and services whatsoever.

In testimony whereof we have caused the seal of our said Province to be hereunto affixed. Witness, Benning Wentworth, Esqr., our Governor and Commander-in-Chief of our said Province, the 19th day of June, in the year of our Lord Christ, 1753, and in the twenty-sixth year of our reign.

B. WENTWORTH.

By His Excellency's command, with advice of Council.
THEODORE ATKINSON, Secretary.

Entered and recorded according to the original charter, under the Province seal, this 21st day of June, 1753.
Per THEODORE ATKINSON, Secretary.

The names of the grantees of the above Charter have already appeared in Mr. Field's address.

His Excellency Benning Wentworth Esq., one tract of land of the contents of five hundred acres, which is to be accounted two of the above shares; one whole share for the incorporated society for the propagation of the gospel in foreign parts; one whole share for the first settled minister of the gospel in the said town; one whole share for a glebe for the minister of the church of England as by law established.

Henry Sherborn, Theodore Atkinson, Richard Wibird, Samuel Smith, John Downing Senior, Lolly Sampson, Sheaffe and Daniel Warner, John Wentworth Junior.

Province of New Hampshire, entered and recorded from the back of the charter of *Fane*, the 21 June, 1753.
THEODORE ATKINSON, Secretary.

The following named persons were the grantees of the second Charter, granted November 3, 1761.

The names of the grantees of New Fane: Benja. Flagg, Mary Sawyer, Jonas Heywood, James Barrat, John Milling, Sam'l Ball, Thomas Barrat, Eben'r Morse, Luke Brown, Sam'l Jones, Isaac Miller, Timo. Brown, Sam'l Jones, Jun'r, John Hazleton, Esq., Sam'l Heywood, Jonas Potter, Ross Wyman, Amos Heywood, Abijah Brown, Charles Brigham, Esq., Charles Heywood, Isaac Glezon, Ezra Sawyer, Jun'r, Joseph Hubbard, John Brooks, James Taylor, Isaac Hubbard, Thos. Sawyer, Inness Sterner, Thos. Davis, David Fiske, Job Cushing, Jona. Fisk, Isaac Davis, Thos. Green, Ezra Sawyer, Simon Davis, John Woodward, Daniel Warner, Esq., Sam'l Potter, Isaac Willard, Mark Hunking Wentworth, Esq., Sam'l Potter, Jun'r, Benja. Stowell, Theodore Atkinson, Esq., Simon Davis, Jun'r, Isaac Barnard, Esq., Maj. John Wentworth, Esq. Ephraim Brown, Joseph Bixby, Ephraim Potter, Edward Brown, Timo. Payne, Esq., Timothy Wheeler, Sam'l Brown, Will'm Young, Simon Hunt, Luke Brown, Jun'r, Thos. Hubbard, Joseph Hubbard, Jun'r, Jona. Heywood, Joseph Hubbard, Jonah Conant, Samuel Brooks, David Wheeler.

FIRST TOWN OFFICERS,

CHOSEN UPON THE ORGANIZATION OF THE TOWN, MAY 17, 1774.

Moderator, Ebenezer Fletcher; Town Clerk, Luke Knowlton; Supervisor, Luke Knowlton; Overseers of Poor, John Wheeler and Ebenezer Fletcher; Trustees, Jonathan Park, Moses Kenney, and Christopher Osgood; Commissioners, Edward Smith, Chirstopher Osgood, and John Wheeler; Assessors, Christopher Osgood, and Luke Knowlton; Collector, Josiah Randall; Treasurer, Luke Knowlton; Constables, Phineas Farrar, John Morse, Edward Smith, and Lemuel Stevens; Overseers of Highways, Josiah Randall, Ebenezer Merrick, Moses Kenney, and Lemuel Stevens; Fence Viewers, Jonathan Thurston, Joshua Morse, Christopher Osgood, and Nathan Pike.

FAMILY GENEALOGIES.

FIELD FAMILY.

John Horne Tooke, in his "Diversions of Purley," suggests that Field in old English was written Feld. Field land or Feld land was open land and was used to designate land where the trees had been felled, in contradistinction to wood or forest land. Feld, Felde and Fielde were common names in England before the fifteenth century.

Hubertus De la Feld came from Colmar, an imperial city during the middle ages, near Strasburg, in Alsatia, on the German border of France. He was of the Counts De la Feld, who resided at Colmar as early as the sixth century. He came to England with William the Conqueror, in 1066, and held lands in Lancashire, in 1068, granted to him by the Conqueror for military services. The De la Felds and De la Feldes were common before the reign of Richard II. During the fourteenth century the prefix " De la " was dropped, in consequence of the wars with France having made it unpopular. In the fifteenth century the name Field seems to have been generally substituted for that of Feld, Felde, or Fielde.

John Field, the astronomer, was born about 1525, and died at Ardsley, England, in 1587. He published the first astronomical tables in 1550 that ever appeared in England, they were calculated upon the basis of the Copernican theory.

The first appearance of the name of Field without the prefix " De la " was in Ardsley and Bradford in the west riding of Yorkshire which borders upon Lancashire, near the lands granted by the Conqueror to Hubertus De la Feld.

Ancient records and documents furnish satisfactory evidence that the name Feld without the prefix "De la" is not to be found earlier than about 1400, and the fact that the Fields appear where the De la Felds were originally located indicates that the families were identical. In addition, the coat of arms of the ancient De la Felds is the same as that of the modern family of Field: "Sable, a chevron between three garbs, argent."

John Field, the Astronomer, married Jane Amyas, of London, in 1560. They had eight sons and one daughter. John Field, Jr., the fourth son, was the father of Zechariah Field, who was born at Ardsley, England, in 1600, emigrated to Boston, in 1632, and settled in Dorchester, where he remained until 1639, when he removed to Hartford, Conn., and from thence, in 1659, to Northampton, Mass., and, in 1663, to Hatfield, Mass., where he died in 1666.

He married Mary ———, and left five children who were all born in Hartford, between the years 1643 and 1658. The youngest son, Joseph Field, remained in Hatfield until 1714, when he removed to Sunderland, and from thence to Northfield, in 1720, to gain a title to his allotment of land. He returned to Sunderland, in 1726, died February 15, 1736, aged seventy-eight years.

He married, first, Joanna, daughter of John Wyatt, of Hartford, Conn., June 28, 1688; second, Mary Belding. She died March 15, 1751, at Northfield, aged eighty-seven years. Joseph Field had by his first wife eleven children. Jonathan Field, youngest son of Joseph Field, was born October 13, 1699, at Hatfield, and removed with his father to Sunderland. He married, first, Mary Billings, of Hatfield, March 30, 1721, by whom he had four daughters. She died in 1736. In 1738 he married, for his second wife, Esther Smith, of Hatfield, by whom he had four sons and two daughters. His oldest son, Seth Field, was born in 1741, and died in 1813. Seth Field married, first, Mary Hubbard, of Sunderland, by whom he had six children. Second, Margery Lotheridge, of Pelham, Mass., in 1815. She was born in the north of Ireland, in 1754, her maiden name was Margery Knowlton. She died at Silver Creek, N. Y., in 1833.

Martin Field, son of Seth Field, was born January 12, 1773, died October 3, 1833. Married Esther Smith Kellogg, of Amherst, Mass., February 21, 1802. She was born February 25, 1780, and died June 6, 1867. They had four children as follows:

Charles Kellogg, born April 14, 1803. Married Julia Ann Kellogg, of Cooperstown, N. Y., June 29, 1828.

Mary Hubbard, born September 13, 1804. Married, first, Theodore F. French, of Troy, July 27, 1824. Died September 11, 1828. Second, Thomas Jones, of Enfield, Mass., December 24, 1835. Died October 21, 1853.

Roswell M., born February 22, 1807. Died at St. Louis, July 12, 1869. Married Frances Reed, of St. Louis, May 30, 1848. She died November 18, 1856.

John F., born September 25, 1808. Died in Wisconsin, August 25, 1847.

Chas. K. Field had five children, as follows:

Julia K., born October 14, 1829. Married Elisha Payne Jewett, of Montpelier, January 15, 1861.

Martin, born April 24, 1831. Died September 3, 1861.

Esther Sophia, born January 5, 1834. Died April 17, 1837.

Mary H., born August 5, 1839. Married Henry C. Willard, of Brattleboro, June 1, 1868.

Henry K., born June 8, 1848. Married Kate L. Daniels, of Hartford, Conn., November 25, 1872.

KNOWLTON FAMILY.

Thomas Knowlton and Margery Goodhue, both of Ipswich, Mass., were married in Watertown, Mass., December 2, 1692. She was the daughter of Deacon William Goodhue, who was in Ipswich, in 1635, and whose wife was Margery Watson. They were probably from England.

Deacon Ezekiel Knowlton, son of Thomas and Margery, was born about 1707. He married Susanna, daughter of Capt. Morgan and his wife, Susanna Pitts, from England; Captain Morgan died on the voyage hither, and his widow married —— Clark. Ezekiel and Susanna Knowlton came to Shrewsbury, Mass., probably from Manchester, as they were discharged from the church there and added to that in Shrewsbury, in 1731.

Luke Knowlton, son of Deacon Ezekiel Knowlton, was born in Shrewsbury, Mass., October 24, 1738, and July 29, 1760, married Sarah, daughter of Ephraim Holland, of Shrewsbury, who married Thankful Howe, of Worcester, Mass., December 11, 1739. Luke and Sarah Knowlton had seven children, three sons and four daughters. Five of their children survived their father. Six were born in Shrewsbury, Mass., and one, the youngest, in Newfane, Vt.

Calvin, born January 22, 1761. Married Sophia Willard, of Petersham, Mass., sister of Samuel Willard, February 3, 1793. Died, at Newfane, January 20, 1800. Their son, Geo. W. Knowlton, born in Newfane, in 1794; now resides in Watertown, N. Y.

Patty, born December 5, 1762. Died in 1814, in Ohio. She married Daniel Warner.

Silas, born December 19, 1764. Married Sarah Holbrook, the sister of his brother-in-law, John Holbrook, November 30, 1786. She died in Canada, about 1800. He also died in Canada, aged 80 years. Their son, Paul H. Knowlton, was born in Newfane, in 1787.

Sarah, born May 2, 1767. Married John Holbrook,

November 30, 1786. She died, in Brattleboro, Vt., March 22, 1851, aged eighty-four years.

Alice, born July 22, 1769. Married Nathan Stone. Died, in Newfane, November 14, 1865, aged ninety-six years.

Lucinda, born August 8, 1771. Married Samuel Willard. Died in Canada, in 1800.

Luke, born in Newfane, March 24, 1775. Married Charlotte Kenney, March 18, 1799. She died in Canada, in February, 1843. He also died in Canada, in 1855, aged eighty years.

THE MORSES OF NEWFANE.

The Morses of Newfane, though of two distinct branches, have a common origin in Joseph Morse, who was born in England, in 1615, emigrated to New England with his father, Samuel Morse, in 1635; first settled at Watertown, Mass., and afterward resided at Dedham and Medfield. The more numerous and earlier settled branch, more immediately descended from Rev. Dr. Ebenezer Morse, of Boylston, Mass., a graduate of Harvard College, a skillful physician and an eminent preacher. Dr. Morse early came into possession of a large tract of land in the southwestern part of the newly chartered township of Newfane, whither his sons, John, Joshua, Ebenezer and Amherst, came to settle.

Dr. John, the oldest son of Rev. Ebenezer and Persis (Bush) Morse, was born July 15, 1746. Married Elizabeth Andrews, of Boylston, May 11, 1769. Removed to Newfane, and settled on the farm now owned and occupied by Elwin Ingram, in the parish, in June, 1774; his family being the twentieth which settled in town. On the night of their arrival they stopped at Luke Knowlton's, on Newfane Hill, and the next day, guided by marked trees, walked to their rude log house which had been constructed by Dr. Morse, during his visit to Newfane the previous autumn. Dr. Morse, or "Dr. John," as he was more familiarly called, was the first physician in town, and for many years the only one. He was poorly paid for his labors, often receiving no remuneration, yet, prompted by his kindness of heart, he allowed no call to go unheeded, whether of the rich or of the poor. His services were therefore of inestimable value to a community largely made up, as was the one in which he lived, of persons possessing but little wealth. He died April 7, 1822, on the farm which he cleared, and on which he had lived for nearly half a century.

Elizabeth, daughter of Dr. John and Elizabeth Morse, was born March 2, 1770. Married Ichabod Merrifield, December, 1793. Died December 6, 1844. Had nine children, viz.:

Lucinda, born September 5, 1794. Married Levi Buel, of Fort Plain, N. Y. Died 1872.

Mary, born September 12, 1796. Married Ephraim Hall, of Newfane. Died September 12, 1849.

John A., born May 9, 1799. Died July 31, 1801.

Elizabeth, born March 3, 1801.

Sarah, born March 19, 1803. Died April 4, 1816.

John A., born October 27, 1808. Married Louisa Williams, January 14, 1842; is a farmer and resides in school district No. 6.

Aaron R., born October 14, 1810. Married, first, Harriet N. Mather; second, Rachel M. Cox. Died at Vicksburg, Miss., September 22, 1851.

Anna, born May 7, 1814. Married, May 13, 1835, Geo. W. Lamb, who is a farmer and resides in school district No. 5.

Fanny, born May 31, 1815. Married John W. Hill. Died, at Chicopee, Mass., July 11, 1858.

John, second child of Dr. John and Elizabeth Morse, was born January 15, 1773. Married Susanna Osgood; settled on what is now known as Timson Hill. Died June 19, 1850. Had eight children, viz.:

Eliakim, born November 3, 1799. Married Roxa Briggs, of Dover; resides at Troy, N. Y.

Charlotte, married Wm. Hall, of Newfane.

Adeline, Calvin and John, residences in Pennsylvania.

Susan, married Lorenzo Estabrooks; resides at Dover.

Mary, married Jonathan P. Hall; resides at Rochester, N. Y.

Sidney, married Janette Rand; was well known as a livery stable keeper, at Brattleboro, at which place he died, May 3, 1869.

Ebenezer, third child of Dr. John and Elizabeth Morse, was born July 14, 1775. Married Sally Goodnow; resided on the farm now owned and occupied by Dea. Joseph Morse, in district No. 8; was a justice of the peace for many years, and died March 29, 1846. Ebenezer and Sally Morse had eleven children, viz.:

Lawson B., born February 4, 1805. Married, first, Elizabeth Gates; second, Mary Ingram. Died, at Philadelphia, January 1, 1870.

John, died young.

Eliza A., born November 11, 1810. Married Dea. Joseph Morse, May 21, 1833. Died February 5, 1868.

Mary F., born February 18, 1815. Married Joseph Dexter; resides at Philadelphia; summer residence at Pondville.

John, died young.

Benjamin E., born December 23, 1816. Married Mary Ann, daughter of Rev. Phineas Howe, April 2, 1840. Is a farmer, and now resides at Pondville. Has been a justice of the peace, or notary public for many years, and has had considerable practice as an attorney in minor courts of law.

Sarah G., born January 31, 1819. Married Russell Mason, January 31, 1854, who is a farmer and resides at Pondville.

Ebenezer, born November 3, 1820. Married, first, Clara Pendleton; second, Lavina L. Warren, and resides at Springfield, Mass.

Ashley W., born August 31, 1822. Married Aurelia Lawton. Died at Dummerston, September 24, 1875.

Charles F., born September 1, 1824. Died in California, February 16, 1854.

Amelia, died young.

Jonathan, fourth child of Dr. John and Elizabeth Morse. was born January 9, 1778. Married Polly Bailey. Resided for many years with his father, but died, June 14, 1838, on the "Lamb Place," so called, now owned and occupied by Emory Dunklee.

George A., son of Jonathan and Polly Morse, was born January 13, 1807. Married Mary P. Merrifield, October 1828; second, Martha Wood, April 8, 1832, and now resides in Philadelphia, where he has been engaged in the baking business. His earlier years were mostly spent as a farmer in the parish, living with his parents the latter part of his father's lifetime, and afterward erecting the buildings on the place where Loima Lamson now lives. He was a distinguished musician, and highly popular as a teacher of singing schools in this and neighboring towns.

Mary, fifth child of Dr. John and Elizabeth Morse, was born September 10, 1782. Married Simon Fisher, of Newfane, and died July 27, 1813. Simon and Mary Fisher had five children, viz.:

Daniel, born August 27, 1805. Married in Maryland, and was killed by the cars.

Mary, born April 25, 1807. Married Pardon T. Kimball, December 9, 1824, now resides at Dubuque, Ia., with her son Nelson.

Simon and Sophia P., died young.

Martha Ann, born April 7, 1812. Married —— Hough, and resides at Lebanon, N. H.

Thomas Andrews, sixth child of Dr. John and Elizabeth Morse, was born March 13, 1786. Married Lucinda Wood, lived, the latter part of his years, and died, July 29, 1840, upon the farm which his father settled. He is said to have been a man of great industry and strict integrity. Thomas A. and Lucinda Morse had six children, viz.:

Caroline, born November 28, 1810. Married Welcome Allen, December 11, 1834. Died Febuary 1, 1843.

Elizabeth A., born June 16, 1812. Married Austin J. Morse, April 9, 1835. Died July 20, 1846.

Frederick J., born October 23, 1814. Married H. A. Adams, October 13, 1840; is a lumber dealer, and resides at Williamsville.

Franklin B., born September 20, 1817. Married Mary Warner. He is a farmer and resides in the parish.

Ann W., born June 8, 1822. Married Laban Dexter, and resides at Springfield, Mass.

Andrews T., born October 17, 1824. Married, first, Emily A. Houghton; second, Sarah (Kelsey) Burt, and resides at Springfield, Mass.

Joshua, son of Rev. Ebenezer and Persis Morse, was born March 8, 1752, married Lavina Holland, of Boylston, a sister of the wife of Hon. Luke Knowlton, came to Newfane with Judge Knowlton, in 1773, first settled on the farm now owned and occupied by Welcome Allen, in the parish; removed to the "Dr. Olds Place," on Newfane Hill, and subsequently to the farm now owned by Sabin Morse, where he died October 1, 1828. Joshua and Lavina Morse had eleven children, viz.:

Tabitha, born September 8, 1773. Died, unmarried, in 1817.

Amherst, born April 25, 1776. Married Abigail Holden, February 11, 1800. Settled on the farm now owned and occupied by Marshall Houghton, in district No. 8, and afterward removed to his father's farm on Newfane hill, where he continued to reside until his death, July 20, 1842. Amherst and Abigail Morse had four children, viz.:

Maria, born May 4, 1804. Married Nathaniel Cheney, of Wardsboro, October 27, 1825; now resides at Brattleboro.

Abigail H., born May 20, 1807. Married Huntington Fitch, April 23, 1832; now resides at Columbus, Ohio.

Austin J., born November 11, 1812. Married, first, Elizabeth A. Morse, April 9, 1835; second, Catherine Miller, March 18, 1847. Resided many years on Newfane Hill and at Fayetteville; has been an extensive farmer and cattle drover, represented the town in the State Legislature in 1863 and '64, and in the Constitutional Convention for 1870, and now resides at Worcester, Mass.

Sabin P., born March 15, 1817. Married Sarah C. Fitts, September 12, 1839, lived on for many years, and now owns, the farm on Newfane Hill, on which his father and grandfather lived and died, but now occupies the residence erected by Gen. Martin Field, at Fayetteville.

Ephraim, third child of Joshua and Lavina Morse, was born May 23, 1778. Married, first, Polly Cook; second, Sally (Keyes) Lamb. Settled on the farm now occupied by Geo. W. Knapp, on Timson hill, but afterward removed to the farm now owned by A. B. Hazelton, in district No. 8, where he died March 24, 1865. Ephraim and Polly Morse had six children, viz.:

William H., born September 25, 1804. Married Mary Hall, April 30, 1828; is a farmer and resides in district No. 8.

Sewall, born January 6, 1809. Married, first, Sarah A. Houghton; second, Electa Stevens. Is a mechanic and resides at Brattleboro.

Amherst, born January 16, 1811. Died December, 1813.

Ephraim, born June 25, 1812. Married Mary Ann Winchester, February 11, 1840; is a farmer and now resides at Williamsville.

Nelson, born August 22, 1814. Married Electa (Keyes) Fletcher, April 16, 1845; is a farmer and resides at Williamsville.

Thomas Parker, born November 29, 1817. Married, first, Martha (Kelsey) Ingram; second, Mary (Alden) Adams; third, Mary Lane. Is a farmer, and now resides at Dummerston.

Joseph, fourth child of Joshua and Lavina Morse, was born September 16, 1780. Died January 26, 1792.

Luke Knowlton, fifth child of the same, was born February 6, 1783. Married, first, Elizabeth Cook, February 29, 1808; second, Clara Cook (now Mrs. Newman Allen, of Fayetteville), May 6, 1824. Lived, and died September 21, 1830, on the farm now owned and occupied by his son, O. P. Morse. Luke K. and Elizabeth Morse had three children, viz.:

Lewis C., born November 19, 1809. Died February 21, 1827.

Oliver Plimpton, born March 4, 1816. Married Lydia L. Stratton, January 1, 1838. Represented the town in the General Assembly of 1845; is a farmer and resides in school district No. 6.

Elizabeth, born October 10, 1820. Died February 22, 1824.

Luke K. and Clara Morse had Jonas C., born February 7, 1825. Died March 17, 1825.

Persis, sixth child of Joshua and Lavina Morse was born January 17, 1785. Died July 9, 1809.

Eunice, seventh child of the same, was born March 28, 1787. Died July 19, 1789.

Eunice, eighth child of the same, was born August 30, 1789. Married Jonathan Adams, of Wardsboro. Died October 15, 1826. Jonathan and Eunice Adams had three children, viz.:

Julia, born December 27, 1818. Married, March 10, 1842, Orwell Stratton, who is a farmer and resides in district No. 8.

Oliver C., born August 8, 1821. Married Aurilla Jackson, April 18, 1844; is a merchant and resides at Shushan, N. Y.

Marcia, born May 16, 1824. Died February, 1847.

Windsor, ninth child of Joshua and Lavina Morse, was born January 9, 1793. Married Arletta Pratt, October 20, 1818; settled about a mile south of Williamsville, on the road leading to Dummerston Hill, where he lived for more than half a century, but moved, in his old age, with his son Charles, to the Pratt farm, in district No. 5, where he died August 31, 1875. Windsor and Arletta Morse had three children, viz.:

Lavina H., born December 31, 1822. Married Joel K. Dickinson, February 16, 1841; now resides at Williamsville.

Hannah Louisa, born January 1, 1829. Died September 6, 1845.

Charles W., born May 25, 1834. Married Jenette F. Brown, November 7, 1865.

Sewall, tenth child of Joshua and Lavina Morse was born April 12, 1795. Died September 3, 1795.

Betsey, eleventh child of the same, was born August 24, 1796. Married Calvin Davis, May 5, 1818. Resided on the place now owned and occupied by L. J. Timson, in district No. 6, and died November 6, 1862. Calvin and Betsey Davis had seven children, viz.:

Rhoda, born October 24, 1819. Married Samuel Hall, May 20, 1835; now resides at Baraboo. Wis.

Alexander H., born November 16, 1821. Married Sylvia Timson, June 10, 1847; now resides at Brattleboro.

Mary B., born February 22, 1825. Married John S. Dutton; resides at Jaffrey. N. H.

Sarah E., born May 7, 1827. Married Leonard J. Timson, August 13, 1846.

Franklin C., born February 5, 1829. Married Mary Ann Downs; now resides at Brattleboro.

Henry H., born March 12, 1833. Married Sarah E. Journay: resides at Brooklyn, L. I.

Ann C., born March 22, 1836. Married Charles Howard; resides at Townshend.

Ebenezer, son of Rev. Dr. Ebenezer and Persis Morse. was born July 10, 1755; married, September 22, 1782, Henrietta Siverly, of New York. a highly accomplished and cultivated lady. and soon afterward removed to Nova Scotia. About the year 1788 he came to Newfane, at the urgent solicitations of his brothers and other citizens of the town, for the purpose of building a gristmill. Selecting for his farm the site of the present village of Williamsville. and the hillside north of it, then a forest, he erected a house on the ground on which the hotel now stands. and built, soon afterward. near the site of the present mill, the first gristmill in the southern part of the town, of which we have any knowledge. He was a good mechanic, worked at his trade, in connection with tending the mill, for many years, and 'died June 30, 1813. Ebenezer and Henrietta Morse had twelve children, viz.:

Abraham, born July 26, 1784. Died young.

Priscilla, born November 15, 1786. Died 1801.

Mary M., born July 28, 1791. Married David Reed, who kept the first hotel at Williamsville. Died April 24, 1826. David and Mary Reed had six children, viz.: Ransford, Charles E., Henrietta M., William N., Martha A., and Lucius E.

Ann D., daughter of Ebenezer and Henrietta Morse, was born October 13, 1793. Married Denzil, son of Rev. Hezekiah Taylor. Carried on the millinery and dress-making business at Williamsville for many years, supported and educated her children, and died September 6, 1858. Denzil and Ann D. Taylor had four children, viz.:

Horace B., born August 25, 1815. Married Abby E. Bryant, July 2, 1844; resides at Boston, where he has accumulated a large fortune in the foreign commission business.

George W., born December 15, 1819. Married Leonice F. Kilton, January 29, 1842; was merchant and postmaster at Jonesboro, Maine, for twenty-two years, and is now a foreign commission merchant at Boston.

Harriet A. E., married Wm. S. Jones and succeeded her mother in the millinery business at Williamsville. W. S. and H. A. Jones had Alfred H., born December, 1852. Entered Harvard College in 1872. Died August 10, 1873. Was a young man of fine natural talent, and took high rank as a scholar.

Henry R. Taylor, born May 31, 1829. Married, first, Amelia Longfellow; second, Laura Smith; is a jeweller, and resides at Machias, Maine.

Harriet S., daughter of Ebenezer and Henrietta Morse, was born November 26, 1797. Married Jonathan M. Dexter, a merchant of Boston. Died in 1841. J. M. and Harriet S. Dexter had seven children, viz.:

Samuel, Frances, Augustus, George, Harriet, Montgomery and Helen. Frances married James P. Tolman and resides at Philadelphia.

Sarah K., daughter of Ebenezer and Henrietta Morse, was born February 22, 1799. Married, first, Chas. K. Gayety; second, —— Oliver, resided in Pennsylvania and Ohio. Died July, 1870.

John G., son of Ebenezer and Henrietta Morse, was born June 23, 1801. Died 1837.

Robert McNeil, son of the same, was born January 8, 1807. Married Sarah M. Clark; is a merchant residing in Boston, and has four children, viz.:
Robert McN., Jr., an eminent Boston lawyer; Charles F., Ellen C., and Mary.

Emily F., daughter of E. and H. Morse, was born July, 1812. Married, first, Alpheus Atherton; second, Samuel Tolman. Died at Watertown, Mass.

Amherst, youngest son of Rev. Ebenezer and Persis Morse, was born November 11, 1760. Married Widow Fisk, mother of Miss Catherine Fisk, the celebrated teacher, resided in Nova Scotia and afterward came to Newfane and settled on the farm now owned and occupied by George Briggs, in district No. 10. Had no children.

Rev. Dr. Ebenezer Morse, while on a visit to Newfane, in 1773, or the early part of 1774, preached from a rock on the premises now occupied by Welcome Allen, the first sermon ever preached in town. In the course of the sermon he used this expression. " The people of this parish " must do so and so. From this circumstance that section of the town has since been called " The Parish."

Jacob Morse, of whom the second branch of Newfane Morses are descendants, son of Joshua and Mary Morse, of Medfield, Mass., was born December 24, 1745. Married, first, Mary Kingsbury; second, Mary Hawes. Came to Newfane from Princeton, Mass., in 1787, settled on the farm now owned and occupied by his grandson, Samuel Morse, in the parish district, and died April 14, 1818. Had nine children, viz:

Catherine, born March 18, 1773. Married William King; resided near the brickyard, opposite Lamson's mills, and died November, 1858. William and Catherine King had four children, viz.:

Lydia, born November 8, 1803. Married Joel Redfield, died at Woodford. September 1, 1841.

William, born July 25, 1807. Married Emily Duncan.

Louisa, born February 10, 1813. Married, first, John Knapp, of Woodford; second, Elnathan Houghton; resides in district No. 8.

Ezra, born September 11, 1820. Married, first, Hannah Bellows; second, Jane O. Benson; resides in district No. 8.

Joshua, second child of Jacob Morse, was born November 20, 1774. Married Sally Phillips, August 12, 1798, resided on the farm which his father settled, and died September 12, 1859. He was a man of many good qualities. Was kind and generous to the poor, and liberal in his contributions to public charities. He built, almost wholly unaided, the first meeting house of the Pondville Baptist Society. That he enjoyed the confidence of his fellow townsmen is attested by the fact that for many years he was constantly called to their service, very often in the capacity of selectman. Joshua and Sally Morse had twelve children, viz.:

Electa, born April 25, 1800. Died November 8, 1800.

Joshua, born September 3, 1801. Married, first, Eunice Kelsey; second, Rheuhama Pierce; is a carpenter and resides in district No. 6.

Willard, born July 23, 1803. Married, first, Polly Goodnow; second, Almira Keyes. Died June, 1838.

Joseph, born June 24, 1805. Married, first, Eliza Morse, May 21, 1833; second, Dolly R. Stratton; is a farmer and resides in district No. 8. Has been a deacon of the Baptist Church for many years.

David, born June 28, 1807. Died in 1811.

Polly, born July 22, 1809. Married Asa Stratton, who is a farmer and resides in district No. 11.

David, born September 19, 1811. Married, first, Louisa Bellows; second, Mary Williams. Died April 10, 1876, at Springfield, Mass.

John, born November 24, 1814. Married Priscilla Ward. Died November 3, 1853.

Sally, born January 9, 1817. Married Harvey G. Whitaker. Died, at Brattleboro, January 29, 1868.

Nathan C., born July 2, 1818. Married Mary Z. Withers; resides at Covington, Ky. Has been somewhat celebrated as a teacher of music, but is now an extensive dealer in and a large owner of real estate.

Samuel, born October 13, 1820. Married Georgiana Goodnow, November 12, 1846. Now owns and occupies the farm which his grandfather settled, and which is the only one in town, with the exception of the Stedman farm at Fayetteville, that has been retained in constant possession of the family by whom it was settled.

Elijah, born January 23, 1823. Married Mary E. Charter, and resides in California.

Unity, third child of Jacob Morse was born February 3, 1777. Died young.

Polly, fourth child of the same, was born December 26, 1778. Married Levi Knowlton of Stukeley, P. Q. Died March 28, 1803.

Sally, fifth child of the same, was born November 15, 1780. Died young.

Joseph, sixth child of the same, was born April 5, 1783. Died young.

James, seventh child of the same, was born March 18, 1785. Married, first, Hannah Bailey; second, Sarah B. Yeaw; third, Eldice Simpson; resided in district No. 11, and afterward at Gouverneur, N. Y. Had thirteen children, viz.:

Julia Ann, born October 9, 1808. Died January 20, 1811.

Horace D., born December 7, 1809. Married, first, Elizabeth Goodell; second, Almira Drake.

Elliot, born March 17, 1812.

Appleton George, born September 17 1813. Married ——— Spaulding; resides at Ellsworth, Ohio.

Chesselden, born October 4, 1815. Married Dolly Ann Ingram.

James, born July 11, 1817. Died October 20, 1821.

Samuel, born April 6, 1819.

Royal, born October 26, 1820.

Lectana, born November 6, 1821. Married Silas Gates, of Marlboro, now of Minnesota.

Polly, born October 13, 1823. Married ―― Spaulding; resides at Ellsworth, Ohio.

Hannah, born October 26, 1825. Married and resides at Cincinnati, Ohio.

Sarah, born March 20, 1831.

James, born November 8, 1832.

Jacob, eighth child of Jacob Morse, was born January 22, 1787. Married Adah Brown; lived on the place occupied by his son, Emerson Morse, in district No. 8. Died September 12, 1838. Jacob and Adah Morse had ten children, viz.:

Emerson, born December 24, 1810. Married Mary Bellows. Died January 11, 1876.

Sally, born May 1, 1812. Died August 6, 1817.

Melinda B., born September 18, 1815. Married Rev. Geo. W. Brewster. Died ―― ―― ――.

Catherine, born January 22, 1818. Married Mason Ingram, December 4, 1845. Died February 28, 1867.

Cynthia, born November 9, 1820. Married Cyrus Hill. Died April 15, 1852.

Sarah S., born March 22, 1823. Married John Howe, April, 1847; resides at Boston.

Hannah P., born July 22, 1825. Married Wm. S. Baker, May, 1844; resides at Boston.

Abby M., born February 5, 1827. Married John Buck, July, 1848; resides at Bucksfield, Maine.

Mary E., born July 18, 1830. Married Lorenzo W. Childs, April, 1847; resides in Iowa.

Albert Mc., born April 22, 1836; resides in Nebraska.

Hannah, ninth child of Jacob Morse, was born December 6, 1789. Married Nathan Phillips. Died May 9, 1840. Nathan and Hannah Phillips had six children, viz.:

Bathsheba H., born March 1, 1811. Married Rev. Denzil M. Crane, formerly of Brookline.

Sidney, born August 23, 1813. Married Abigail Atwood: resides at Boston.

Adin, born February 6, 1816. Married Rebecca Sanborn.

Aurelia, born January 11, 1818. Married Warren Lazell. October 29, 1839; resides at Dover.

Nathan O., born October 20, 1822.

Mary H., born March 6, 1827. Married Edwin F. Sherman, of Dover, September 23, 1846. Died March 11. 1848.

The name of Morse is less common in Newfane to-day than it was forty years ago. It does not follow, however, that the race is running out. Many have gone forth into other towns and states. The family name has been largely merged in others. And four of the five men mentioned in this article as original settlers of the town, and somewhat prominent in its early history, were represented, at the date of its first centennial, by fully five hundred living descendants.

PARK FAMILY.

Dea. Jonathan Park, born in Milbury, Mass., September 22, 1743. Died July 18, 1827.

Elizabeth Fletcher, his wife, born January 14. 1750. Died February 14, 1787.

Sarah Scott, his second wife, born June 29, 1751. Died May 11, 1789.

Mariam Fiske, his third wife, born in 1758. Died March 26, 1841.

Children of Jonathan Park and his wives.

1. Elizabeth Park, born February 20, 1768. Died September 26, 1773.

2. Lucy Park, born August 20, 1769. Died September 18, 1773.

3. Jonathan Park, born June 17, 1771. Married Caroline Locklin, March 14, 1799. Died at Lyndon, June 17, 1829.

4. David Park, born November 27, 1772. Died September 30, 1773.

5. Submit Park, born October 26, 1774. Married Thurstin Holman, February 19, 1801. Date of death unknown.

6. Samuel Park, born October 6, 1776. Married Rachel Chase, January 27, 1802. Died September 17, 1863.

7. Lydia Park, born July 12, 1778. Married Thomas Downs, November 19, 1798. Died May 5, 1857.

8. Ephraim Park, born March 29, 1780. Married Hannah Whitcomb, September 20, 1802. Died February 6, 1861.

9. Rhoda Park, born February 18, 1782. Married Thomas Cook, February 21, 1802. Died March 1, 1873.

10. Moses Park, born August 17, 1788. Died February 29, 1796.

11. Nathan F. Park, born June 1, 1794. Married Almena Bennet, October 29, 1818. Died March 18, 1860.

12. Sarah Park, born February 26, 1796. Married Jasper Stone, March 16, 1817. Still living, aged 81.

13. Miriam Park, born July 27, 1797. Married Thomas Sherwin, March 8, 1818. Died November 1, 1850.

STEDMAN FAMILY.

Nathaniel Stedman, born April 18, 1746. Died October 16, 1812.

Ruth Stedman, born April 3, 1750. Died December 22, 1843.

Children of Nathaniel and Ruth Stedman:

1. Billey Stedman, born July 5, 1773. Died September 14, 1777.

2. Betty Stedman, born November 14, 1774. Died September 10, 1777.
3. Mary Stedman, born September 15, 1776. Died September 20, 1777.
4. William Stedman, born March 26, 1778. Died December 27, 1864.
5. Lucinda Stedman, born March 12, 1780.
6. Luritta Stedman, born November 19, 1781. Died October 9, 1817.
7. Huldah Stedman, born October 10, 1783. Died 1860.
8. Betty Stedman, born March 10, 1785.
9. Mary Stedman, born August 13, 1788. Died 1860.
10. Ruth Stedman, born March 26, 1790.
11. Sarah Stedman, born February 7, 1792. Still living.

DANIEL TAYLOR'S FAMILY.

Daniel Taylor, Jr., was born at Concord, Mass., in 1767. Married Elizabeth Wheeler, of Newfane. They had twelve children, four of whom died young.

Nathan Bigelow, born in 1786. Married Hannah Bixby, of Dummerston, and settled in Newport, N. H.

Elizabeth, born in 1788. Married Roswell Elmer, of Claremont, N. H.

Arad, born in 1796. Married Hannah L. Robinson, of Newfane, settled in Claremont, N. H.

Daniel, born in 1798. Married first, Mary Ann Ainsworth, of Claremont, N. H. Second, Lucia Chase, of Weathersfield, Vt. Settled in Waterloo, Que.

Luke, born in 1800. Married Nancy Newman, of Newfane. Settled in Newfane, but afterwards removed with his family to Shefford, Que.

Luther, born in 1802. Married Louisa Rice, of Winchester, N. H. Settled in Boston, Mass.

Mary, born in 1804. Married, first, Dan Bailey, of Brattleboro. Second, Wright Porter, of Hartford, Vt.

Laura, born in 1807. Married Charles Allen, of Chester, Vt. Settled in Waterloo, Que.

Daniel Taylor and Charles Allen went to Waterloo, Que., with Hezekiah Robinson, or shortly after, and entered into co-partnership, under the firm name of Allen & Taylor, Iron Founders and Merchants. The firm is still in existence under the same name, the business being conducted by the sons of the original partners.

HEZEKIAH TAYLOR'S FAMILY.

Parson Taylor was born on Wednesday, November 28, 1748. Died August 23, 1814.

His wife, whose maiden name was Sarah Frost, was born May 24, 1751. Died March 3, 1840.

They were married March 31, 1774.

May 20, 1775, their first child, a son, Hollis, was born, who died at Rotterdam, in Holland, August 14, 1793.

The second child, Simon, was born January 25, 1778. Died July 23, 1818.

The third, Pardon, was born May 28, 1780, and was drowned in the Connecticut river, at Brattleboro, July 2, 1797, the day upon which the late well-known Gen. Kimball was born, and it was this sad ending of a young life, on the day his began, that gave him the name of Pardon Taylor Kimball.

The fourth son, Frost, was born December 4, 1781. Died September 23, 1802.

The fifth, Sally, born November 3, 1783. Married Moses Sabin, April 24, 1814. Died October 25, 1819.

The sixth, Patty, born November 2, 1785. Married Josiah L. Holden, November 2, 1806. Died May 10, 1825.

The seventh, Denzil, born January 21, 1787. Died May 13, 1868.

We extract the following from Mr. Taylor's private church notes:

He baptized 446 children, the first of whom was John Farrar, son of Phineas Farrar, July 10, 1774.

Attended 328 funerals, the first of which was an infant son of Moses Kenney, November 22, 1774.

Married 111 couples, the first of whom was Joseph Gleason and Sarah Ball, July 1, 1774.

March 12, 1775, Nathaniel Stedman and his wife united with the church, the first after its organization.

Fourteen were admitted to the church during the year 1775.

From November 22, 1774, to July 2, 1778, he has recorded the deaths of twenty-four children under fifteen years of age.

A FUNERAL SERMON

PREACHED AT NEWFANE;

OCCASIONED BY THE DEATH OF MR. HENRY SAWTELL, HIS WIFE AND FIVE CHILDREN, WHO WERE ALL CONSUMED BY THE FLAMES OF HIS HOUSE, WHICH TOOK FIRE ON THE OF 2D FEBRUARY, 1782.

BY THE LATE

REV. HEZEKIAH TAYLOR,

FORMERLY PASTOR OF THE CHURCH IN THAT PLACE.

St. Luke, Chap. XIII—part of the 2d, 3d, 4th, and 5th verses.

"Suppose ye that these Galileans were sinners above all the Galileans, because they suffered such things?—I tell you, Nay; but except ye repent, ye shall all likewise perish. Or those eighteen upon whom the Tower in Siloam fell, and slew them; think ye that they were sinners above all the men that dwelt in Jerusalem?—I tell you, Nay; but except ye repent, ye shall all likewise perish."

These words of our blessed Saviour, which by divine leave have now been read, and are designed for the subject of our present meditation, need no other introduction than the melancholy occasion, and the sorrowful dispensation of God's holy and righteous providence, in taking suddenly away a whole family from our neighborhood and parish; both parents and children all perishing together, whose remains are reduced to the contents only of that coffin!

The circumstances and manner of their deaths is an exhibition of a most tragical scene! such an afflicting instance as cannot, perhaps, be found, except among God's special providences; and our blessed Saviour teaches us in the text what improvement we are to make of such disasters, both negatively and positively.

1. Negatively, he forbids our imputing the awaking judgments, which befall some of the children of men, and the awful end some are brought to, and carried out of the world by, to the effects of God's wrath, or our supposing those who suffer by such things to be the special objects of the divine indignation.

It is the case of some to draw such false conclusions from such awful providences, as did those who discoursed with our Saviour, as is mentioned in the context, respecting those poor mortals, whose lot it was to fall victims to Pilate's rage, and cruelly have their blood mingled with their sacrifices; and also those unfortunate ones who were crushed to death by the fall of a tower. But Christ, by his answer to them in the text, forbids their entertaining such uncharitable thoughts as these, and expressly tells them, that their being brought to such an awful, untimely end, was not because they were greater sinners than others that lived around them. So neither are we to suppose, that this unhappy family, that we are now called to mourn the loss of, were destroyed thus suddenly in this sorrowful manner, because they had provoked God more than we had; or that he was more displeased with them, and hereby intended to make manifest to us his anger and indignation towards them. No, it may be we are more deserving his wrath and displeasure, and have more highly and aggravatedly sinned against him.

Let us be deeply impressed with humiliation and due penitence to almightly God, for we behold here in his severity and goodness—severity towards them and goodness towards us, that we are yet the objects of his sparing mercy, and forbearing goodness; and "despise not the riches thereof, and his long suffering; otherwise thou also shalt be cut off." [See Romans xi.: 22.]

The manner of one's death is no proof of his being a good or a bad man. But we are all born to die! The decree has gone forth, and it is unavoidable by the righteous and the wicked. Death is entailed to us by the fall of our first parents. By one man sin entered into the world, and death also came by sin, for all men have sinned.

The manner and circumstances of our deaths depends upon God's sovereign will and pleasure. There are many ways in which God is pleased to take us out of the world, and there is no difference nor distinction made of the good or bad; it is the certain fate of both. The manner is no ways essential, and does not effect the future state of the soul. Some of the brightest saints have died the most cruel and tormenting deaths. Our Saviour died upon the cruel cross! Many of his faithful followers have patiently and courageously ended their lives in the pains and agonies of the flames! Outward circumstances in life, nor at death, are any certain tokens of the divine special favour, or displeasure of almighty God. "No one," the wise man tells us, "knows love or hate by these things;" as is the good, so is the bad in this respect. The same befalleth them both; as dieth the one so dieth the other. The saint hath no preference above the sinner, as to the circumstance or temporal part of his death.

As our text forbids our condemning what befalls, or the manner of one's death; so also it forbids condemning any persons, on account of their unfortunate vicissitudes in life. Some are so censorious as to impute the hard fortunes and frowns which many meet with, to their being more wicked, and greater sinners. Thus Job's friends, or pretended comforters, disputed his innocence and uprightness, upon the account of his sore trial, and condemned him as being only an hypocrite: for who, said they, ever perished and suffered such things, being innocent; and who but the wicked were thus afflicted? and ask Job to which of the saints he would turn for an instance of the like calamity that he was visited with; as though the wicked only suffered thus. "Though I have seen," says Eliphaz, "the foolish taking root, yet I suddenly crossed his habitation, for his children are far from safety, and they are crushed in the gate, and there is none to deliver them." But Job tells us that he had seen the reverse; both the righteous suffer and the wicked flourish and prosper. He had seen these live to be old, and become mighty in power. "Their houses," saith he, "are safe from fear, neither is the rod of God upon them. Their children dance, take the timbrel and harp, and rejoice at the sound of the organ, they spent their days in mirth, and at last die an easy death, in a moment go down to the grave." [See Job, chap. xxi.]

Let us not, therefore, entertain the thought, that these our deceased neighbors were greater sinners than we, on account of what they have met with in the dealings of God's providence towards them in life or in death; in their being all cut off together, and suffering, as we may suppose, in the greatest agony of body. But in the positive sense of our text, let us improve this sad disaster, this awakening, affecting dispensation as our blessed Lord teaches us to our own repentance; for, "except ye repent," saith he, "ye shall all likewise perish."

Our Saviour is not to be understood in a literal sense altogether, that they would perish in the same manner, either by being made a sacrifice, or by the fall of a building; but hereby taught them their exposedness, and that they were liable to meet with the like disaster; they might be taken out of the world as suddenly, and with as little warning. That they were not so specially interested in God's love and mercy as that they had reason to expect any more favor in this regard than the other; and the same also we are taught, and are loudly called upon hereby to repentance. This important duty is presented to you, my hearers! From this providence, and the motive to excite you hereunto is greater than that which is body temporal; it is greater than that you may escape a sudden and sorrowful death; it is greater than that you may escape being consumed in your houses, burnt alive in the flames of an earthly fire; but that you may escape the flames of that "fire that never shall be quenched. Where the worm dieth not, and the fire is not quenched."

Let us realize and consider how we are exposed every day and every hour to be called for, to be called off this state of trial and probation, and to appear before God our Judge; for we know not what hour our Lord will come, whether at the second or third watch, whether at eve or midnight.

When we reflect on the frailty and uncertainty of life, of what vast importance and concern does it appear to us, to be ready, to be always ready and prepared for death, and not to have the whole and great work of our souls undone, and all to do, at the last moment. O, how great is the danger, and how very hazardous it is to live one day in sin, and in a state of impenitency: without God, without a reconciled God, while our peace is not made with him; while we have no Saviour, no saving interest in Christ. How dangerous I say to live one day in a state of sinful nature! How dangerous to go out or come in, to lie down or rise up. How awful is the state of such, that are instantly called out of the world. And what a poor time it is also to prepare for eternity upon a death-bed; or when we have but a few moments warning. These our deceased friends, it is probable, had a short space allowed them to cry unto God for mercy in: inasmuch as it appears evident from the places where their remains lay, that they awoke and arose out of bed, and fled to that part of the house most distant from where the fire then raged. But if it was their unhappiness to have misimproved their former opportunities of the day and seasons of grace, what a poor time was that for them to prepare for eternity in; for any in such deplorable circumstances, being encompassed about with the flames of fire and smoke!

Such was the unfortunate construction of the building in which they lived, it seems they had no chance of escaping. No one escaped to relate the mournful tale, no one to describe the agonizing groans of parents, and the doleful cries of children for help! or how long they remained in agony before death closed the scene! They have " gone to that bourne from whence no traveler returns." And how it is with them now is not for us to determine; but we may rely upon this, that they have gone to a just God, that will do them no wrong.

If they died in Christ, their bodies, though reduced to a few sad remains, will be raised in incorruption and immortality.

In the times of the persecutions of the Christians, when many laid down their lives as faithful witnesses for Jesus, the persecutors undertook to gather up the ashes of the saints that were burnt, and strew them in the air, that they might be all dispersed by the wind, in order to prove the impossibility of the truth of their doctrines, that their bodies would be raised again. But God our maker is able by his almighty power, to re-animate and raise these bodies in their former shape.

Without being particular in portraying the lives of the heads of the deceased family, in justice to their memory it may be observed of him, that he was a good neighbor, a kind, obliging man, uniformly disposed to live in peace, ever ready to afford relief and assistance to the needy and distressed, to the utmost of his ability, honest in his dealings, and punctual in the perfomances of his promises and engagements.* She, the wife of Mr. Sawtell, seemed to be a well-disposed woman, to have a regard for religion, for God's house and worship; and considering their situation and circumstances, it appeared they both did not willingly forsake the assembling themselves with us in the adoration of God, and in the solicitation of his needed mercies: and have pretty constantly attended through this inclement winter season. It was but lately they were here present, joining with us in the public worship of almighty God, and little thought, perhaps, that they and their little ones should be so soon in eternity; and be brought here in this deplorable situation, exhibiting an awful pile of the relics of mortality!

These bodies, though dead, and nearly consumed, seemingly speak to us, and are calling upon us by a voice not to be equalled by any human living tongue, and plead with us the great necessity it is, to be ready one and all of us, old and young. These remains teach us the frailties of our nature, and the uncertainty of our lives, and the importance of our being prepared for a dying hour, and for the eternal world: and also our wisely improving our present time, and not to put far away the evil day; "for in a thoughtless hour, our final and fatal summons may arrive," to appear before that tribunal, from whence there is no appeal.

*" An honest man 's the noblest work of God."

These our poor friends and neighbors, who were so recently alive, and in good health, are gone to be here no more. However like a dream it may to any seem, yet they have enough left for testimony, and to prove it to a demonstration. They have done forever with the things of this world; no more to be worried and perplexed with the cares thereof. No more to be found in a state of trial and probation. They have had their day and seed-time for repentance, and the means and necessaries of grace. They are now in that state where there is no obtaining the divine pardon of one sin, for

> "There is no act of pardon passed
> In the cold grave to which we haste;
> But darkness, death, and long despair
> Reign in eternal silence there."

Jesus our mediator has taught us to "love our neighbor as ourself." In this sorrowful loss of one of our neighbors, how deeply ought we to be impressed with our Saviour's pious and benevolent precepts. However remiss we have been in performing those Christian and charitable duties in times past, to these our deceased friends, we too well know that our time of performance is now over, as relates to them. Divine revelation teaches us to do unto others as we may wish them to do unto us. And whenever duty and charity may hereafter call us to perform any necessary act of kindness towards our neighbors and fellow mortals, we ought ever to bear in remembrance that it may be the last in our power to do. And this ought to induce us to the performance thereof, with a willing heart.

In the death of the younger branches of this family (the children) we have a loud call to such as are young, in the sorrowful instance of their being taken out of the world in the morning of life. How apt it is for youth to expect to live to grow up, or arrive at manhood; and live wholly thoughtless about death; easily led away by the world and its temptations. But, my young friends, don't think you are so safe one day, as that it is safe for you to live in sin. Death frequently passes by the decreptitude of old age, and levels its fatal shafts on youth.

Here is also a call to parents and guardians, in attending to those incumbent duties they owe to their children, and those under their immediate care. When our children are taken from us by death, the day is past; it hath gone over: we can do no more for them; and however we may lament our neglect of past duty to them, in not training them up in the "nurture and admonition of the Lord." there is no remedy, no future opportunity for us to perform these important duties to them. Let us therefore see that we embrace and improve the present, as it is the only certain time we have.

To conclude, let us all be directed to view the hand of God, and wisely improve his dispensations. for he frequently calls on us, and loudly, too, by one and another of his special providences.* And may our hearts be softened under his divine reproofs. O that we may become "heirs of God, and joint heirs with Christ:" that we may repent of our sins, and shun the sinner's way. That God would quicken us by his all-powerful grace, in every duty that will enable us to obtain a saving interest in his divine favor. And then we shall be ready, however soon or suddenly, or in whatever manner we may be called for. Which may God of his infinite mercy grant. Amen.

Mr. Sawtell was a native of Templeton, Mass. Mrs. Sawtell's maiden name was Hudson; she was born in Petersham, Mass.

The names and ages of this family are as follows:

Mr. Henry Sawtell, aged 41 years.
Mrs. Jerusha   "   " 37 "
Henry, aged 14 years.
Levi,   "   12   "
Jerusha, "   10   "
Rufus,   "   7   "
Thomas,   "   4   "
Joel,   "   2   "

* The winter before this disaster, February 17, 1781, Mr. Benjamin Fuller, aged 24, perished in the woods, at the northwest part of Newfane. In 1779, Mr. Ebenezer Merrick, aged 75, a spry, hearty man of his age, was killed by the fall of a tree, at the southeast part of the town. Same year Mr. Jonas Cook had a child scalded to death.

Levi, the second son, was living with friends in Templeton, and thus escaped the sad fate of the rest of the family. He afterwards married and lived in Marlborough, where he died a few years since, leaving a wife and children.

LONGEVITY, LONG MARRIED LIFE, ETC.

The first white woman and undoubtedly the oldest person that ever lived in town, was Mrs. Jane Hazleton, who died on the Franklin farm, February 16, 1810, at the advanced age of one hundred and three years, eleven months and eleven days. A venerable lady who well remembers this centenarian, says of her, that the day she was one hundred years old she spun a full day's work, and then called her son and told him to set her wheel away, as she had spun her last thread. Tradition says that Mrs. Dyer was the first white woman that ever wintered within what was then supposed to be the chartered limits of Fane. We find her death recorded November 27, 1789, at the age of eighty-nine, and that of Joseph Dyer, September 2, 1790, at the age of ninety. The name of Ebenezer Dyer, who is reported in Thompson's Gazetteer as one of the original trio of settlers, is not mentioned in the town records or Hezekiah Taylor's notes; but, inasmuch as the early historian has handed down the name, it is probable that there was such a name in the family. We have been able to obtain the least authentic knowledge of this family of either of the original three.

Isaac Goodnough and wife lived in the married state sixty-six years. She died October 8, 1804, aged eighty-seven, having been a member of the church seventy-two years. He died July 6, 1805, aged ninety-two. Thomas Green and wife lived together sixty years, dying July 10 and 24, 1804, at the age of eighty. Artemas Bruce and wife were married fifty-five years. He died July 31, 1811, aged eighty-four. She died the 29th of August, following, aged seventy-eight. The first grown person whose death we find recorded by the Rev. Mr. Taylor, is that of Ebenezer Merrick, who was killed by a falling tree, January 9, 1779, aged seventy-five. April 20 and 21, 1795, five children died in town under twelve years of age.

ROADS AND BRIDGES.

As is well known, all the social and business intercourse between the first settlers of our New England forests was conducted by the aid of marked trees. By their aid the beaten path was formed, and as the people and their wants increased, the trees along the line were cut, and a track that marked the advent of civilization formed. In this town there were, undoubtedly, two of these paths leading from the north and south part of the town, to a point near the mouth of the South Branch, as we find an undoubted record that there was a bridge over the stream at this point, before 1782, but the records fail to show by whom or by what means this bridge was built.

We find the first record of a regularly surveyed and laid out road to be in June, 1782, when it appears that the selectmen, Moses Kenney, Charles Evans, and Jonathan Park laid, and Lieut. Ward Eager surveyed, three roads. The most important and undoubtedly the first of these roads, commenced at the east side of the common and run eastwardly down the hill in and near the track already improved, to a point near the house of Thomas Higgins, thence in a northerly direction to Townshend line. In September following, a road was laid, commencing at a point near the house of Artemas Bruce and running south by marked trees and monuments, to and across the bridge at the mouth of the Branch, to Dummerston line. During the following twenty years a great number of roads were built throughout the town. The first vote on record for building a bridge was taken April 13, 1789, when it was voted to build a bridge over the South Branch near its mouth.

In 1791 Thomas Wheeler took a contract to furnish red beech and birch plank three inches thick, for the Phillips bridge, at the rate of one shilling and sixpence for every fourteen feet of plank used.

In 1794 it became necessary to rebuild the east bridge over the Branch, and the town voted to raise forty pounds for the purpose, a sum, according to their manner of reckoning, equal to one hundred and thirty-three and one-third Spanish milled dollars. In 1796 they voted to grant the sum of fifty pounds to Darius Wheeler to build a bridge across the Branch, near his mills. In 1802 the county road was laid and surveyed, four rods wide, from the court house to the north line of the county, the distance from the court house to Townshend bridge being four and three-fourths miles, and forty-seven rods.

In closing these notes it is perhaps proper for us to designate a few points of location, for the benefit of the future reader. The house of Thomas Higgins, mentioned in the survey of the first road, stood upon the farm now owned and occupied by Chas. Nichols. This farm is on the road leading to Brookline, upon the upper or oldest river flats, the second one from the bridge. From it you have a complete and beautiful view of the broad flats in Brookline, composing the meadow lands of the farms at this day owned and occupied by Timothy Albee, Luther Osgood and A. T. Barnes. The Bruce farm is situated at the foot of Newfane Hill, upon the brook to which his name has been given. From the date of its first settlement to the present it has remained in the possession of the family, and is now owned and occupied by a great grandson, Wm. T. Bruce.*

*We were in error in stating elsewhere that the farms now owned by Samuel Morse and Wm. A. Stedman were the only ones in town which have remained in continuous possession of the families by whom they were originally settled.

Wheeler's mills were in the present village of Williamsville, upon the mill-site owned at this date by H. H. Hoyt, just above where the stream rushes through the deep gorge in the rocks, over which the present bridge stands. Tradition says the old bridge stood above the mills, opposite the spot where now stands the residence of the late Wm. H. Williams. From the location of the old road, it appears that the east bridge near the mouth of the Branch, stood some rods further up the stream than the present one.

EXTRACTS FROM THE FIRST TOWN RECORDS— VOTES FOR COUNTY AND STATE OFFICERS— NATIONAL REPRESENTATIVE.

In March, 1782, the town voted to grant the sum of four pounds, silver money, to pay Luke Knowlton for a book which he had procured to register deeds, and in April they accepted from him the gift of a book for town records, and ordered all their former records copied therein.

March 27, 1781, the town cast its first vote for County officers, and Luke Knowlton was chosen to carry the vote to Putney, as pointed out by act of the Assembly, but how many, or what officials were voted for, the records fail to show.

The first vote on record for Governor, Lieut.-Governor, and Treasurer, was taken on the first Tuesday of September, 1794, and stood as follows: Governor, Thomas Chittenden, 29; Isaac Tichenor, 44; Nath'l Niles, 3. Lieut.-Governor, Jonathan Hunt, 64. Treasurer, Calvin Knowlton, 28; Sam'l Cutler, 16; Dea. Moses Kenney, 1.

On Tuesday, the 30th of October following, we find the first vote recorded for a Representative in Congress—Jonathan Hunt, 48; Stephen R. Bradley, 1; Lewis R. Morris, 1;

Nath'l Niles, 2. Not until September, 1797, do we find any record made of the election of a Town Representative, when we find Ebenezer Allen elected to the General Assembly. Yet it appears from the State records that the town was represented at a much earlier date, and why no record was made of the fact, we are unable to give even a reasonable conjecture. Doubtless many facts that would be of especial interest now, have been lost in the same manner.

COLLECTION OF TAXES.

The first record we find referring to the sale of the office of tax collector to the lowest bidder, is March 24, 1788, when it appears that Artemas Bruce, Jr., bid off the position of first constable for two pounds, and that of collector of town rates for two pounds and sixteen shillings. In 1799 the office of first constable was bid off by Luke Brown, he treating the town to ten mugs of *flip*. For collecting town rates he received $9.75. As time passed on the contest for the first constable's office waxed warm, and in 1810 Zatter Butterfield paid $3.00 for it, and in 1811 Ebenezer Morse gave $10 for the office. In those days the custom of warning people out of town, to prevent their becoming legal paupers, was almost universal, and we suppose it was the fees that accrued to the constable in that business that made the office so desirable.

SCHOOL DISTRICTS AND SCHOOLS.

The first recorded action of Newfane in regard to schools was taken March 15. 1784. when it was voted to divide the town into five school districts, and the following committee were chosen to hire teachers for the several schools: Charles Evans, 1st district; John Morse, 2d district; Daniel Taylor, 3d district; Jonathan Park, 4th district; Jonas Cook, 5th district. At a meeting held September 7, 1790, the town was divided into seven districts, and March 20, 1792, it was again divided into eight districts. March 4, 1799, the 9th district was added to the list, and the sum of one hundred pounds voted for the support of schools. March 22, 1802, the 10th district was formed; March 20, 1809, the 11th district, and March 10, 1817, the 12th and 13th districts.

We have not space in this article to mention the various changes which have been made, from time to time, in the boundaries of the different districts. It is sufficient to say that they have been so numerous and complete that but little idea of original locations can be formed from present names. There are, at present, ten organized school districts in town.

District No. 1 comprises Whitakerville, and the immediate surrounding territory; No. 2 includes the village of Fayetteville; No. 3 is situated midway between Fayetteville and Williamsville; No. 5 is known as the parish district; No. 6 includes the village of Williamsville; No. 7 occupies the northwest corner of the town; No. 8 includes the village of Pondville; No. 9 is the first district north of Fayetteville; No. 10 embraces the Adams neighborhood; No. 11 takes in Stratton Hill, now called, and is a joint district with No. 14 in Marlboro. In addition may be mentioned several small notches in the town, embracing only four families in the aggregate, connected with districts in Townshend, Dummerston and Dover. District No. 4, embracing Newfane Hill, was dissolved and annexed to other districts, by vote of the town, March 31, 1873, having been unable to support a school for many years previous to that date

Prior to 1815 the schools of Newfane were supported, most of the time, by direct appropriations from the town treasury. Since about that date the districts have received some aid from the town, varying in amount at different times according to the different laws in force, but have supported schools, in the main, by direct taxes upon their separate grand lists. The law in force at the present time requires the town to appropriate, annually, a sum equal to nine per cent. of its grand list, for a school fund, to be divided among the several districts, one-half of said amount equally, and the balance in proportion to the aggregate attendance of scholars.

The following table may be of interest as showing the number of scholars attending the common schools of the town in 1824 and in 1874, the fiftieth and one-hundredth years, respectively, of its existence as an organization:

Districts,	Scholars, 1824,	Scholars, 1874.
No. 1	23	26
" 2	26	34
" 3	42	14
" 4	58	
" 5	65	12
" 6	80	35
" 7	47	19
" 8	62	33
" 9	50	28
" 10	31	9
" 11	25	6
" 12	9	
Townshend and Newfane,		5
Dummerston and "		2
Dover and "		2
Totals,	518	225

Decrease in attendance, 56 per cent.
Population of town, 1820,   1506.
     "   "   "   1870,   1113.
Decrease in population, 26 per cent.

The following table shows the number of weeks of school sustained by the several districts in 1874, the rates per cent. raised on the grand list for support of the same, and the population of the town, by districts, in January, 1877:

Districts,	No. of weeks, 1874.	Rate per cent. of tax.	Pop., 1877.
No. 1	20	57	73
" 2	24	12	255
" 3	24	24	71
" 5	20	22	41
" 6	30	15	175
" 7	20	45	60
" 8	24	50	121
" 9	24	50	104
" 10	22	60	42
" 11	20	50	25
Towns'd and Newfane,	24	22	6
Dum'st'n " "	24	112½	6
Dover " "	24	25	9

Population of town, January, 1877.   988

As will be seen from the above figures the burden of school district taxation is one which falls very unequally upon the inhabitants of different sections of the town ; and it is a question now considerably agitated by some of our citizens, whether the present system is an improvement upon that formerly in use, of paying all school expenses by orders drawn upon the common treasury.

The practice of school supervision by a committee chosen by the town, commenced in 1828. At the annual March meeting held in that year, Chandler Bates, Roswell M. Field, Geo. A. Morse, Roger Birchard and Huntington Fitch, were chosen a committee to superintend schools. This practice evidently soon came into disrepute, as men of a lower standard of intellect were chosen at each successive election till 1833, when the office was filled by persons said to be chiefly noted for ignorance.

In 1847 the practice was renewed, and Foster Hartwell, Otis Warren and Darwin Adams were chosen superintendents. Since the latter date the position has been occupied by the following persons: 1851, Otis Warren; 1852,'53, O. S. Morris and Otis Warren; 1854, George Fisher and Phineas Howe; 1855, J. P. Huntington; 1856, George Arnold; 1857, Phineas Howe; 1858, '59, Solomon Bixby; 1860 and 1866, D. B. Morse; 1861, W. W. Hayward; 1862, '63, '65, '68, R. M. Pratt; 1864, Benjamin Ober and J. W. Willmarth; 1869, J. W. Croker; 1870, '71, '72, J. H. Merrifield; 1873, '74, '75, A. M. Merrifield; 1876, Charles Burnham.

The inhabitants of this town, quick to detect a necessity for better educational facilities than were afforded by their common schools, took measures, at an early date, to secure the establishment of an academy. An act incorporating the Windham County Grammar School was granted by the legislature, October 31, 1801, in which the following persons were named as the first board of trustees: Luke Knowlton, Jason Duncan, Asa Wheelock, Samuel Fletcher, Jonas Whitney, James Shafter, Martin Field, Esqrs., and Mr. Joseph Ellis. A suitable building was erected, and for several years the institution enjoyed high repute. Many persons who afterward occupied honorable positions in the affairs of the county and state, received their education at this place. This school had a run of about fifteen years, and then became a subject of that general decline which about that time began to attach itself to all the public enterprises of the village on the hill. The academy building was used for several years for district school purposes and was finally taken down and removed to Fayetteville.

For many years the inhabitants of the town have supported one or more select schools for a portion of the time, which, though not of an academic character, have been very useful as aids to the common school work.

The following is a list of the natives of Newfane who have graduated from colleges:

Ephraim Holland Newton,	Middlebury,	1810.
Luke Whitcomb,	"	1813.
Charles K. Field,	Middlebury,	1822.
Roswell M. Field,	"	1822.
Chesselden Ellis,	Union, N. Y.,	1823.
Lewis Grout,	Yale,	1842.

Hollis Reed,	Williams,	1826.
Admatha Grout,	Dartmouth,	1845.
Henry M. Grout,	Williams,	1854.
Henry K. Field,	Amherst,	1869.

The following, though not natives, have received a collegiate education while residents of the town. Calvin Knowlton moved to Newfane with his father in 1772, fitted for college here, and graduated, at Dartmouth, in 1784; Edward J. and Samuel R. Warren, sons of Dr. John P. Warren, graduated,—Edward at Dartmouth in 1846, and Samuel at Yale in 1860.

William H. Hodges, graduated at Colby University, Waterville, Maine, in 1851.

Four young men from Newfane are now obtaining a collegiate education:

Webster Merrifield, at Yale, class of 1877.
Aaron C. Dickinson, at Tufts, " " 1878.
R. Morton Sherman, " " " " 1880.
John N. Shipman, at Madison University, Hamilton, N. Y., class of 1880.

THE PONDVILLE BAPTIST CHURCH,

FORMERLY CALLED MARLBORO AND NEWFANE.

This church was organized October 29th, 1794, from members of the Dummerston Church, fifteen males and seven females. The council was composed as follows: Eld. Whitman Jacobs, Moderator, and Deas. Barney and Carpenter, of 2d Guilford Church; Eld. Asa Hibbard, and Brn. Lewis Allen and Ebnr. Brown, of Putney Church; Eld. Perley Hicks, Dea. Darius Bullock, and Brn. Jos. Carpenter and Benj. Ballou, Scribe, of 3d Guilford Church. There were added to these, Nehemiah Fisher, of 2d Guilford Church, and Eld. Freeman, Dea. French and Br. Wakefield. This council met at the house of Nehemiah Fisher, in Newfane.

At the close of the council, the infant church met and elected John Phillips, Jr., as clerk, who served them in that capacity, with the interruption of only two or three years, till 1840, when the present incumbent, Joseph Morse, came into office. The above is all that can be gathered of the history of this church for the first six years, as its records were not preserved.

In 1802, Nehemiah Fisher is called deacon, and the membership doubled in two years.

In 1803, Eld. Benj. Cole is preacher, and is still with them in August of 1804, and, after an absence of one or more years, returns with a letter from the Halifax Church.

In November, 1804, Matthew Bennett is authorized to improve his gifts. A Deacon Thomas Baker is mentioned in 1805, who prepared the Circular Letter for the Association, was licensed to preach in July, 1806, called to the pastoral care of the church on trial, and declining to be ordained, was dismissed to the Windham Church.

In 1806, James Ball and Mansfield Bruce were chosen deacons, the latter of whom, with twenty others, were added to this little church during the last seven months of this year.

In March, 1807, the church " *Voted*, That it is the deacons' duty to call on brethren that do not go to meeting, to know the reason and invite them to their duty." In May of the same year, Br. Achalaus Dean was appointed leader of singing.

In July, 1809, Dea. N. Fisher was licensed to preach, and Brn. John Phillips and Stephen Otis chosen deacons. In September of the same year, Dea. M. Bruce was ordained and became the first settled and salaried pastor of the church, and remained such till the close of 1818. During the last years of his pastorate, he did not preach all the time to this people; the rest of the time was occupied by their licensed deacon, Nehemiah Fisher. Elder Bruce baptized into this church 85 converts. There were present at the ordination of Elder Bruce, Eld. J. Huntley, Moderator, and Brn. Saml. Guernsey and Jesse Manley, of Dummerston Church; Eld. Lewis Allen, Dea. Jacob Stoddard and Br. Saml. Nichols, of the united Guilford Church; Eld. Benj. Buckland and Br. John Greene, of the 4th Guilford Church; Eld. Thomas

Baker, Dea. Aaron Knapp and Br. Wm. Holmes, of Windham Church, and Eld. Elijah Hall and Br. Jas. Tucker, of Halifax Church. To these were added Elds. John Rathburn, Asa Hibbard and Joseph Elliot; and Brn. John Spalding and Jonathan Wilson. Elder Elliot preached the sermon, Elder Hibbard made the ordaining prayer, Elder J. Rathburn gave the charge and Elder Allen gave the right hand of fellowship.

The following vote, passed September 5, 1810, shows the early practice of the church on the subject of the Lord's Supper:

"*Whereas,* The church has formerly given liberty to those members that were received into this church to commune with an unbaptized denomination, we now see our error; and now, *Voted,* to unfellowship the practice."

October 7, 1811. Simeon Jones was chosen deacon, and served the church about two years. In 1816 the membership of the church was ninety-six.

In 1817 the church built their first meeting house within the limits of the town of Marlboro.

The church was supplied by Dea. N. Fisher during 1819 and a part of 1820, when Eld. Paul Hines became pastor and served as such for two years. The church was prospered during this pastorate, and forty-three were added by baptism. From the close of Eld. Hines' labors till the ordination of Phineas Howe, the church was supplied with preaching by Dea. N. Fisher, assisted, in 1823, by N. McCullock.

September 10, 1824. Ira Ingram was chosen deacon.

October 28, 1824. Phineas Howe was ordained pastor by a council, composed of Elds. M. Bruce, Wilmington, who preached the sermon; Asahel Wood, Putney, moderator; A. Lamb, Guilford (united), clerk; Linus Austin, Whitingham, ordaining prayer; and Eld. Goodenough, right hand of fellowship.

With the exception of three years, from 1832 to 1835, when D. H. Grant and other licentiates supplied the church, Eld. Howe was pastor till 1842. During this pastorate the church enjoyed, at least, four periods of revival, and nearly one hundred and seventy-five were added by baptism, and had numbered as many as one hundred and ninety-five in 1841. He afterwards returned to this people and spent his last days with them.

February 24, 1834, John Goodnow was elected deacon.

From January, 1838, till March, 1839. Rev. Calvin Keyes was a member of this church. He was dismissed to Conway, Mass.

In 1838 a man ninety-seven years of age was baptized, who had waited sixty-seven years to become fit for the ordinance.

In 1840 Joseph Morse was chosen clerk and deacon, and Luke Sherwin licensed to preach. About this time a new meeting house was built, and the location changed to Pondville. This change created a dissatisfaction in a part of the membership, who, for a time, held a separate meeting. This same meeting house has lately been extensively repaired, and rededicated May 30, 1872.

From the close of Eld. Howe's pastorate till the commencement of Foster Hartwell's, in October, 1844, the church was supplied one year by a licentiate named Caleb Smith. Eld. Hartwell closed his labors about September, 1848. They were destitute a short time, when Rev. C. L. Baker supplied them till the fall of 1849; and, sometime before September, 1850, Rev. A. H. Stearns became pastor, and was pastor three years. During this time he received into the church thirty-six by baptism and nine by letter.

In 1852 the church passed the following resolution:

"*Resolved*, That we disapprove of all secret societies, whether it be Odd Fellowship, Freemasonry, or called by any other name."

After a destitution of about one year, Rev. J. P. Huntington became pastor, and was pastor till about the last of 1856. In January, 1857, Bro. Baldwin labored as an Evangelist. In March following, I. C. Carpenter became pastor. Twenty-two baptisms were reported in the association letter as the result of this revival. Eld. Carpenter remained pastor till March, 1862, and was followed in the pastorate by C. D. Fuller in July next. The latter was pastor till March, 1864, when J. M. Willmarth succeeded him in this office till April, 1867.

From the last date till December, 1868, the church was destitute of a pastor, but not destitute of revival interest, as several were converted and added to the church. At that time, S. S. White became pastor, closing in April, 1871. During the winter of 1870 and 1871 the church was refreshed, and nine were added by baptism. From April, 1871, to June, 1872, they were without a regular preacher, but were supplied at intervals. During this time they repaired their house of worship at an expense of about $1500. In June, 1872, John A. Rich became pastor and continued in that relation till September, 1873. He was succeeded in February, 1874, by A. J. Walker, who preached two years. During Mr. Walker's pastorate twenty-six were added to the church. The present pastor, Wm. Beavins, commenced his labors in April, 1876. Since 1802, there have been added to this church, by baptism, four hundred; eight have been licensed to preach, the most of whom were subsequently ordained, and eight have been called to the deacon's office, two of whom still remain to serve the church, viz.:—John Goodnow and Joseph Morse. James Charter, formerly deacon in a Baptist church at Somerville, Mass., has acted in that capacity in this church since 1870.

FIRST UNIVERSALIST SOCIETY.

The present society was organized in 1825. That Universalism existed in town, in an organized form, at a much earlier period, however, is shown by the following extract from the first volume of town records:

"NEWFANE, AUGUST YE 14, 1787.

This may certify all persons whom it may concern that the following persons, whose names are herein inserted, are professors of the doctrine of Universal Salvation by

Jesus Christ, and are constant attenders to hear the preaching of the same, and also do contribute to support the preaching of that doctrine, viz.:

Tilley Wilder,	Ebenezer Robinson,
Ebenezer Ober,	John Pike,
Benjamin Fuller,	Asa Houghton,
Ephraim Fuller,	Joseph Wilder,
Abel Fuller,	Edward Smith,
Thomas Higgins, Jr.,	Stephen Fuller,

All belonging to Newfane.

Witness our hands,

THOMAS BARNS, Teacher in said Society,
EDWARD SMITH. Society Clerk."

It also appears, from the same source, that there was inserted in the warrant for the annual March meeting, in 1820, an article which reads as follows:

"8th. To see if said Town will vote to permit the Universalists to occupy the Meeting House four Sabbaths in each year;" which article, according to the record of the meeting, it was voted to dismiss. These extracts, together with recollections by our older inhabitants of occasional preaching in school-houses and halls, constitute all the information that we now have relative to the history of this denomination in town prior to 1825. In November, 1825, a new society was organized by Charles Hudson, under the name of "The First Restorationist Society in Newfane," the constitution being signed by Josiah Taft and seventy others. In regard to the early preachers of the society, and their terms of service, the records give but little information, and the recollections of the older members are alike indefinite and conflicting. It seems to be agreed, however, that Jonathan Whitcomb was the first regular minister, but there is nothing to indicate the dates of the commencement and expiration of his term. At the annual meeting of the society, November 23, 1827, it was "Voted that the Committee should hire Mr. Wm. S. Balch to preach one-fourth of the Sabbaths in eight months, to commence in March or April, on condition that Mr. B. does not want more than five dollars per Sabbath, and his boarding." From information received from Mr. Balch, it seems that he preached his first sermon in Newfane, and the fifth in his ministry, at the schoolhouse in Williamsville, September 23, 1827, and, occasionally, at other places in town till the following April, at which time he commenced a regular engagement with the society for one-half the time, which was continued till November 15, 1829. From the latter date to 1836 the society was supplied for short periods by A. L. Pettee. —— Maynard, Matthew Hale Smith, and others, but was destitute of preaching the greater portion of the time. Otis Warren became pastor in 1836, which relation he occupied till 1859, with the exception of a portion of 1858, when, during his illness and absence from town, the pulpit was supplied by Warren Bassett.

At a meeting of the society, held December 10, 1839, it was voted that the old constitution be considered null and void, and a new constitution was adopted, under the name of "The First Universalist Society of Newfane."

W. W. Hayward was preacher in charge from May, 1860, to March, 1862; M. B. Newell from June, 1862, to June, 1863; and Joseph Barber during the summer of 1865, from which time till the summer of 1871, the society was wholly destitute of preaching. In 1870 the meeting house at Williamsville—the portion of which belonging to the Williams estate having become the property of the society—was extensively repaired, and was dedicated June 28, 1871, as a Universalist house of worship. N. C. Hodgden was preacher from July, 1871, to September, 1872; D. C. White from the latter date till the spring of 1874. From the close of Mr. White's term the pulpit was supplied by different persons till October, 1874, at which time Mrs. R. A. D. Tabor commenced her labors, which were terminated in April, 1876.

The pulpit is supplied at the present time, September, 1876, by T. B. Gregory, a student from the theological seminary at Canton, N. Y.

Most of the public services of the society, prior to 1836, were held at Fayetteville, at first in the court house, but in the Union church after its dedication in 1832. From 1836 to 1854, the time of the preacher was divided between the two villages, meetings being held one-half the time in each, respectively. During the latter year regular services by this society were discontinued at Fayetteville, but have been sustained at Williamsville with the exception of the period from 1863 to 1871, to the present time.

METHODISM IN NEWFANE.

Methodism never obtained a very enduring foothold in this town. It has been many years since the denomination has been able to support preaching here with any degree of constancy. There was once an organized society, however, possessing, for a while, considerable strength. It was formed in 1830, under the direction of Guy Beckley and James M. Fuller, members of the Vermont Conference, who, for about two years, divided their time between Fayetteville, Williamsville and Wardsboro. They were succeeded in this town, in 1832, by Wm H. Hodges, who preached at the two villages, alternately, most of the time till 1838. Then followed Elder Guernsey, till May, 1839, after which time, till 1848, the society was destitute of preaching, with the exception of occasional supplies. E. B. Morgan was stationed at Williamsville, by Conference, in 1848, followed by John A. Wood in 1850, O. S. Morris in 1851 and '52, C. D. Ingraham in 1853, and Simeon Spencer in 1862. In addition to the above, the society was often supplied by local preachers, for short lengths of time. The public services of the society were held, at Fayetteville, in the Court House and in Union Church; at Williamsville, in Wm. H. Williams' hall, and afterward in the church, a half interest in which, until its sale to the First Universalist Society in 1868, was controlled by this denomination.

CEMETERIES.

As has been noted in the proceedings of the Centennial Anniversary, the old Common on Fane hill was one of the first pieces of land cleared in town, and Dea. Jonathan Park one of the first men that had occasion to make use of it as a burial ground ; and, as by common consent, it soon became the general burying ground, so that in 1789 the north part was set off by the town for that purpose. And it was here that the remains of the unfortunate Sawtell family were buried. As early as 1794 it became evident that it would soon be necessary to have new grounds, and a committee was chosen to make the necessary arrangements for a new lot, and we suppose that the present yard on the hill is the result of their plans. Our Fayetteville Cemetery was first occupied by Dea. Park in the burial of a son, Moses, Feb. 29th, 1796. and soon after he gave the ground for a public lot, on the condition that the people should build and maintain a good wall around it. About 1830, Anthony Jones added a donation of some four rods of land across the south end, on condition that the people remove and rebuild the wall. For many of the first years the graves were made without any regard to form or order, and it was not laid out into lots until 1832, when a plan was made and the lots mapped out 10x30 feet. In 1854, P. T. Kimball, F. Sawyer, S. W. Bowker, and Mrs. C. C. Merrifield, purchased of A. Birchard the land lying between the original lot and the Stedman farm, Mr. B. reserving unto himself and his heirs a one-fifth interest ; the first-mentioned parties to build and maintain a good wall, in a direct line from the south wall of the old yard to the Stedman land. About this time the ladies' sewing circle took the matter in hand, and caused the double bank walls to be built facing the road, and the stone stairway to be laid. For years they have kept a small deposit in the savings bank for the benefit of the yard, and in the fall of 1875 they expended a portion of this fund in building the carriage track around the old lot.

In the yard are tablets sacred to the memory of the following named soldiers: Lieut. Jonathan Park, who served at Bennington in 1777, and the boys of the late war of 1861, '5, as follows: Sardis Birchard, Wayland E. Fairbanks, Alvin G. Higgins, Frederick Miller, Morris Miller, James Newton, Samuel Ray, John S. Ward. May 16, 1868, the Hon. John Roberts, a venerable barrister of four score and seven was buried here, and some three years and a half after, his remains were removed to Jacksonville, Vt., by a nephew, Mr. Henry Roberts. Upon opening the grave the coffin was found to be a severe lift for four men, on examination the body was found slightly darkened in color, but hard and nearly as perfect as when buried.

The Williamsville Cemetery was used as a private burying-ground as early as 1793, or thereabouts, by the owners of the farm of which it was a part. It was not, however, till 1830 that measures were taken to set it apart for public use. In July of that year it was deeded by the owner, Samuel Ingram, to Aaron C. Robinson, Benj. Prescott, and others, to be used as a public burying-ground forever, with the provision that they would cause it to be inclosed by a good stone wall. It was inclosed accordingly, laid out into lots, and soon came into general use by the inhabitants of that section of the town. In 1857, with a view to its more efficient management, an act of incorporation was obtained under the name of the Williamsville Cemetery Association. A new survey was immediately had and such changes made as to secure the desired uniformity in lots and walks. In 1862, chiefly through aid rendered by the ladies' sewing society, the stone wall on the south side was removed and a picket fence erected one rod nearer the road, thus enlarging the ground sufficiently for an extra tier of lots. In 1865 a receiving tomb was built. The ground is kept in order by the avails of a tax of twenty-five cents assessed annually upon each lot. The affairs of the Association are managed by a board of trustees, constituted, at present, as follows: D. D. Dickinson, D. A. Dickinson, E. R. Lincoln, S. W. Bowker, and G. B. Williams.

Here may be found the graves of seven soldiers of the late war, viz: Myron Pratt, Frank Cook, Linus P. Miles,

Samuel B. Lincoln, Henry C. Blashfield, Everett F. Gould and Lewis G. Brown; also the grave of Ephraim Hall, a soldier of the Revolution.

The land for the older portion of the Pondville Cemetery was contributed by Amherst Morse, second, while a resident of the farm of which it was originally a part, and was walled in by the inhabitants of the vicinity, in fulfillment of a condition of the gift. The time of its first use for burial purposes is not definitely known. The oldest gravestone bears the date of 1813, but there are several unmarked graves which may have been made at an earlier period. Situated near the dividing line of the two towns, this yard early came into general use by the inhabitants of the northern part of Marlboro as well as the southwestern part of Newfane, and in 1864 it was found necessary to have it enlarged. Accordingly, in August of that year, three-fourths of an acre of land adjoining the old yard, on the east, was purchased of Ephraim Morse, then owner of the surrounding farm, by Orison Bruce, was transferred by him to Dana Morse, and has now come into the possession of Samuel Morse who disposes of lots, to individuals, as they are needed. It does not now appear that there was ever an organization having for its object the supervision of this yard; and, in consequence, in the older portion the lots were taken up with too little regard for that uniformity deemed so desirable in cemeteries at the present day. In the newer portion the lots are regularly laid out. Here may be found the graves of two soldiers of the Revolution, Robert Timson and Justus Augur.

The cemetery in the parish is now but little used. Like the one on Newfane Hill it contains the graves of many of the early settlers of the town. Like it, as the more immediate descendants of its inmates are passing away, it is becoming more and more neglected. It would seem a highly appropriate act at this time, and one in which our town would do her early settlers no greater honor than she would herself, should she assume the care of their last resting places.

FAYETTEVILLE.

The first framed house in Fane was built in the summer of 1768 by Jonathan Park, in the yard in front of what we term the old Parks house, just north of the Fayetteville hotel. The ground was so thickly wooded at the time that when the sills were laid there were several stumps within the space they enclosed. The frame is still in existence in the house of Mrs. Orison Johnson. Its original cover was hemlock bark.

We have not been able to learn the date when Nathaniel Stedman left Fane hill and took up his farm near Fayetteville, but it was not until after Park had taken the land on which the village stands. His first log house stood a little northeast of the barns occupied by his grandson, Mr. Wm. A. Stedman, who has pointed out the spot to us. A few traces of the old foundations being still discernible.

Thomas Higgins, Artemas Bruce, Ephraim Fuller, and Thomas Green were among their early neighbors. Fuller settled on the first farm north of the village, now owned and occupied by M. O. Howe. Green came from Worcester and built his cabin on the hill about half a mile west of Park, upon land now owned by W. A. Stedman, and known as the Judge Allen farm. This farm has long since been vacated, nothing now remaining but the foundation of the old buildings.

Artemas Bruce came September 22, 1776. He built the first saw mill in this part of the town, of which we find any authentic record, on the brook just south of his house. Of his family we find but little reliable information. Yet it would seem that there were at least three sons; Ephraim, Artemas Jr., and Elijah, from the latter of whom Mansfield Bruce, the Baptist divine, is a descendant. Samuel, a son of Ephraim, a carpenter by trade, built a dam and first occupied the privilege, where now stands F. O. Burditt's cabinet shop, about 1820. He rented a portion of the shop to a clothier.

From them the line of occupancy descended to Ide, Kidder and Burditt. About 1815 Thomas Cook built a dam and trip-hammer shop near the bridge south of the village. From him it passed to Newman & Newton, scythe manufacturers. And from them to Joseph Green, in 1823, who continued the scythe business until 1839. In 1840 he erected a grist mill with a sash and blind shop on the second floor. From him it passed to its present owner, E. C. Walker, in 1851. The county buildings were located on the Parks flats, so called, in 1825. Mr. Park giving the land to the county for a common so long as the buildings remain here. It was proposed to call the place Parkville, but Mr. Park was decidedly opposed to the plan, and at the suggestion of Gen. Field it was named Fayetteville, in honor of Gen. Lafayette, who visited this country for the last time in 1824. As a matter of economy several houses in the village on the hill were taken down, moved and rebuilt here. The Fayetteville hotel and the Dr. Olds house, now standing on the right hand of Main street, fronting the common from the south, were among the number. Also, the two houses standing south of the Dr. Olds house, and one now owned by Mrs. S. K. Holland on the west side of the street, south of the Field place.

During the early growth of the village, religious meetings were held for several years in the court house. About 1830 the several religious sects united under the following title: "The Liberal and Charitable Christian Society of Newfane," and erected the Union church, in 1831. One of the articles of the association provided that each sect should have the right to occupy the desk, in proportion to the number of slips said sect owned in the house. This union was dissolved in 1838, and the Congregationalists erected their new house in 1839. The Universalists continued to occupy the old house until about 1853, when they found themselves unable to sustain a pastor. From that time the house began to decay, and in 1872 it had reached that stage that it must be repaired, or sink to utter ruin. It was repaired and remodeled into a hall by a public subscription and is now called Union Hall.

In 1845 the enterprising farmers of the county organized and established the Windham County Fair at this place, and with the exception of a year or so at Brattleboro, and six at Westminster, it has remained here, and as a whole been a successful and prosperous society. The Windham County Savings Bank was chartered in the fall of 1853. Upon its organization the Hon. Austin Birchard was chosen treasurer, the duties of which position he faithfully discharged for twenty years, retiring January 1, 1874, at the advanced age of eighty, leaving the institution with a capital of $184,500, in round numbers; he and his brother Roger Birchard were the first merchants in Fayetteville.

In the further tracing of our business interests we find the following interesting facts in regard to the history of our post-office:

Daniel Kellogg was the first postmaster, and began to render accounts at Newfane on the first of October, 1811. It is probable, therefore, that the office was established during the summer, or early in the fall of 1811, but the exact date is not known. The following lists give the names of the several postmasters at each office, together with the dates of their appointments, as found in the record books of the P. O. Department at Washington, D. C.

NEWFANE, WINDHAM COUNTY, VERMONT.

The office was established, probably, in July, 1811.

Daniel Kellogg, appointed postmaster,		July, 1811.
Jonathan Nye, " "		February 24, 1812.
Adolphus Wing, " "		October 23, 1815.
Henry Kellogg, " "		June 2, 1817.
Martin Field, " "		November 2, 1818.
David W. Sanborn, " "		" 17, 1819.
Charles K. Field, " "		June 21, 1825.

On the twenty-fifth of November, 1825, the name of the office was changed to Fayetteville.

Charles K. Field, appointed P. M.,		November 25, 1825.
Roswell M. Field, " "		May 1, 1826.
Ira McCollom, " "		April 26, 1830.
Dexter Holbrook, " "		November 25, 1831.
Wright Pomeroy, " "		" 4, 1834.

Jacob Dunklee, Jr., appointed P. M.			December 27, 1837.
Franklin Sawyer,	"	"	May 10, 1841.
Jacob Dunklee, Jr.,	"	"	May 16, 1845.
John P. Warren,	"	"	September 29, 1849.
Jacob Dunklee, Jr..	"	"	October 20, 1853.
Samuel P. Miller,	"	"	August 5, 1861.
Chandler Wakefield,	"	"	October 26, 1864.
Amherst Morse,	"	"	" 24, 1865.
Francis W. Fairbanks,	"	"	January 6, 1868.
William H. Goodnow,	"	"	August 26, 1868.
Elliott W. Blodgett,	"	"	February 12, 1874,

who is the present incumbent.

It is so common to speak of every severe storm or other unusual feature of the weather, as being the highest or unlike anything that ever occurred before, that we think it proper to make the following notes on high water:

October 5, 1869, the New England states, and especially the Connecticut River valley, was visited by one of the severest and most extensive freshets ever known since the country was settled. The damage in this town to roads and bridges was immense, to say nothing of the loss sustained by individuals. Smith Brook overflowed all known bounds, and, for the first time within the memory of man, came flowing over the highest point in the road above Fayetteville, in a depth of from six to ten inches, into the village, occasioning a good deal of alarm, and not a little dismay. West River was many feet higher than it had ever before been seen, coming up and striking the Brookline covered bridge its entire length, and extending into the meadow some twenty rods or more, entirely surrounding an oak tree that stands in Mr. Albee's meadow, upon the side of one of the ancient river banks.

May 24, 1875, Fayetteville was visited with the most terrific thunder shower ever known, raising Smith's and Bruce's brooks several inches higher than in 1869, the water flowing down the street and covering the east side of the common. The shower did not continue more than two hours. A cloud broke over the head waters of these brooks and caused the unusual flood.

Smith brook is a short and rapid stream. In the early days when its hillsides were covered with timber it furnished a stable and abundant water power, but as the forests have been cleared away it has become unreliable, and consequently our manufacturing interests have failed to keep pace with those of our sister village. At one time Anthony Jones conceived the idea of erecting a woollen factory here, and sought to increase the flow of the stream by drawing the waters of the Kenney pond this way, and opened a canal for that purpose, the course of which is still plainly visible in land now owned by J. J. Green. Mr. Jones was a man whom some of the wise heads called visionary. But it is only simple justice to his memory to say that he had higher hopes for the future prosperity of this place than almost any other man, and bent all his energies toward bringing about a full realization of those hopes, building, as he did, not only several private dwellings, but the long building, the Fayetteville hotel and the Exchange, the latter of which stood upon the site now owned by L. I. Winslow. It was the largest building ever erected in town and was designed for a store and hotel; in this enterprise he over-stepped his mark and failed. About 1844 he gathered up the remains of his shattered fortune, and broken in health and spirit sailed to Sicily, in the employ of a brother-in-law, Mr. Chamberlin, of New York city, from whence he returned to Rochester, N. Y., where he died soon after.

Thus we have noted the origin and growth of our village, with its incidents of flood, and the natural causes that have prevented it from becoming a prosperous manufacturing center, and perhaps we cannot better close this sketch than by appending hereto a list of those who have represented the mercantile interests of this part of the town. The date when the first store and hotel were opened can only be approximated at about 1780. The tavern was kept by Luke Brown, and the store by Luke Knowlton. They united in trade under the firm name of Knowlton & Brown, but soon dissolved, and Knowlton took, as a second partner, Ezekiel Knowlton. Then followed, as near as can be ascertained, in the following order: John Holbrook, from 1785 to '90,

Capt. Adams, Dr. Brooks, Oliver Chapin and Zutter Butterfield, under the firm name of Chapin & Butterfield, Joseph Ellis, David W. Sanborn and Anthony Jones. In 1822 the firm of A. & R. Birchard opened a store on the hill and continued business until 1825, when they began business here, dissolving in 1836, then it was A. Birchard, alone, until 1841; then Birchard & Sawyer until April 1, 1850, when Mr. Birchard retired from business, selling his interest to S. P. Miller. The firm of Sawyer & Miller dissolved in the spring of 1853. Franklin Sawyer then took a partner, Geo. Smith, and continued the business until 1858, when they dissolved and Sawyer removed his goods into the Jones Exchange, and carried on business alone until 1861, when he sold to F. D. Sawyer and Chas. Goodhue; upon the expiration of their lease, F. Sawyer took the business again and kept it until the spring of 1869, when he sold to Winslow & Park. In 1871 they sold to Holbrook & Co., who sold to the Winslow brothers, in 1873. In March, 1874, L. I. Winslow bought out his brother's interest and the first of April following, the building, the original of the Jones Exchange, was destroyed by fire. Mr. Winslow re-built in the summer of 1876, and kept a store until the spring of 1877, when he sold his goods and rented his store to N. M. Batchelder, the present occupant. Thus we have noted the line of trade established by the Birchard brothers, and now we will trace the competing line founded by Anthony Jones, who began trade very soon after the Birchards. He was succeeded by Geo. A. Morse; in 1833 came Phelps & Sanford; in 1835 it was Sanford & Baker; from 1836 to 1840 Baker & Merrifield; then H. E. Baker alone until 1847, who sold to Wm. L. Williams; in 1849 the Eager brothers purchased his stock; in 1851 it was Dunklee & Lamb; in 1853 S. P. Miller, whose dissolution with Sawyer has already been noted, took up the line and continued business until 1864, when he sold to Goodnow & Morse; in 1865 this firm dissolved and W. H. Goodnow kept the business until 1874, when he sold to the present owner, E. W. Blodgett.

WILLIAMSVILLE.

This village derived its name from William H. Williams, in early years the owner of the larger portion of its business interests. It doubtless owes its origin, and, in a large degree, its subsequent growth, to the natural advantages afforded by the stream upon which it is situated. The development of these advantages commenced at a very early date, as the natural result of their being more available than any other to the inhabitants of the village on the hill. The time and place of the erection of the first mill on the South Branch, and the circumstances connected therewith, are matters more of tradition than of definite knowledge; and the different stories are of so conflicting a nature as to seem to be entitled to but little credit. Referring to the town records we find that the first conveyance of mill property was made in 1790, in October of which year John Wheeler sold to Winslow & Jones, a grist mill and saw mill standing where Hovey's carding mill now does. This property frequently changed hands till it came into the possession, soon after 1800, of Wm. H. Williams, who built the first carding mill in 1810, and soon afterward conveyed it to John Robinson, from whom it passed to Hezekiah Robinson. The grist mill is not mentioned in the deeds given after 1800. The saw mill was owned at different times by John Robinson, John Rider and David Newman, and prior to 1830 the whole property came again into the hands of Wm. H. Williams, who retained it until his decease. It is now owned by S. M. Hovey, and operated by Isaac Hovey, who has had charge of the works for twenty-five years.

During the war of 1812–15 a small woolen factory was erected near the carding mill, by William H. Williams and Hezekiah Robinson, but was run but a few years, the venture not proving a successful one.

In April, 1794, Thomas and Darius Wheeler purchased of Abner Merrifield and Thomas Farr, for twelve pounds, the mill privilege now owned by H. H. Hoyt, together with one and one-half acres of land, and built, during that or the following year, a fulling mill and an oil mill. These mills were sold by the Wheelers, in February, 1801, to Wm. H. Williams, who had previously operated them for a few years, and who soon established a reputation for doing first-class work in the cloth-dressing line, and received a large and remunerative patronage until home made cloth began to be superseded by the products of the factory. W. H. Williams continued the business until his decease, with the exception of a few years in which it was carried on by his son, George Williams, and others. He continued the oil making business till 1852, when it was discontinued on account of the difficulty attached to obtaining flax-seed. The mills were entirely swept away during the great freshet, September 23, 1815, but were immediately rebuilt. This property was purchased in 1874, by H. H. Hoyt, who put in, and now runs, a circular saw mill and other wood-working machinery.

A grist mill was built, near the site of the present mill, about the year 1786, by Ebenezer Morse. It was a small structure containing but a single run of stone, and was set upon the rocks, near the middle of the pond as it now is. It was run by Mr. Morse until his decease, in 1813, and was sold by his widow, in 1814, to Darius Norcross. From Norcross it passed to Samuel Dutton, Jr., in 1816; from Dutton to Wyman Richardson, in 1817; from Richardson to Roswell Ingram, in 1831; from Roswell to Samuel Ingram, in 1832; from Samuel Ingram's estate, through A.C. Robinson, James Eastman and Richmond Dunklee, in 1837, to Wm. H. Williams, who built the present mill in 1839, and retained its ownership till 1864, when it was purchased by D. B. & D. J. Lamson. From the Lamsons it passed to J. E. Benson, in 1865, and from Benson to S. W. Bowker, the present owner, in 1873. In 1874 the mill was thoroughly repaired at a large expense, and is now considered one of the best in this section of the state. Captain Ira Blashfield, who had tended this mill for several years previously, was killed March 1, 1855, by being drawn through the gearing attached to one of its wheels. In former years a saw mill was connected with this mill.

Amasa Lincoln came to this village in 1817 or 1818, and built, about that time, a small tannery in which he continued business till 1840. In the latter year, in company with his son, O. L. Lincoln, he built the upper or western section of the present structure. The property soon afterward passed into the hands of O. L. Lincoln, who became associated in business, in 1846, with Gilbert C. Brown, the new firm putting up the eastern section of the building the same year. The business was continued by the Lincolns and Goodwin, and Merrifield & Goodwin, from 1847 to 1852. Wm. L. Williams purchased the building in 1851, and sold the same, in 1855, to Amasa and John G. Wood, who carried on the business from the latter date till 1874. The building was purchased by O. L. & E. R. Lincoln, in December, 1874, and occupied by them for about a year and a half, but is not now in use. As a means of furnishing employment to several men, and a ready market for bark, wood and other products, this business has contributed largely to the prosperity of the village and its vicinity.

The building now used by Wheeler & Morse, in the manufacture of butter tubs and kegs, was built by Ephraim Hall, Jr., and used by him for a number of years, partly as a carpenter's shop, and partly as a grist mill. It was purchased by John S. Emery, in 1845, and fitted up with machinery for making pails. In 1850 it came into the possession of Dana D. Dickinson, who added new machinery, and commenced the manufacture of tubs and kegs. Mr. Dickinson continued the business till 1873, when he sold it to E. P. Wheeler and L. O. Morse, the present proprietors. About six thousand tubs and kegs are annually made at this shop.

In 1848, O. L., L. A. & E. R. Lincoln erected a large building near the present residence of Geo. T. Allen, and engaged in the manufacture of pails, employing, for a few years, from eight to twelve men. From the Lincolns the property passed to J. A. Merrifield, in 1851; from Merrifield to Gardner C. Hall, in 1852; and from Hall to A. H. Stearns, in 1853. During the great freshet of 1856, August 20, the building was carried away—the water at the same time cutting through the Goodnow flat above—as were also several bridges, including the covered bridge then standing near the Bingham mill, at Pondville.

In 1854, W. R. Davenport purchased the premises just west of the present residence of F. J. Morse, on which a house and barn were then standing, constructed a shop and commenced the manufacture of bobbins. In 1856 Mr. Davenport was succeeded in the business by Lucius Halladay. In the early morning of June 29, 1857, the shop was discovered to be on fire, and, with the house and F. J. Morse's barn, was entirely consumed. The fire was thought to have been caused by friction created by machinery in motion. The shop was immediately rebuilt by Mr. Halladay, who conducted a successful business for several years. It is now unoccupied.

The saw mill now owned by D. D. Dickinson, was built by D. D. Dickinson and E. P. Wheeler, in 1859, to replace the one built by them in 1857, and which was carried away, July 13, 1859, during a heavy shower which swelled Baker Brook to a greater height than it was ever before remembered to have reached, sweeping off nearly every bridge on the brook, including the one near Dr. Blakeslee's, and doing a great amount of damage to private property. Mr. Dickinson obtained the entire control of this mill in 1866, and has since furnished a ready market for a large amount of oak and ash timber, by working it up into carriage stock and other salable lumber.

The manufacture of wagons and sleighs was commenced here, in 1858, by H. H. Hoyt, who built, the same year, the carriage shop now standing. Geo. W. Dickinson purchased an interest in the business in 1869, after which time, till 1872, it was conducted under the firm name of H. H. Hoyt & Co. Mr. Dickinson became sole proprietor in the latter year and has since continued the business. A large number of wagons and sleighs have been manufactured at this shop.

No sketch of the business enterprises of this village would be considered complete, by the older portion of its inhabitants, without the mention of the hatting business conducted by Isaac Cutler from about the year 1820 to 1833 or 1834.

It was commenced in the store building now occupied by O. L. Sherman, which was built by Mr. Cutler for the purpose, but sold to John R. Blake & Co., in 1824. It was afterward carried on in the tall, yellow house now occupied by Eli Tyler. Mr. Cutler is said to have been a skillful workman, and to have built up a large trade in silk and wool hats.

The manufacture of potash, though now foreign to this section, was a branch of industry of much importance at the commencement of the present century. It was almost the only business of a manufacturing nature engaged in by the inhabitants of the village on the hill. It was also carried on in this village for nearly fifty years, by Wm. H. Williams, in a long, low, rough-boarded building which stood nearly south of the present residence of Geo. B. Williams, and the appearance of which, together with that of the old red house opposite, is inseparably connected with every recollection of the village as it existed in former years.

The mercantile business was commenced here, in 1814, by Wm. H. Williams and David W. Sanborn, in the old red house which was torn down in 1868 to make room for the present residence of Geo. B. Williams. The first store was built, in 1815, by Williams & Sanborn, who continued business till 1820, when Sanborn retired. Huntington Fitch was admitted in 1826, and retired in 1829. The store and goods were entirely destroyed by fire, October 8, 1829, the loss being estimated at ten thousand dollars. The store was rebuilt by W. H. Williams, the following year, and the business continued by him till 1838, when his son, Wm. L. Williams, was received as a partner. W. L. Williams retired from the business in 1844, but returned in 1849, purchased the entire stock of his father, and traded till 1851, when he was succeeded by H. F. Houghton and Lucius Walker. Mr. Houghton retired from the business in 1855, and John D. Blake was received as a partner about a year thereafter. Walker & Blake closed out their stock in the spring of 1857, after which time, till 1868, the store was unoccupied. Amherst Morse commenced trade in June, 1868, and continued till 1875. Since the latter date the building has not been occupied for purposes of trade.

The store now occupied by O. L. Sherman was opened in January, 1824, by John R. Blake, C. H. Cune and Francis Goodhue, of Brattleboro, who continued in business, under different firm names, with Jason Duncan, Jr., as agent, till the spring of 1838. Henry Wheelock and John A. Merrifield were the next to occupy the store, commencing in 1839, and continuing two or three years. H. N. Miller and George Clark commenced trade about 1844. The firm of Miller & Clark was succeeded in 1847 by that of Miller & Ward, the interest of Clark being purchased by Abel S. Ward. Miller & Ward were succeeded, in 1851, by Martin Perry and G. L. Howe, who continued together for a few years, when Perry sold his interest to S. H. Sherman, who in turn sold to O. L. Sherman, in 1855. Howe & Sherman traded together for ten years. The whole business then passed to O. L. Sherman, who has since continued it.

Abel S. Ward opened a store, in 1846, in his dwelling house, then standing on the site of the present residence of F. J. Morse. The building and goods were entirely consumed by fire, April 7, 1847.

The main portion of the hotel in this village was built by Ebenezer Morse for a private residence. It was first opened as a public house by David Reed, in 1815 or 1816. The property passed from Mr. Reed to Emory and Asa Wheelock, in 1829, and was occupied from 1829 to '35 and from 1837 to '39, by Henry Wheelock; from 1835 to '37, by Geo. A. Morse; from 1839 to '46, by Luke A. Wright; from 1846 to '51, by Clark Adams and Samuel Hall; from 1851 to '56, by Richmond Dunklee; from 1856 to '58, by A. L. Howard; from 1858 to '60, by Fred Thompson; from 1860 to '70, by Lucius Halladay; from 1870 to '72, by H. E. Harris; S. W. Bowker has been proprietor and occupant since 1872. The owners of the property, since 1835, have been as follows: Henry Wheelock, Aaron C. Robinson, Marshall Newton, Clark Adams, Caroline Dunklee, Dr. C. S. Blakeslee, L. Halladay and S. W. Bowker.

Chas. K. Field came to this village in March, 1826,

engaged in the practice of law, remained two years and then removed to Wilmington. Returning in 1855, he remained till 1861, when he sold out to Kittredge Haskins, and removed to Brattleboro. Hon. Hoyt H. Wheeler, late of the Vermont Supreme Court, and the newly appointed U. S. District Judge for this state, commenced the study of law with Mr. Field, in this village.

Mr. Haskins remained here in the practice of his profession till September, 1862, when he enlisted, and entered the army. In the fall of 1863 he removed to Brattleboro.

Geo. W. Davenport opened a law office here in May, 1865, and remained till January, 1867.

Dr. Simon Taylor, son of Rev. Hezekiah Taylor, was the first physician to settle in this immediate vicinity. He commenced practice here in 1813, and died in 1818. Dr. James Cutler came here about 1817, but remained only a few years. Dr. Sewall Foster came the same year, and remained till 1823, when he removed to Shefford, P. Q., where he became highly distinguished as a physician, and received many political honors. Dr. John Wilson settled in this village about the year 1820, and remained till 1835, when he sold out to Dr. Orville P. Gilman, and removed to Brattleboro. Dr. Gilman remained but a short time. Dr. Elihu Halladay practiced here from about 1833 to 1838. Dr. C. S. Blakeslee became established here in May of the latter year, and soon built up, and now retains, an extensive and successful practice. Dr. H. B. Chapin came here in 1856, and remained in this village and vicinity about fifteen years. Dr. Geo. H. Harvey located here in 1873, and Dr. John Heard in 1874, both of whom now remain.

School District No. 6, of which this village is now a part, was formed Sept. 7, 1790, but embraced, as originally constituted, none of the territory on the north side of the Branch. The territory embraced within the present village limits, and on which, as late as 1812 or 1813, only four houses were standing—the old house of Wm. H. Williams, the red house previously alluded to, the hotel building, and a house on the Chester Perry farm—was originally attached, a portion to district No. 3, and a portion to the parish district.

Changes were made in the boundaries of the district from time to time, and prior to 1820 it assumed very nearly its present proportions. The first school house stood on the east side of the road leading to Dummerston Hill, about twenty rods south of where J. A. Merrifield now lives. The second school house was built, in 1836, in the woods, on the west side of the brook, near where the road leading to the cemetery separates from the river road to Brattleboro. The present commodious and convenient school building was erected in 1861.

The meeting house in this village was built in 1834 and 1835, under the direction of a society representing different denominations, and was dedicated December 17, 1835, by the Methodists and Universalists. It was controlled by these two denominations, one-half the time each, respectively, till 1868, when it became wholly the property of the latter. As originally built it was set up some six or seven feet from the ground, on brick walls, with the intention of having the basement finished off for a town house. In 1870 it was lowered several feet, moved further back from the road, and otherwise remodeled.

In the matter of postal facilities this section of the town was tributary to Newfane Hill, so long as an office was kept there. Upon the removal of the office to Fayetteville, active measures were taken to secure the establishment of one in this village, which were soon successful. It is said that the inhabitants of the hill felt none of their losses more keenly than that of their post office. As expressive of this feeling, it is related of one of the older inhabitants, that, when he heard of the removal, he remarked that he would never take a letter from the new office, even though one should come for him covered with seven black seals. The Williamsville post office was established May 20, 1826, with Chas. K. Field as postmaster, and was first kept in the building now occupied by Geo. W. Dickinson as a residence. For a number of years after the establishment of the office the mail was received here but once a week, and was carried, for some time, by Jonathan Wood, of Dover, who went down Friday and back Saturday, in a kind of wide seated gig, carrying occasional passengers. It was afterward carried, for several years, by Daniel Brown, of Dover. A mail route was then established between Bellows Falls and Wilmington, and a coach passed through this village, carrying the mail, twice a week, each way. This route was continued for some time after 1850, the mail being carried, for several years, by Ransom King. Since its discontinuance a coach has run between this place and Brattleboro, carrying the mail,—at first semi-weekly, and afterward tri-weekly and daily. A daily mail was established by the Government, at this place, April 25, 1872, but had been maintained by private contributions for several years previously. The following is a list of the persons who have been postmasters at this office, together with the respective dates of their appointment:

Charles K. Field, appointed P. M.	May 20, 1826.
Jason Duncan, Jr., " "	November 30, 1826.
Charles W. Joy, " "	April 16, 1838.
Horatio N. Miller, " "	June 28, 1847.
John A. Merrifield, " "	July 9, 1851.
Henry F. Houghton, " "	August 27, 1853.
Oscar L. Sherman, " "	October 18, 1856.
Gardner L. Howe, " "	July 20, 1861.
Charles E. Park, " "	September 13, 1865,

who is the present incumbent.

March 25, 1833, after repeated attempts, as shown by the records of several previous meetings, the town voted to hold its town meetings thereafter at Williamsville and Fayetteville, one year in each place, alternately.

At the time that arrangements were being made to remove the shire from Newfane Hill to some place more convenient of access, strong efforts were made by the inhabitants of the south part of the town to secure its location in this village. The interest taken in the matter is best shown by a subscription paper, now in existence, on which was pledged the sum of nearly four thousand dollars for the purpose of aiding in the erection of suitable buildings, should Williamsville have been selected as the site of the new shire.

PONDVILLE.

The Baptist Society at this place was formerly called "The Baptist Society of Marlboro and Newfane," and worshiped for many years in a meeting house standing on the farm now owned by A. & A. Williams, in the extreme northern part of the former town. The present site was selected on account of its more central location, and the church building now standing was erected in 1841. Upon the completion of the new house, a bell was presented to the society by Caleb Pond, then a wealthy merchant of Hartford, Conn., but formerly a member of this church. From him the village derived its name.

The first mills in this section of the town are said to have been a grist mill and a saw mill which stood on the opposite side of the stream from the Bingham mill, and a short distance below the bridge. The ownership of these mills can be traced back to Isaac and Oliver Goodnow, who transferred them, in July, 1797, to Amos Perry. From Amos Perry's estate they passed to Samuel Dutton, Jr., in 1814; from Dutton to Wm. and Nathaniel Hills, about 1816; from W. & N. Hills to Asa Worden, Jr., in 1833; from Worden to Asa H. Marsh in 1839; from Marsh to Lyman Burr; from Burr to Windsor Goodenough; from Goodenough to Ransom King; and from King to Clark Adams and Cyrus Hill, who built, about 1850, the saw mill now standing. The property afterward passed from Adams & Hill to D. B. & D. J. Lamson; from the Lamsons to Zina G. Bailey, and from Bailey to W. E. & M. W. Bingham, the present proprietors.

The spot on which D. B. Lamson's carding mill now stands was first used for mill purposes, by Mr. Lamson, in 1834, in which year he built a saw mill and grist mill. The mills were afterward owned by Asa Marsh, Nahum Houghton and Joshua Morse, respectively, and were finally destroyed by fire. The carding mill now standing was formerly connected with the lower Lamson mills and was moved to this spot in 1876.

A saw mill was built several rods above the lower Lamson mills, in 1834 or thereabouts, by John D. Moore. The property soon came into the possession of David B. Lamson, who added a grist mill and a carding mill, and moved the buildings to their present site. These mills have been operated for nearly forty years by D. B. Lamson and his sons.

The building now occupied by W. E. and M. W. Bingham as a dwelling house, was built for a store, in 1840, by Linus A. Phillips, James Charter, and Ira Pierce, who commenced trade in December of the same year, under the firm name of L. A. Phillips & Co. James Charter became sole proprietor in 1841, and continued business till 1849. From the latter date till 1856, the business was conducted for short periods by Ira Pierce, Joshua Morse, Moses Merrifield, Lawson B. Morse, and Abel Gould, respectively. In 1856 the building was purchased by Ira Ingram, Mason Ingram and D. J. Lamson, and a company formed under the "Union Plan" then so common in this section of country. This company was succeeded, in February, 1859, by B. E. Morse, who continued in business till May, 1862, then selling his stock to D. J. Lamson and Edward Adams, who removed it to one of the Lamson houses near the mills, and traded for a short time. The store was next occupied by Wm. H. Goodnow, who commenced business in the spring of 1864 and continued about a year. It was lastly occupied, for purposes of trade, by Thomas A. Morse, who opened in September, 1865, and closed out his stock in the spring of 1868.

Many of the early settlers and older inhabitants of the southern part of the town have been already mentioned. There are others who are equally entitled to notice.

Joshua Davis was born at Barre, Mass., March 1, 1750. Came to Newfane and settled on the farm now owned by Leonard J. Timson. Married Rhoda Balcom. Died June 29, 1838. His son, Calvin Davis, was born April 17, 1794. Married Betsey Morse, May 6, 1818. Died April 25, 1871.

Moses Saben was born at Uxbridge, Mass., August 24, 1782. Married, first, Sarah, daughter of Rev. Hezekiah Taylor, April 24, 1814. Came to Newfane, in 1814, to live on Mr. Taylor's farm. Married, second, Ruth, widow of Chas. Lamb, November 9, 1820. Resided until his decease, on the farm now owned, partly by his son D. S. Saben, and partly by James Charter. Died January 31. 1872.

Samuel Brown was born at Buckland, Mass.. July 4, 1783. Married Gertrude Glyde of Boston, February 16, 1812. Came to Newfane in 1812, and operated, for a few years, a grist mill and saw mill then standing on the site of Alvin Gates' chair shop. Was afterward engaged, for a long time, in running a freight team between Williamsville and Boston. Died April 5, 1870.

George Williams was born at Chester, Mass.. March 23, 1769. Married Orilla Pease, June 30, 1803. Came to Newfane in 1816. Resided on the farm now occupied by J. A. Merrifield. Died March 18, 1846.

Robert Cook was born in 1730. Came to Newfane, with his family, from Worcester, Mass., in 1798, and settled on the farm now occupied by Alanson Stone. Died April 27, 1808.

John Cook, son of Robert and Elizabeth Cook, was born March 17, 1781. Married Polly Elmer, December 8, 1808. Resided on the farm on which his father settled. Died December 5, 1845.

Stephen Bowker was born October 18, 1788. Married Sarah Whitney, April 7, 1814. Came to Newfane from Fitzwilliam, N. H., soon afterward, and settled on the farm owned by himself or his son, S. W. Bowker, for nearly sixty years, but now occupied by H. A. Carpenter. Died September 22, 1860.

Elijah Elmer was born at Hinsdale, N. H., in 1753. Married, first, Grace Gould, of Winchester, N. H.; second, Amy (Wood) Wheeler. Came to Newfane, about 1792, and settled on the farm now occupied by George Wheeler. Died December 28, 1833. His son, Ozias Elmer, was born in 1793. Married Susan Edwards, of Claremont, N. H. Resided on the farm now owned by S. W. Bowker. Removed to Pennsylvania, about 1848.

George Wheeler, son of Thomas Wheeler, was born in this town, March 2, 1799. Married Ferona Williams, December 3, 1829. Has resided, since 1823, on the farm which he now occupies.

Daniel Taylor was born in 1767. Came to Newfane from Dummerston, and settled on the farm now owned by Ozearl Attridge. Married Elizabeth Wheeler, of Newfane. Died November 13, 1839.

Moses Aldrich came to Newfane from Rhode Island, where he was born in 1768 or 1769. Settled on the farm now occupied by his grandson, H. N. Aldrich. Married Elizabeth Taylor, of Dummerston. Died May 21, 1841. His son, Daniel Aldrich was born in 1796. Married, first, Betsey Whipple; second, Laura Whipple. Resided on the farm on which his father settled. Died May 23, 1857.

Amasa Lincoln was born at Norton, Mass., July 10, 1787. Married, first, Lucy Richardson, April 14, 1814; second, Mary Hastings, January 26, 1830. Came to town about 1817, from Dummerston. Was engaged in the tanning business for many years. Died January 9, 1858.

Ephriam Hall was born at Rutland, Mass., September 8, 1762. Married Hannah Spears, of New Ipswich, N. H., November 26, 1789. Came to Newfane and settled on the farm now owned by O. P. Morse. Afterward lived on a portion of the farm now owned by C. W. Morse. Died January 18, 1847. Was a soldier of the Revolution.

Richard Pratt was born at Malden, Mass., September 2, 1770. Married Lydia Spears, of New Ipswich, N. H., in 1795. Came to Newfane in 1802, and settled on the farm now owned by Chas. W. Morse. Died August 23, 1856.

Ichabod Merrifield was born at Medford, Mass., April 15, 1768. Married Elizabeth Morse, of Newfane, in December, 1793. Settled on the farm now owned by William Boynton. Afterward removed to the farm now owned by Geo. W. Lamb, where he died, April 22, 1836.

James Lamb was born at Spencer, Mass., in 1750. Married, first, Charlotte Howard; second, Lydia (Cushing) Stearns. Came to Newfane at a very early date and settled on the farm now owned by D. A. Dickinson. Afterward removed to the farm now owned by Emory Dunklee, where he died, January 11, 1836.

Silas Gates was born in 1757. Was one of the earliest settlers of the town. Cleared the farm now owned by Oliver Dexter. Married for his second wife, Hannah Cook, of Newfane. Died August 21, 1828.

Ethan Durrin, was born in 1747. Came to Newfane in 1774. Was married, the same year, to Millescent Parmenter, of Sudbury, Mass. Occupied the farm now owned by H. C. Sparks. Died, July 7, 1823. His wife, Millescent, died, December 5, 1848, at the age of one hundred years.

Capt. William Bartlett was born at Northboro, Mass. Married Azubah Gleason, of Westboro, Mass., about 1790. Came immediately to Newfane, and settled on the farm now owned by Welcome Allen. Removed to Winchester, N. H., in 1837. Capt. Bartlett was a man of much prominence in town affairs.

John Timson was born at Brattleboro, October 4, 1794. Married Julia Knapp, of Brattleboro, in 1813. Came to Newfane in 1819. Resided for more than forty years on the farm now owned by C. E. Tyler, on Timson Hill, so called. Died August 13, 1866.

Daniel Stratton was born at New Ipswich, N. H., March 23, 1773. Married Jane Stickney of New Ipswich, N. H., February 16, 1800. Came to Newfane, the same year, and settled on the farm occupied by himself or his sons, for more than seventy years, but now owned by J. H. Worden. Died October 11, 1850.

Ira Ingram was born in Massachusetts, December 19, 1786. Married, first, Sally Miller; second, Lydia Putnam. Came to Newfane from Marlboro, in 1813, and settled on a farm now owned, partly by Mason Ingram, and partly by Russell Mason. Was chosen a deacon of the Baptist Church, in 1824, and held the office until his decease, April 5, 1860.

Nahum Houghton was born in Newfane, March 17, 1785. Married, first, Mary Holden, January, 1812; second, Lydia Stratton. Resided on the farms now owned by Mason Ingram, Marshall Houghton, and Welcome Allen, respectively. Died, May 12, 1854. Was a justice of the peace for many years, and transacted much public business.

John Goodnow was born in Newfane, August 17, 1797. Married, first, Sally Stratton; second, Charlotte Gould; third, Sarah H. Chase; fourth, Hannah (Charter) Bruce. Settled, and resided for more than forty years, on the farm now owned by Anna Frost. Has been a deacon of the Baptist Church since 1834.

THE REVOLUTIONARY WAR.

When our military stores at Bennington became in danger, and the call came for the Green Mountain Boys to rally for the rescue, Lieut. Jonathan Park and others from this grant, volunteered, and after a two days' march reached Bennington in time to participate in the glorious struggle of that memorable day. In returning after the battle, Park, worn by the fatigues and hardships of the campaign, sickened and was several days in reaching home. We can find no record, or reliable tradition, of the names or number of men who accompanied Lieut. Park on this expediton. But the fact that our minute men responded to the call to arms, is vouched for by one who has often heard the venerable Lieutenant recount the trials of that eventful day and the weariness of the homeward march. From Mrs. Baker's biographical sketch of her grandfather, we doubt not that Ward Eager was one of the number.

The following is all the official record we have been able to find that in any way connects this town with the war for our independence. "March 8, 1781, they voted to raise the soldiers, for the defense of the frontiers, by a town tax." But who or how many soldiers ever enlisted under that vote, or in any other manner went from this town to serve in the struggle for our national independence, the records showeth not.

WAR OF 1812-15.

September 29, 1812, a town meeting was called to see if the town would vote to raise the wages of the Cavalry and Militia, that should be compelled to march. to ten dollars per month. They voted to dismiss the article and adjourned without day.

There is a tradition that at one time the militia expected to be called to Plattsburg, and the company volunteered. Many of the men worked all night, before the day of their expected march, running bullets, making cartridges, etc. But the order came the next day to disband, instead of march. This would seem to explain the second article in the warrant for a town meeting, May 31, 1813, which reads as follows: "To see if the town will raise a sum of money to make compensation to Andrew Grimes, Jr., for damage done said Grimes, by the failure of a certain contract made with him by said town, for the transportation of military stores to Burlington in 1812." They voted to dismiss the article. The soldiers who actually enlisted from this town were Lyman Holden, a man by the name of Gambel, a Mr. Bullard, and Nathaniel Holland, who died at Plattsburg, October 6, 1814. The venerable Isaac Hovey, now of Williamsville, enlisted in January, 1814, from the town of Craftsbury, and served for a period of eighteen months in the engineers' department. He was in only one engagement, the battle of Bridgewater. He now draws a pension of $96 per year.

SOLDIERS OF 1861–65.

It would naturally be supposed that a history of the soldiers who served in the war for the suppression of the slaveholders' rebellion, could, at this time, when so many of the veterans are still living, be easily and correctly written. But in fact we have found it one of the most serious and difficult tasks of the entire work. After corresponding and conversing with many of the soldiers and their friends, and spending days in carefully searching, analyzing and comparing the various names and dates in the Adjutant-General's Reports, the following are the results, which we feel justified in presenting as historical facts:

Company C, 2d Vt. Regiment.

Miller. Frederic F., aged 24. Enlisted May, 1861. 3rd Corp. Promoted Sergeant. Killed at Spottsylvania, May 10, 1864. He fought in seventeen battles without receiving a wound, but was instantly killed by a Minie ball over the left eye, just at night-fall on the first day of the eighteenth engagement, which commenced at Spottsylvania, May 10th, and closed on the 18th. The story of his death, as told by his comrades, is as follows: The Regiment was massed upon a hillside, in an undergrowth of bushes and small trees, in a position that it was evident must soon be abandoned. Sergeant Miller and his men were lying in a hollow behind a knoll, when he crept carefully to the top and fired upon the enemy, time and again handing back his empty gun, and receiving a loaded one from his companions, until, as was supposed, he was sighted and picked off by a sharpshooter. His comrades pulled him back by the legs, and took from his pockets $64.00, a knife and tobacco-box, and sent them to his mother, then cut his clothing so that the enemy should not avail themselves of its use, and left his body on the field. The eulogium pronounced upon him by his Captain and comrades, who served with him to the day of his death is, that he was one of the bravest, truest men that ever wore the blue.

Carpenter, Edwin J., aged 18. Enlisted Aug. 10, 1861. Wounded in the leg and taken prisoner at Savage Station. June 29, 1862; carried to Richmond, exchanged and discharged from the General Hospital at West Philadelphia, Penn., Jan. 28, 1863.

Howe, Edmund P., aged 22. Enlisted May, 1861. Promoted Sergeant. Mustered out of service June 29, 1864.

Lamb, Henry L., aged 22. Enlisted May, 1861. Taken prisoner at Savage Station, June 29, 1862. Reported to the War Department as a deserter, Oct. 19th, 1862, when in fact he was a prisoner, and was afterwards exchanged and sent to the General Hospital at Washington, D. C., where he was discharged by order of the surgeon, January 25, 1863.

Mason, Albert, aged 21. Enlisted May 18, 1861.

Taken prisoner near Spottsylvania, May 21, 1864. Exchanged Nov. 19, 1864. Discharged Dec. 24, 1864. His was the first name on the roll from this town. In speaking of his life as a prisoner, he says: "I marched eight days after I was captured, with the rebel army, and was well treated." Upon leaving the army he was confined two weeks in Libby Prison, where all his greenbacks were confiscated; from there he was sent to Andersonville, where, he says: "I suffered what no pen can tell. When I was exchanged I could not walk nor straighten either of my legs. I was almost dead with the scurvy."

Miller, Morris, aged 40. Enlisted May, 1861. Discharged June 2, 1863.

Pratt, R. M., aged 22 years. Enlisted May, 1861. Discharged Nov. 1, 1861. He was severely wounded in the right arm, early in the first battle of Bull Run. In attempting to go to the rear, he fainted from fatigue and loss of blood, and not recovering himself until after the day was lost, he was captured by the victorious rebels and taken to Libby Prison, where he suffered a foretaste of all the horrors in store for our unfortunate prisoners of war. While in prison his arm was amputated near the shoulder. A portion of the winter after his discharge, he spent with a comrade in lecturing in various towns in Vermont, upon the horrors and sufferings of his prison life, and showing up to the North with what zeal, fiendish spirit and intent the rebels were engaged in the great rebellion.

Company H, 3d Vt. Regiment.

Allison, Everett M., aged 23. Enlisted June 1, 1861; re-enlisted Dec. 22, 1863. Killed at the battle of the Wilderness, May 5, 1864.

Company I, 4th Vt. Regiment.

Cooley, Geo. C., aged 20. Enlisted Aug. 21, 1861, 2d Corporal. Reduced to the ranks. Re-enlisted Dec. 15, 1863, promoted Sergeant, and transferred to Co. F, Feb. 25, 1865; mustered out July 13, 1865.

Company F, 4th Vt. Regiment.

Hall, James, aged 29. Enlisted Sept. 2, 1861. Discharged March 14, 1862.

Perry, Daniel, aged 25. Enlisted Sept. 5, 1861. Discharged Oct. 22, 1862.

Perry, Henry, aged 22. Enlisted Sept. 3, 1861; re-enlisted Dec. 15, 1863. Taken prisoner June 23, 1864; transferred to Co. F, Feb. 25, 1865. Mustered out July 13, 1865.

Nelson, Stephen H., aged 38. Enlisted Dec. 6, 1863. Mustered into service Jan. 4, 1864. Taken prisoner on the Weldon Railroad, June 23, 1864. Died in Andersonville, Ga., Dec. 13, 1864.

Sexton, Thomas B., aged 21. Enlisted Dec. 6, 1863. Captured June 23, 1864. Died at Andersonville. Sept. 11, 1864.

COMPANY F, 6TH VT. REGIMENT.

Green, Geo. E., aged 34. Drafted July 13, 1863.

COMPANY F, 1ST VT. CAVALRY.

Betterly, Frank W., aged 26. Enlisted Sept. 21, 1861. Mustered out Nov. 18, 1864.

Donohue, Patrick, aged 39. Enlisted Jan. 3, 1864. Mustered into service the 7th, and missed in action at Ashland, Va., June 1. Died at Andersonville. Aug. 17. 1864.

Goodnow, Orwell S., aged 21. Enlisted Sept. 16, 1861. Discharged Sept. 20, 1862.

Pond, William W., aged 21. Enlisted Dec. 15, 1863. Missed in action at Ridley's Shop, June 30, 1864.

COMPANY F, 2D VT. (FRONTIER) CAVALRY.

Brown, Lewis G., aged 18. Enlisted Jan. 3, 1865. Mustered out June 27, 1865.

COMPANY G, 7TH VT. REGIMENT.

Hazleton, Edward L., aged 24. Enlisted Nov. 30, 1861; promoted 2d Serg't. Re-enlisted Feb. 17, 1864; promoted 1st Lieut., July 31, 1865. Mustered out March 14, 1866.

COMPANY H, 8TH VT. REGIMENT.

Franklin, Alvin B., aged 23. Enlisted November. 1861; commissioned 1st Lieut., Jan. 17, 1862; promoted Capt., Oct.

27, 1863; promoted Maj., Nov. 24, 1864; promoted Lieut-Col., March 8, 1865. Mustered out June 28, 1865. In June, 1862. Co. H were stationed at Des Almands, La., and on the 22d inst., Lieut. Franklin was ordered to take a detachment of thirty-two men, all told, and with an engine and car proceed carefully up the railroad on a reconnoissance. When slowly nearing Raceland station, they were ambuscaded by the enemy, who fired a heavy volley from the thicket on either side of the road, killing three men and wounding several. Franklin received a number of buckshot in the arms and chest and was supposed to be mortally wounded. At the seige of Port Hudson, from May 25 to July 9, he was hit several times but not injured. At the battle of Cedar Creek, Va., six balls passed through his clothes, one of which wounded him slightly.

Company I.

Holland, Geo. N., aged 27. Enlisted November, 1861; commissioned 1st Lieut., Jan. 17, 1862. Resigned Oct. 25, 1862.

Morse, Joshua C., aged 30. Enlisted Nov., 1861; commissioned 2d Lieut., Jan. 17, 1862; promoted 1st Lieut., Oct. 25, 1862. Resigned July 10, 1863.

Betterly, Thomas F., aged 21. Enlisted Nov. 26, 1861; 4th Serg't. Deserted June 30, 1863. Returned under the president's amnesty proclamation, May 6, 1865; dishonorably discharged June 12, 1865.

Hudson, Bonaparte, aged 20. Enlisted Nov. 30, 1861; 2d Corp. Died in the hospital at New Orleans, May 24, 1862.

Warren, Francis E., aged 23. Enlisted Dec. 23, 1861; 5th Corp.; promoted Serg't. Re-enlisted Jan. 5, 1864; promoted 1st Serg't, June 8, 1864. Wounded at Winchester, Va., Sept. 19, 1864. Promoted 1st Lieut., Feb. 23, 1865; promoted Capt., April 18, 1865. Mustered out June 28, 1865.

Bemis, Leonard C., aged 36. Enlisted Nov. 30, 1861; promoted Corp. Re-enlisted Jan. 5, 1864. Transferred to the Vt. Reserve Corps, April 25, 1865.

Alls, Horace, age 25. Enlisted Dec. 11, 1861. Mustered out June 22, 1864.

Betterly, Alfred, aged 19. Enlisted Nov. 29, 1861. Re-enlisted Jan. 5, 1864. Mustered out June 28, 1865.

Betterly, Geo. S., aged 19. Enlisted Nov. 30, 1861. Discharged May 4, 1863.

Betterly, Gilbert W., aged 18. Enlisted Nov. 29, 1861. Discharged July 16, 1862.

Blashfield, Henry C., aged 18. Enlisted Dec. 2, 1861. Killed at the seige of Port Hudson, June 14, 1863.

Brown, Clark, aged 23. Enlisted Dec. 3, 1861. Discharged July 17, 1863.

Carpenter, Eben B., aged 18. Enlisted Dec. 2, 1861. Re-enlisted Jan. 5, 1864. Mustered out June 28, 1865.

Charter, Samuel, aged 32. Enlisted Jan. 16, 1862. Mustered out June 22, 1864.

Church, Henry, aged 33. Enlisted Dec. 15, 1861. Mustered out June 22, 1864.

Davis, Eros L., aged 18. Enlisted Dec. 9, 1861. Died March 18, on board the ship Wallace, while on her passage to Ship Island.

Davis, Hiram, aged 44. Enlisted Dec. 9, 1861. Discharged July 15, 1862.

Downs, Henry W., aged 18. Enlisted Nov. 28, 1861; promoted Corp.; promoted Serg't, Dec. 13, 1863. Re-enlisted Jan. 5, 1864; promoted 1st Serg't, March 21, 1865; promoted 2d Lieut., April 18, 1865. Mustered out June 28, 1865.

Estabrooks, Sydney J., aged 19. Enlisted Aug. 11, 1864. Mustered out June 28, 1865.

Forbush, William F., aged 15. Enlisted Jan. 13, 1862; musician. Discharged July 15, 1862.

Fairbanks, Wayland, aged 21. Enlisted Dec. 24, 1863. Died Jan. 27, 1865. We extract the following from a biographical sketch published soon after his death:

Wayland Fairbanks enlisted in Co. I, 16th regiment of nine months' men, Sept. 6, 1862, at Williamsville. He was mustered in at Brattleboro, Oct. 23. Left Brattleboro for Washington the 24th. Crossed the Potomac into Virginia, Oct. 30, and up to June 10, 1863, was on picket duty at Fairfax Court House, Union Mills. Capt. Knapp, in writing to Mr. Fairbanks' father, says: "Your son is a fine boy.

From his past conduct I can assure you of his fidelity, bravery and ability." The long marches and terrible battles culminating in the defeat of the rebel horde at Gettysburg, so impaired his constitution, that it was nearly four months after his discharge and return home before he regained his health. And when the call came, Dec. 6, 1863, for more men, he responded by enlisting. Upon his friends remonstrating against his re-enlisting, he replied: "I cannot stay at home when more men are needed. I will not shirk my duty." When told that he could get more money by enlisting for some other town, his answer was: "I shall go for my own town, county and state, if I go at all."

He was mustered into the U. S. service the second time Jan. 7, 1864, and left for New Orleans the twenty-eighth of the same month. Here he was promoted Orderly for the company, and so continued to their entire satisfaction. After the company had a furlough, upon re-enlisting, they were sent to the Shenandoah valley, and Fairbanks went to the hospital at Harper's Ferry, and from thence was transferred to the general hospital, at Annapolis; while there some prisoners were brought in from Andersonville, from whom he took a fever of a malignant type, and died Jan. 24, 1865.

Gates, Alvin, aged 21. Enlisted Dec. 28, 1861. Re-enlisted Jan. 5, 1864. Mustered out June 28, 1865. Detailed to serve as Bass Drummer in the Regimental Drum Corps.

Ingram, Chas. E., aged 18. Enlisted Dec. 6, 1861. Discharged Sept. 30, 1863. Re-enlisted Aug. 10, 1864. Mustered out June 28, 1865.

Ingram, John H., aged 19. Enlisted Aug. 15, 1864. Mustered out June 28, 1865.

Ingram, Jonathan M., aged 38. Enlisted Aug. 10, 1864. Mustered out June 28, 1865.

Lamson, Daniel, aged 27. Enlisted Nov. 27, 1861. Died March 10, 1863.

Mills, Alonzo, aged 21. Enlisted Dec. 24, 1863. Mustered out June 28, 1864.

Morse, Luke J., aged 23. Enlisted Nov. 27, 1861. Mustered out June 22, 1864.

Park, Otis, aged 20. Enlisted Dec. 6, 1861. Discharged Nov., 1863.

Park, Oscar E., aged 18. Enlisted Dec. 5, 1863. Mustered out June 28, 1865.

Peavey, Augustus C., aged 18. Enlisted Nov. 30, 1861. Discharged Nov. 28, 1862. Re-enlisted in the regular army.

Plummer, Geo. F., aged 17. Enlisted Dec. 2, 1861. Re-enlisted March 1, 1864. Mustered out June 28, 1865.

Stearns, Henry M., aged 19. Enlisted Dec. 14, 1863. Mustered out June 28, 1865.

Stratton, Asa H., aged 22. Enlisted Jan. 16, 1862. Mustered out June 22, 1864.

Tyler, Stephen M., aged 28. Enlisted Feb. 7, 1862. Mustered out June 22, 1864.

Warner, Frank R., aged 22. Enlisted Jan. 13, 1862; promoted Corp; promoted Serg't. Re-enlisted Feb. 18, 1864; promoted 1st Serg't; promoted 2d Lieut., Feb. 20, 1864; promoted 1st Lieut., April 18. 1865. Mustered out June 28, 1865.

COMPANY F, 9TH VT. REGIMENT.

Allen, Warren, aged 33. Enlisted Aug. 23, 1864. Mustered out June 13, 1865.

Waller, Edgar G., aged 19. Enlisted Aug. 18, 1864. Transferred to Co. D, 4th regiment, Jan. 20, 1865. Mustered out June 19, 1865.

COMPANY K.

Newton, James H., aged 18. Enlisted June 9, 1862; 3d Corp.. promoted 4th Serg't, Dec. 6. Discharged May 20. 1863. Re-enlisted at the age of 20, Oct. 15, 1863, in Co. F, 17th regiment; promoted 1st Serg't. Killed at Spottsylvania, May 12, 1864.

In a letter to a friend he says, " I was captured in that *disgraceful* surrender at Harper's Ferry, Sept. 15, 1862." His regiment was paroled and ordered to Chicago to guard rebel prisoners, where it remained until April 1, 1863, when it was ordered east and exchanged at City Point. Va. From here he went into the Regimental Hospital at

Suffolk, from which he was discharged in what was considered the first stages of consumption. Upon the partial recovery of his health he re-enlisted, remarking to his friends that he was as good to be shot at as a well man.

Sergent Newton is spoken of by his commander, Capt. Knapp, as a brave, cool, thoroughly competent officer and a perfect gentleman. From the Captain we learn the following as to Newton's death: several times during the day we had charged on the enemy losing heavily, during the intervals between the charges we lay flat on the ground, only when it was necessary to change our position. Late in the afternoon we were lying in an open field under a galling fire, with the protection of only a few rails in the most exposed part of the line, Newton watching the enemy closely to improve every opportunity to send home a shot, at length the order came, forward, and as the line rose and moved on in the last grand charge of the day, Newton fell.

Company E., 11th Vt. Regiment.

Morse, Amherst, aged 23. Enlisted July 29, 1862; promoted 3d Serg't; promoted 1st Serg't, Sept. 6. 1862; promoted 1st Lieut. of Co. K. May 3, 1863. Captured on the Weldon railroad, June 23, 1864. Discharged May 8, 1865.

Lieut. Morse was first engaged at Spottsylvania from May 15 to the 18. 1863; next at North Anna River; next at Cold Harbor, June 1 to the 12. Early in this great battle his Captain was severely wounded, and the command devolved upon him. He came unscathed out of that terrible charge, June 3, when in less than thirty minutes full ten thousand brave men lay dead, wounded and dying on the field. June 23 he was ordered early in the forenoon out upon the skirmish line on the Weldon railroad, where he continued skirmishing until nightfall, when his ammunition, seventy rounds, having failed, and no support reaching him, he attempted to fall back; when near Reams Station he found himself surrounded by a large body of rebels and was obliged to surrender himself, two Lieuts. and fifty-four men. From the field he was taken to Libby, Richmond, and from thence to the following prison pens in the order named: Salisbury, N. C., Macon, Ga., Savannah, Ga., Charleston, S. C., Columbia, S. C., Charlotte, N. C., Raleigh, N. C., and Goldsboro, at which place he signed the parole and came into our lines at Wilmington, March 1. 1865.

Patch, Albert, aged 19. Enlisted Aug. 9, 1862; promoted Corp., Jan. 11, 1863; promoted Serg't, Jan. 21, 1864; promoted 1st Serg't, March 1, 1865; promoted 2d Lieut., June 4, 1865. Mustered out June 24, 1865. During the entire active service of his regiment, Serg't Patch was never off duty, never fell out of the ranks on a march, and nightfall, whether fighting or marching, always found him at his post.

Carpenter, Henry A., aged 21. Enlisted Aug. 9, 1862; promoted Corp., Jan. 23, 1864. Mustered out June 24, 1865.

Miles, Linus P., aged 20. Enlisted Aug. 9, 1862. Died Feb. 8, 1863.

Parsons, Geo. W., aged 29. Enlisted Aug. 9, 1862; promoted Artificer, Dec. 28, 1863. Mustered out June 24, 1865.

Johnson, Edward H., aged 21. Enlisted Nov. 13, 1863. Transferred to Co. D, June 24, 1865. Mustered out Aug. 25, 1865.

Mullett, Daniel A., aged 37. Enlisted Dec. 4, 1863. Transferred to Co. D, June 24, 1865. Mustered out Aug. 25, 1865.

Park, Otis, aged 21. Enlisted Dec. 5, 1863. Transferred to Co. D, June 24, 1865. Mustered out Aug. 25, 1865.

COMPANY L, 11TH VT. REGIMENT.

Birchard, Sardis, aged 21. Enlisted June 27, 1863; 1st Serg't. He was taken prisoner on the Weldon railroad, June 23, 1864, and carried to Andersonville, Ga., where he died Aug. 20, and was buried in grave number 6334. His last message to his aged parents, delivered to a comrade, while suffering and dying with all the horrors and pangs of starvation, was, "Tell my father and mother that I die a Christian; tell them I am not sorry that I enlisted"

Newton, Chas. M., aged 17. Enlisted July 6, 1863; promoted Corp., June 2, 1865. Transferred to Co. C, June 24, 1865. Mustered out Aug. 25, 1865.

Company I, 12th Vt. Regiment.

Smith, Everett N., aged 18. Enlisted Oct. 4, 1862. Mustered out of service July 14, 1863.

Company H, 2d Vt. Regiment U. S. Sharp Shooters.

Mullett, Chas. M., aged 21. Enlisted Oct. 20, 1861. Discharged March 22, 1862.

Robbins, Geo. W., aged 37. Enlisted Oct. 20, 1861. Discharged July 2, 1862.

Willis, Daniel H., aged 23. Enlisted Oct. 14, 1861. Killed in action at Sulphur Springs, Va., Aug. 26, 1862.

16th Regiment Nine Months' Men, Mustered into the United States Service Oct. 23, 1862. Mustered out Aug. 10, 1863.

Company I.

Haskins, Kittredge, aged 26. Enlisted Sept. 20, 1862; 1st Lieut. Resigned March 19, 1863.

Dunklee, Addison R., aged 19. Enlisted Sept. 20, 1862; 3d Serg't.

Wallen, Harrison, aged 26. Enlisted Sept. 20, 1862; 5th Serg't. Reduced to the ranks July 4, 1863.

Goodnow, Wm. H., aged 19. Enlisted Sept. 20, 1862; musician.

Adams, Adin, aged 26. Enlisted Sept. 20, 1862.

Brooks, Wm. A., aged 23. Enlisted Sept. 20, 1862.

Cook, James F., aged 20. Enlisted Sept. 20, 1862. Killed at the battle of Gettysburg, July 3, 1863. He was shot through the vitals and dropped with the exclamation upon his lips, "I am a dead man." In the evening after the battle, two of his comrades, William Brooks and John Kelsey, sought out his body and buried it.

Corbitt, John N., aged 24. Enlisted Sept. 20, 1862.

Donahue, Patrick, aged 38. Enlisted Sept. 20, 1862.

Fairbanks, Wayland E., aged 19. Enlisted Sept. 6, 1862; promoted Corp. May 9, 1863.

Jones, John D., aged 25. Enlisted Sept. 20, 1862.

Lincoln, Samuel B., aged 18. Enlisted Sept. 20, 1862. Taken prisoner at Gettysburg, July 3. Died in Richmond, Nov. 20, 1863.

The story of his capture, as told by Corporal Wilson, is as follows: "My squad were on picket duty, at break of day we saw another picket line just in advance which we supposed were our men, they shouted to us to come down out of our exposed position, and some of the boys started. Instantly I saw that they were Rebs, and ordered the boys back, but it was too late to save Lincoln and another young man, for the shot were flying like hail."

Morse, Chas. E., aged 31. Enlisted Sept. 20. 1862.

Morse, Wm., aged 25. Enlisted Sept. 20, 1862. Died April 26, 1863.

Powers, Jeffrey, aged 21. Enlisted Sept. 20, 1862.

Stone, Henry B., aged 26. Enlisted Sept. 20, 1862.

Sexton, Thomas B., aged 19. Enlisted Sept. 20, 1862.

Willis, Monroe C., aged 19. Enlisted Sept. 20, 1862. Shot through the wrist and forearm at the battle of Gettysburg, July 3, 1863.

Company E, 17th Vt. Regiment.

Coburn, Chas. H., aged 18. Enlisted March 10, 1864. Mustered out July 14, 1865.

Taylor, Franklin J., aged 18. Enlisted March 26, 1864. Absent and wounded July 14, 1865. Discharged Nov. 4, 1865.

Thompson, Thomas, aged 40. Enlisted March 25, 1864. Deserted July 1, 1865.

Company F.

Day, Henry A., aged 21. Enlisted Oct. 24, 1863. Killed at Petersburg, Va., June 24, 1864.

Strong, Lewis aged 41. Enlisted March 20, 1864. Mustered out May 13, 1865.

Company H.

Magraw, John, aged 30. Enlisted March 31. 1864. Deserted May 22, 1864.

United States Navy.

Fairserois, Robert; Green, James; Ham, Geo W.; Merrick, Nicholas; Shaw, Benj. F.; Smith, William.

NAMES OF MEN WHO FURNISHED SUBSTITUTES.

Bowker, S. W.; Dunklee, A. B.; Lamson, J. D.; Redfield, Geo. W.; Sherman, O. L.; Bemis, W. L.

NAMES OF MEN WHO PAID COMMUTATION MONEY.

Adams, Jos. O.; Merrifield, Hollis R.; Mixer, Chas.; Morse, Thomas A; Russell, Sylvanus; Walker, Henry W.; Wheeler, E. P.

Number of soldiers who served and were not credited to the town by name, six.

It is but truth to say that those who served in the navy, and several of the infantry, were not citizens of the town, but as many at least of our sons served elsewhere, as were employed from abroad to fill Newfane's quota.

NATIVES OF NEWFANE WHO ENLISTED FROM OTHER TOWNS AND STATES.

Aldrich, Harrison, enlisted at Petersham, Mass., and joined a company formed at Barre, which went into camp at Worcester, July 19. 1861, as Co. K, 21st Regiment, Mass. Volunteers. The regiment left Worcester in August, for Annapolis, Md., where it performed garrison duty and guarded the Annapolis and Baltimore railroad until January, 1862. It was then attached to Burnside's expedition to North Carolina, where it was engaged in the following battles: Roanoke Island, Feb. 8; Newbern, March 14; Camden, April 19. The regiment left North Carolina in July, 1862, for Virginia, and was engaged in second Bull Run, Aug. 29 and 30; at Chantilly, Sept. 1; Antietam, Sept. 17; Fredericksburg, Dec. 13. In April, 1863, the Twenty-First, having suffered very severe losses in its numerous engagements, was ordered to be consolidated with other regiments, and the Colonel and several line officers, including Capt. Aldrich, resigned and were honorably discharged. Capt. Aldrich enlisted as private, served in Co. K as Serg't, 2d Lieut. and 1st Lieut., and was appointed Capt. of Co. I, same regiment, Dec. 13, 1862. Was wounded in the shoulder at the battle of Newbern, N. C. It is said of Capt. Aldrich that in the various battles in which he was engaged he was particularly noted for coolness and bravery.

Bennett, Henry L., enlisted at Royalston, Mass., in 1864.

Davis, David H., aged 18. Enlisted from Dummerston, in the 8th Reg., Co. D, Jan. 2, 1864. Mustered out June 28, 1865.

Gould, Lyman W., son of the late Dea. Lyman Gould, of Newfane, enlisted Aug. 12, 1862, as a private soldier, at East Boston, Mass., and was immediately detailed on recruiting service in the city of Boston, by Gov. Andrew, Aug. 20, 1862, was commissioned 2d Lieut. in the 41st Mass. Infantry, and Captain in the same regiment Sept. 15, 1862; was transferred June 17, 1863, to 3d Mass. Cavalry, with same rank, and mustered out of service, on resignation, by reason of disability, Oct. 19, 1863. The Forty-first, under Col. T. E. Chickering, was attached to Gen. Banks' Louisiana Expedition, arriving at New Orleans Dec. 17, 1862, and proceeding with Gen. Grover's command to recapture Baton Rouge. Captain Gould remained at the latter place during the winter, on detached service, serving on Board of Court Martial, and as Assistant Provost Marshal. In the spring of 1863 he participated in the Bayou Teche campaign until the arrival of the army at Opelousas, when he was ordered by Gen. Banks to take command of a force, proceed outside the lines, and secure the products of the country. He succeeded in capturing, and turned over to the Government, a large amount of property, including five hundred bales of cotton. While engaged in this duty he received a severe wound in the left side, from which he suffered intensely while being brought back through the country to headquarters. Joining his regiment, June 4, 1863, in front of Port Hudson, he was assigned to the command of the outpost cavalry pickets, a line some five miles long, which position he held until the surrender of the place, July 6. On arriving at Boston, after resigning, he was offered a commission as Lieut. Col., with the promise of the command of a regiment as soon as he should be able to assume it, but was unwilling to draw pay for services not rendered. Besides numerous skirmishes Capt. Gould was engaged in the following battles: Comek River, Baton Rouge, Franklin, Irish Bend and Port Hudson.

Higgins, Samuel B., aged 26. Enlisted May 9, 1861, in the first Wisconsin Reg. Re-enlisted Oct. 21, 1862, for three years, as first-class musician in the band of the 16th, U. S. regular infantry, and served under Rosecrans, Thomas, Grant and Sherman.

Higgins, Ira S., aged 26. Enlisted Sept. 6, 1861, in the band of the 4th Vt. Discharged June 23, 1862.

Ingram, Ira O., enlisted at Ripon, Wisconsin. Oct. 17, 1861, in Co. K, First Wisconsin Cavalry. In 1862-63, with his regiment, he was engaged in fighting guerrillas in Missouri and Arkansas. While in this dangerous and exciting service he came in contact with the enemy in numerous skirmishes and minor engagements, and had many narrow escapes. Was often in command of foraging and other expeditions. Was taken prisoner at Languille Ferry, Arkansas, Aug. 3, 1862. Was mustered out of service at Milwaukee, Wis., May 12, 1864.

Johnson, Henry C., enlisted for the defence of the national capital, at the time of Gen. Early's raid in the Shenandoah Valley, in 1864, but the 6th corps arriving the same day, his brigade was immediately discharged.

Kenney, John C., enlisted in the 101st, Illinois Reg., at Joliet, Aug. 12, 1862. Died at Nashville, Tenn., Jan. 21, 1863.

Newton, John, enlisted at Lancaster, Ohio, in the 18th U. S. regular infantry, and served in all the engagements of the 14th army corps, until detailed to act as clerk at the division headquarters.

Newton, John, son of Sir Isaac Newton. Enlisted in the 2d Wisconsin Reg., at Stevens Point, Jan. 4, 1864. Discharged at Mobile, Ala., Oct. 9, 1865.

Newman, John L., aged 21. Enlisted from Brattleboro, Aug. 28, 1862, in Co. B, 16th Reg. Promoted Corp. Feb. 14, 1863.

Pratt, Myron, son of R. P. Pratt, formerly of Newfane, enlisted as a private soldier at Monson, Mass., September 7, 1861, in Co. E, First Mass. Cavalry. He received a commission as 1st Lieut. in December, 1861, and as Captain of Co. G, same regiment, in July, 1862. Accompanying the regiment to Beaufort, S. C., he served for a while in the capacity of Quartermaster, and was engaged in the battle of James Island, at which place he narrowly escaped by swimming the river. Ordered to the Army of the Potomac, he participated in the battles of South Mountain and Antietam, and the numerous skirmishes incident to the cavalry branch of the service in the pursuit of a retreating enemy. In October, 1862, he was detailed, with his company, to act as Maj. Gen. Porter's escort.

He was killed Nov. 3, 1862, in a skirmish at Snicker's Gap, Va., by a bullet from a rebel sharpshooter, which struck him a little below the heart, and came out at the shoulder blade. In letters to his widow one of the members of his company wrote of him:

"Capt. Pratt was the first man to lead us. He came to the front and said, ' Follow me, boys. I will lead you.' He was a good and brave officer, and much loved by all who knew him. His memory will be long cherished by the boys of Co. G. He was their pride. He was ever ready to do any duty which might devolve upon him, and he never was sick when there was any dangerous duty to perform. He died respected and regretted by all of the officers in his command."

Ray, Samuel B., aged 22. Enlisted at Jamaica, in Co. I, 4th Vt. Aug. 14, 1861. Mortally wounded in the lungs and one thigh, in Burnside's disastrous assault upon the heights of Fredericksburg, Dec. 13, 1862.

In his dying hour, after speech was gone, he placed his money in his Chaplain's hands, and when the good man asked, " Shall I send this to your mother?" he nodded yes, but who she was or where she lived he could not tell. The mother was searched out, and the dying soldier's request fulfilled.

Sibley, Isaac H., enlisted from Dummerston, Aug. 12, 1862, in Co. E, 11th Vermont Reg. Promoted Corp. June 8, 1864. Fought at Coal Harbor, Spottsylvania, Winchester, and in numerous other engagements, was wounded in the arm and face at Winchester. Mustered out June 28, 1865.

Ward, John S., enlisted in the 3d Minnesota regiment, in the summer of 1861. Taken prisoner with his regiment near Murfeesboro, Tenn., in the spring of 1862. The regiment were paroled and ordered against the Sioux Indians.

He was sick and discharged at Fort Snelling, in August, 1862. Re-enlisted at the age of 24, Jan. 30, 1865, in the 7th Vt., Co. G, and was stationed on the Rio Grande, Texas. His health again failing, he was discharged in August.

In 1866 he completed his law studies with the Hon. B. F. Rice, of Little Rock, Ark., and was admitted to practice, but his health was so thoroughly impaired that he was compelled to return home, where he died, Feb. 25, 1871.

Worden, James C., of New York, a son of the late Asa Worden, was in the service a while as a member of Co. E, 71st N. Y. Reg.

SENATOR TWITCHELL AND THE SONS OF NEWFANE MURDERED IN LOUISIANA, 1874.

Among those who enlisted upon the breaking out of the war of 1861, was a Townshend boy who entered the 4th regiment. At its close he held a Captain's commission and a position on Gen. Sheridan's staff. That man, to-day, is known as Senator Twitchell, of the State Senate of Louisiana. Upon the close of the war he decided to make the South his home and married the daughter of an ex-rebel planter. Establishing himself at Coushatta, on Red river, in the district known as Red River Parish, he applied himself to business with all his Yankee energy, and soon amassed wealth and political power, for he was the freedman's friend. In 1870 his brother Homer, mother, and three sisters, with their husbands, M. C. Willis, C. Holland, and Geo. King, all of Newfane, removed to Coushatta and established themselves in business under his direction. They remained undisturbed until the political canvass began, in August, 1874, when the old rebel element determined to establish its political supremacy, and drive all the leading republicans from the Parish. Twitchell, Willis and Holland being office-holders were marked men. Capt. Twitchell at the time, fortunately, was in New Orleans. On the evening of Aug. 27 there was a large, noisy and threatening crowd upon the street. When young Twitchell inquired for the cause of this disturbance, he was told that a rising of the blacks was feared, but if he and the republican leaders would surrender themselves it would prevent a massacre of the negroes and allay all political irritation. Upon consideration they accepted the proposition, and surrendered themselves and their arms, when they were further told that if they would leave the country their lives should be protected and they should be guaranteed a safe escort to Shreveport.

They accepted the conditions of life, and on the night of the 30th, under a guard of thirty mounted men, who promised them a safe escort, they started upon their last earthly march. After a ride of thirty miles, a second body of armed men came dashing upon them from another quarter, and the guard, with a treachery unequalled even by Indian perfidy, abandoned their victims to be shot down like dogs. But in the hour of their extremity, their courage, their honor, did not fail them. Holland, being supervisor of registration, they desired to retain for a while and told him to flee for his life, but he, believing that they simply intended to shoot him in the back, with the coolness of a veteran answered, "No, you have murdered my friends, now take me," then walking to the spot where he had seen Willis shot, he calmly opened his coat, folded his arms upon his breast and gave the order to fire, exhibiting a spirit that touched even the hearts of some of his murderers. Thus perished two of the sons of Newfane in her centennial year; one a soldier who had faced the foe at Gettysburg, the other a martyr, who gave the order for his own execution. The story of their captors is, that young Twitchell, being mounted upon the fleetest horse of the party, was only brought down after a wild ride of ____ miles for life. And as a fitting close to this dark and awful tragedy, their friends were denied the boon even of their mutilated bodies, until after decomposition had removed all traces of abuse. Nay, not until Capt. Twitchell obtained a military order for a company of cavalry, could he remove them and bury them like men. Homer Twitchell was 26. Clark Holland 24, and Monroe C. Willis 28 years of age.

TOWN OFFICERS, 1774—1876.

MODERATORS OF ANNUAL MARCH MEETING.

Allen, Ebenezer, 1799, 1800.
Bartlett, William, 1804, '16, '18, '19, '21, '24.
Bowker, S. W., 1869.
Boyden, Hezekiah, 1775, '79, '80.
Burditt, F. O., 1865.
Dunklee, Richmond, 1838, '40, '43, '45, '48, '49, '53, '58, '62.
Eager, Walter, 1831.
Elmer, Elijah, 1809.
Field, Martin, 1811, '12, '17.
Fisher, George, 1842, '47, '50, '51, '52.
Fletcher, Ebenezer, 1774.
Houghton, Nahum, 1836.
Jones, Anthony, 1837.
Kenney, John, 1815.
Kimball, Pardon T., 1832.
Knowlton, Luke, 1777, '89, '90, '94, '96, '98, 1801, '02, '03, '05.
Merrick, Ebenezer, 1781, '82.

Merrifield, J. A., 1860.
Morse, Austin J., 1867, '71, '74.
Morse, Ebenezer, 1822.
Morse, Geo. A., 1844.
Morse, Dr. John, 1785, '95, '97.
Newton, Marshall, 1854, '55, '59. '61, '63.
Newton, Sir Isaac, 1833.
Ormsbee, Benj., 1839, '41, '46.
Osgood, Christopher, 1776, '78.
Osgood, Willard E., 1856, '57.
Ransom, Ezekiel, 1791-93.
Sanborn, David W., 1827.
Sherman, O. L., 1864, '66, '68, '70, '72, '73, '75, '76.
Sherwin, Silvanus, 1806, '07, '08, '10, '13, '14, '26, '28, '30, '34.
Tainter, Benjamin, 1786.
Ward, William, 1783, '84, '87, '88.
Williams, Wm. H., 1820, '23, '25, '29, '35.

SELECTMEN.

Allen, Amos, 1800, '01.
Allen, Ebenezer, 1790-92, '94-99.
Arnold, George, 1845-49, '55-58.
Bartlett, William, 1809, '10, '13, '14, '15.
Bowker, S. W., 1872.
Boyden, Hezekiah, 1799.
Boynton, William, 1850.
Bruce, Artemas, 1832, '33, '50.
Bruce, Wm. T., 1876.
Burditt, F. O., 1868-74.
Cook, Jonas, 1792, '93, 1809, '10.
Cook, Park F., 1860.
Davis, Joshua, 1790, '91, '94-99.

Dickinson, Dana D., 1865, '66, '75, '76.
Dunklee, Emory, 1859.
Dunklee, Richmond, 1855.
Durrin, Ethan, 1778.
Eager, Nahum, 1839-42.
Eager, Walter, 1824, '25, '30 '31, '35, '36, '37, '38.
Eager, Ward, 1777, '82, '83, '84, '85, '86, '88.
Eddy, Isaac, 1835.
Eddy, Jonathan, 1861, '62, '74, '75.
Elmer, Elijah, 1801, '02, '03, '07 '08.
Evans, Charles, 1781.

Field, Martin, 1804, '11, '17, '18.
Fisher, Daniel, Jr., 1807, '08, '11, '12, '15.
Fisher, George, 1839-44, '51-56, '59, '64-66.
Franklin, Alvin B., 1866, '67.
Gates, Silas, 1793.
Hall, Samuel, 1843, '44.
Hitchcock, David, 1777.
Holden, Josiah, 1790.
Holland, Ephraim, 1789.
Holland, James, 1836-38.
Holland, Lot, 1818.
Holland, Paul, 1805, '06, '25.
Houghton, Nahum, 1847, '48.
Howe, Gardner L., 1860, '61.
Kenney, John, 1813, '14, '15, '20, '21.
Kenney, Moses, 1775, '76, '78, '79, '80, 81.
Kenney, Silas, 1824, '27.
Keyes, Ashley, 1816, '17.
Kimball, Pardon T., 1830, '31, '52, '53.
Knowlton, Calvin, 1793.
Knowlton, Luke, 1779, '82, '84, '85, '86, '87, '88.
Knowlton, Luke, Jr., 1812.
Knowlton, Nathan, 1809-15.
Lamb, James, 1800.
Lincoln, O. L., 1863.
Merrick, Ebenezer, 1781.
Merrifield, David, 1816, '17, '18, '34.
Merrifield, Chas. C., 1846, '51.
Miller, Horatio N., 1849.
Moore, Franklin, 1862, '63.
Morse, Amherst, 2d, 1819, '20.
Morse, Amherst, 1867.
Morse, Austin J., 1859-61.
Morse, Benj. E., 1854, '55, '70, '71.
Morse, Joshua, 2d, 1819, '22, '23, '24, '26, '27, '28, '29.
Morse, Oliver P., 1845.

Morse, Sabin P., 1852, '53.
Morse, Samuel, 1864.
Newman, John, 1843, '44.
Newton, Marshall, 1800, '01.
Newton, Marshall, 1854.
Newton, Sir Isaac, 1832-34.
Osgood, Christopher, 1774, '78.
Park, Ephraim, 1818, '19.
Park, Jonathan, 1776, '81, '91, '92, '94-99.
Plimpton, Holland, 1870-72.
Pomeroy, Chester, 1802-04, '20, '21, '26-29.
Redway, J. D., 1864, '65.
Rice, Hazleton, 1875, '76.
Rice, Henry, 1857, '58.
Robinson, Aaron C., 1821-23, '28-30, '35, '36, '51.
Robinson, Hollis T., 1857, '58.
Robinson, Samuel, 1775, '80, '81.
Rutter, Philip, 1775, '85-89.
Saben, Moses, 1831, '32, '37, '38.
Sherman, William, 1845, '46.
Sherwin, Silvanus, 1802, 03, '04, '22, '23.
Smith, Edward, 1774.
Sparks, Chas. E., 1868, '69, '73, '74.
Stedman, Nathaniel, 1780.
Stevens, Israel, 1805, '66.
Stratton, D. O., 1850, '62, '63.
Taylor, Daniel, 1783, 1805, '06.
Tuthill, W. J., 1873.
Ward, Calvin, 1847-49.
Ward, William, 1782, '83, '84, '87.
Wheeler, E. P., 1867-69.
Wheeler, George, 1839-42.
Wheeler, John, 1774, '76, '77.
Wilder, John, 1825.
Willard, Samuel, 1789.
Williams, George, 2d, 1833, '34.
Williams, Wm. H., 1807, '08, '18, '26.

TOWN TREASURERS.

Allen, Ebenezer, 1803–05.
Bruce, Artemas, 1840–59.
Burditt, F. O., 1865–77.
Eager, Ward, 1787–1802.
Evans, Charles, 1783.
Field, Martin, 1819–25.
Knowlton, Luke, 1774–82, 1784–86.

Kenney, John, 1818.
Knowlton, Luke, Jr., 1806.
Newton, Marshall, 1863, '64.
Park, Nathan F., 1839.
Sherwin, Silvanus, 1807–17, 1826, –38.
Warren, Otis, 1860–62.

LISTERS.

Allen, Amos, 1792, '98.
Allen, Newman, 1834, '35.
Bailey, Zina G., 1861, '62, '65, '76.
Baker, Haynes E., 1848, '49.
Bartlett, William, 1791, '97, 1805.
Bowker, S. W., 1850, '51, '52, '53, '55, '70.
Boyden, Hezekiah, 1782, '85.
Brooks, Ephraim, 1800, '07.
Brooks, John, 1813.
Brown, Alexander, 1813.
Brown, Luke, 1796.
Brown, Samuel, 1834, '35.
Bruce, Artemas, 1822, '28.
Butterfield, Zatter, 1807.
Chamberlain, Nathaniel, 1801.
Chamberlain, Thaddeus, 1803, '06.
Chamberlain, Thaddeus, Jr., 1811.
Chamberlain, Wm., 1804.
Cook, Jonas, 1803.
Cook, Nathan, 1808.
Cook, Park F., 1845–48.
Cook, Thomas, 1808.
Cowing, Henry, 1865.
Cushing, Warren, 1814.
Cushing, Warren, Jr., 1843, '44.
Cutler, David, 1816.
Davis, Joshua, 1782, '86, 1802.
Dexter, Joseph W., 1857.
Dickinson, D. A., 1860, '61.

Dunklee, Richmond, 1843, '44, '49, '59.
Durrin, Ethan, 1788, 1810.
Eager, Benj., 1817.
Eager, Walter, 1819, '27, '29, '41, '42.
Eager, Ward, 1775, '77, '79, '81, '91, 1805.
Eastman, James, 1831.
Ellis, Joseph, 1799, 1806, '13, '33, '34, '35.
Evans, Charles, 1780, '83.
Field, Martin, 1803, '10, '19.
Fisher, Daniel, 1790, 1810.
Fisher, Daniel, Jr., 1812, '15.
Franklin, O. E., 1870, '71, '73, '74.
Fuller, Benjamin, 1777, '83.
Fullerton, Edward, 1793.
Gates, Silas, 1792, '95, 1804, '11.
Grout, John, Jr., 1818, '22.
Hall, Jonathan, 1794, 1810.
Hall, Jonathan, Jr., 1818.
Hall, Samuel, 1840, '41.
Hall, Silas, 1806.
Higgins, Nathaniel, 1836, '38, '39, '40, '41, '45, '46, '54.
Holbrook, Dexter, 1831.
Holbrook, John, 1786.
Holden, Josiah, 1788.
Holland, Ephraim, 1802.
Holland, Jonah, 1793, '98.
Holland, Joseph, Jr., 1813.
Holland, Lot, 1814, '19, '20.

Holland, Paul, 1799.
Houghton, Nahum, 1817, '28.
Hunt, William, 1815.
Ingram, Ira, 1837.
Ingram, Mason, 1858.
Jackson, Nathaniel H., 1812.
Kenney, John, 1809.
Kenney, Moses, 1783, '87.
Kenney, Silas, 1816, '20, '21, '26.
Keyes, Ashley, 1796, 1812.
Kimball, Asahel, 1794, 1808.
Kimball, Nelson W., 1859.
Kimball, Pardon T., 1825, '32, '37.
Knowlton, Calvin, 1789.
Knowlton, Ezekiel, 1795.
Knowlton, Luke, 1774, '76, '78, '79, '80, '81.
Knowlton, Luke, Jr., 1801.
Knowlton, Nathan, 1806.
Lamb, Chas. P., 1856, '57, '73, '74.
Lamb, James, 1799, 1806.
Lamb, Silas, 1815, '23.
Lothrop, Thomas, 1812.
Lyman, James, 1875.
Merrifield, Chas. C., 1842-44.
Merrifield, David, 1820, '21, '24, '30, '32.
Merrifield, John H., 1874-76.
Moore, Franklin, 1865, '68.
Moore, John M., 1875.
Morse, Amherst, 2d, 1814, '23, '26.
Morse, Austin J., 1849-56, '68, '72.
Morse, Benj. E., 1872.
Morse, Jason, 1804.
Morse, Dr. John, 1775, '85, '98.
Morse, Jonathan, 1819.
Morse, Joshua, 2d, 1808, '21.
Morse, Lawson B., 1839.
Morse, Nelson, 1872.
Morse, Oliver P., 1858-60.
Morse, Samuel, 1854, '68.
Newman, John, 1836, '42.

Newton, Marshall, 1789, '97, 1810.
Newton, Marshall, 1847, '50, '51, '52, '53, '55, '60.
Newton, Sir Isaac, 1831, '36, '38, '39, '40.
Olds, Chester, 1828.
Osgood, Christopher, 1774, '76, '78.
Park, Ephraim, 1809, '17, '25.
Park, Jonathan, 1784, '87, '88.
Park, Nathan, F., 1816, '30.
Pomeroy, Chester, 1794, 1800, '09, '15.
Pomeroy, P. Ashley, 1805, '11.
Pratt, R. M., 1869, '71.
Rand, Richard, 1785.
Ransom Ezekiel, 1790.
Rawson, Paris, 1869.
Redway, J. D., 1862, '63.
Reed, Thomas 1811, '19, '22.
Rice, Hazleton, 1871.
Rice, Moses, 1813, '23, '26.
Robbins, Thurston, 1817, '29, '33.
Robinson, Aaron C., 1824, '27, '32, '47.
Robinson, Hezekiah, 1814.
Robinson, John H., 1812.
Robinson, Jonathan, 1787.
Rutter, Philip, 1784.
Rutter, Stephen, 1815.
Saben, Daniel S., 1863, '64.
Saben, Moses, 1818, '33.
Sanborn, David W., 1818.
Sherwin, Silvanus, 1797, 1824, '27.
Smith, Edward, 1782.
Sparks, Chas. E., 1863, '64, '66, '67.
Stedman, William, 1818.
Stedman, Wm. A., 1856, '57, '58, '64, '66, '67.
Stevens, Israel, 1792, '94, 1802.
Stevens, Jacob, Jr., 1796.
Stone, Nathan, 1786, 1811, '16.

Stratton, Daniel, 1899.
Stratton, D. O., 1866, '67.
Taft, Josiah, 1807.
Tainter, Benjamin, 1784.
Taylor, Arad, 1825.
Taylor, Daniel, Jr., 1800, '08.
Taylor, Simon, 1814.
Timson, Clark, 1876.
Tuthill, W. T. 1869, '70.
Warren, Albert T., 1876.
Wheeler, Darius, 1790.
Wheeler, George, 1830.

Wheeler, John, 1781.
Wheeler, Thomas. 1793, 1807.
Wheelock, Henry. 1837, '38.
Whitcomb, Jonathan, 1795.
Wilder, John, 1807, '16.
Willard, Samuel, 1789.
Williams, George, 2d, 1829.
Williams, John W., 1848.
Williams, Wm. H., 1801, '09, '17.
Williams, Wm. L., 1845, '46.
Wiswell, Ebenezer, 1861, '62.

FIRST CONSTABLES.

Bowker, S. W., 1860, '65, '66, '67, '69.
Brooks, John, 1816.
Brown, Luke, 1799.
Bruce, Artemas, 1776.
Bruce, Artemas, Jr., 1777, '78, '87, '88.
Butterfield, Zatter, 1803, '10.
Carter, Chas. S., 1861.
Chamberlain, Thaddeus, Jr., 1806-08.
Davis, Joshua, 1783.
Durrin, Ethan, 1779, '84, '85.
Farrar, Phineas, 1774.
Fisher, Simon, 1817.
Fuller, Benj., 1775.
Grout, John, Jr., 1821.
Hall, Silas, 1809.
Holbrook, Dexter, 1827.
Holden, Josiah, 1786.
Holland, Paul, 1789.
Hoyt, Henry H., 1874-76.
Jones, Anthony, 1819, '24, '25.
Knowlton, Silas, 1791.
Lamb, Charles, 1812.
Lamb, Charles P., 1842, '70, '71, '72.
Merrifield, Aaron, Jr., 1792, '93.

Merrifield, David, 1813, '14.
Merrifield, Ichabod, 1790.
Merrifield, J. A., 1833, '34, '35, '49, '50, '52.
Morse, Austin J., 1853, '68, '73.
Morse, Benj. E., 1851, '54.
Morse, Ebenezer, 2d, 1804, '05, '11, '15.
Morse, George A., 1828.
Morse, Dr. John, 1781, '94-98, 1801, '02.
Morse, Jonathan, 1819, '26.
Morse, Joshua, 1780, 1800.
Morse, Lawson B., 1843, '44.
Newman, John, 1836, '37, '38, '40.
Newton, Marshall, 1839, '41, '45, '46, '47, '48.
Pratt, R. M., 1862-64.
Stedman, Wm. A., 1855-59.
Taylor, Denzil, 1818.
Townsley, Calvin, 1822.
Willard, Josiah, 1823.
Williams, George, 2d, 1831, '32.
Williams, Wm. H., 1830.
Wood, Solomon, 1782.
Wood, Warren, 1829.

GRAND LIST OF NEWFANE, 1874.

School District No. 1.

Adams, M. W.,	$20 23	Haskins, Luther,	$ 2 00
Alls, Horace,	4 46	Lord, L. W.,	2 00
Brown, Alvin,	8 67	Moore, Asahel,	9 82
Brown, Levi,	4 65	Moore, Henry W.,	3 14
Brown, Clark L.,	2 00	Moore, Lucius,	75
Bruce, Emory F.,	2 00	Mundell, Mary,	4 86
Cannon, Franklin,	2 00	Staples, R. S.,	3 65
Cannon, Chloe J.,	2 03	Warner, F. R.,	3 65
Cheney, Jeduthan,	16 37	Whitaker, Joseph,	2 81
Coan, Charles D.,	3 83	Whitaker, Walter A.,	2 81
Davis, Joseph,	2 43	Whitaker, Wm. R.,	6 05
Elmore, Emily,	3 24	Whitaker, Henry J.,	6 05
Fessenden, A. D.,	40	Worden, Asa,	1 62
Fuller, George A.,	3 42	Worden, George C.,	2 00
Gould, Henry,	2 00	Worden, Isaac,	1 22
Harris, Madison,	1 22	Worden, J. J.,	5 36
Hastings, George L.,	3 75		

School District No. 2.

Allen, Clara,	$ 9 00	Chase, A. B. & Wife,	$ 8 89
Allen, Newman's Est.,	9 72	Chase, H. T.,	12 03
Barrett, Shubel,	20 00	Chase, W. N.,	2 25
Bemis, Alanson,	1 81	Cook, Sarah,	6 59
Bemis, Levi,	2 00	Converse, Caroline E.,	6 48
Birchard, Austin,	80 92	Cowing, H. C.,	12 61
Blodgett, Eliot,	7 00	Croker, J. W.,	3 00
Bolles, Nelson,	8 08	Cushing, Lucy C.,	24 46
Bowles, Charles,	2 30	Downs, H. W.,	3 65
Boynton, William,	52 15	Eager, Chas. H.,	30 96
Brigham, L. H.,	6 24	Fairbanks, Alexander,	7 67
Bruce, William T.,	23 92	Fish, F. A.,	13 34
Burditt, F. O.,	11 72	Fitts, Mary,	6 00
Burnham, Geo. W.,	6 80	Fitts, Sophia,	2 50

Green, J. J.,	$20 02	Perkins, Jane,	$ 9 58
Hayden, Loren,	8 10	Pettee, H. W.,	3 22
Higgins, L. B. & M. H.,	6 08	Pratt, Mary,	3 65
Higgins, Nathaniel and Wife,	68 76	Redway, J. T. & A. F.,	24 94
		Redfield, Joel & Wife,	3 65
Hildreth, Warren R.,	2 00	Rand, Chester,	2 38
Holland, Sophia K.,	11 80	Ranney, Mary A.,	11 00
Hopkins, Augustus,	2 00	Rawson, Paris,	17 39
Howe, M. O.,	18 77	Rice, Henry,	29 88
Johnson, Annette,	3 24	Rice, Nelson W.,	23 47
Johnson, Orison's Widow,	2 84	Robbins, David & Lucy,	4 86
Kidder, Asa,	16 94	Root, Sophronia,	5 27
Kimball, Mary,	53 46	Sherwin, George,	2 00
Knowlton, Miles,	29 67	Sherwin, Silvanus,	2 00
Knowlton, S. W.,	6 00	Small, J. W.,	9 06
Leonard, F. W.,	4 06	Stedman, Wm. A.,	38 46
Lowe, Martin L.,	10 29	Stone, C. P.,	4 30
Mason, Elbridge,	9 72	Stone, Lucinda W.,	18 00
Merrifield, Hollis R.,	16 00	Tuthill, W. J.,	31 75
Merrifield, Nathan,	31 70	Waite, S. M.,	5 10
Miller, Clarissa,	2 23	Wakefield, Chandler,	15 39
Miller, Marshall's Est.,	8 00	Walker, E. C.,	12 38
Miller, Samuel P.,	16 31	Walker, Abby L.,	3 00
Moore, Franklin,	19 82	Walker, Chas. S.,	2 00
Morgan, Harriet,	2 84	Ward, Calvin,	15 38
Morse, Austin J.,	39 45	Ware, O. T.,	26 05
Morse, Sabin P.,	21 85	Warren, A. T.,	19 23
Newton, Nancy,	10 94	Whitney, S. F.,	9 26
Newton, Fanny W.,	10 00	Windham Co. Savings Bank,	14 32
Nichols, Chas. E.,	13 34		
Park, Elihu,	7 88	Willis, Harriet,	13 13
Park, Otis,	2 00	Winslow, L. I.,	4 00
Park, Walter,	2 10	Winslow, Mary R.,	4 86
Parsons, George W.,	2 00	Witt, Willard,	4 45
Patch, Mirriam,	6 48	Woodward, Romanzo,	2 00

SCHOOL DISTRICT No. 3.

Amsden, S. L.,	$ 3 62	Brown, S. G.,	$ 3 83
Amsden, E. N.,	2 00	Best, Chas. J.,	2 00
Brown, G. C.,	5 27	Coleman, Chas.,	6 86

Coleman, Mary,	$ 4 86	Newell. H. F..	$ 6 66
Fisher, Austin B..	31 97	Phillips, Simon,	11 38
Fisher, George,	50 00	Plimpton, Holland,	17 04
Fisher, Solon,	16 20	Powers, Silas D..	11 72
Gates, Alvin,	5 85	Sewall, L. B..	3 42
Gates, William,	2 00	Sibley, Isaac T.,	11 72
Higgins, Stephen's Est..	23 47	Sibley, William B.,	7 67
Holland, Sarah,	11 53	Stiles, Eugene C..	15 37
Holland, Wm. H..	2 00	Stiles, Oren.	2 03
Holland, Charles.	2 00	White, Geo. B.,	17 00
Hudson, Lydia,	2 23	White, Joseph,	4 86
Johnson, G. B. & Wife,	34 40	Wilder, Lyman,	2 19
Kenney, Henry S..	40 95	Wilson, S. S..	1 83

School District No. 5.

Allen, Welcome,	$27 33	Lamb, Geo. W.,	$10 10
Betterly, Geo. W.,	8 48	Lamson, L. B.,	14 87
Betterly, Geo. C.,	61	Morse, Chas. W..	22 25
Betterly, William C.,	1 22	Morse, F. B.,	15 15
Charter, G. H. K.,	2 92	Morse, F. B. & A. T.,	1 62
Dunklee, Emory,	25 53	Morse, Samuel,	27 30
Hall, Emory U..	2 00	Pratt, R. M..	1 42
Ingram, Elwin,	3 30	Sparks, Herbert C.,	12 13
Ingram, J. M.,	3 00	Timson, Geo. W.,	90

School District No. 6.

Aldrich, Aaron's Est.,	$ 7 70	Cooley, E. K..	$ 5 00
Aldrich, John W.,	9 52	Dickinson, D. A..	47 67
Aldrich, H. N.,	5 71	Dickinson, D. D..	36 82
Allen, Geo. T. & Wife,	6 06	Dickinson, Geo. W..	11 77
Attridge, Ozearl,	28 39	Duncan, Daniel,	6 86
Benson, John E.,	9 70	Goodnow, John,	18 60
Benson, D. C..	3 00	Hall, George P..	2 00
Bixby, Elizabeth,	2 23	Halladay, Lucius,	13 46
Blakeslee, C. S..	14 85	Halladay & Sherman,	6 93
Bowker, S. W..	34 61	Harvey, Frank K..	3 00
Bowker, Charles,	2 00	Harvey, George H.,	2 00
Brown, G. C..	4 86	Harvey, Marcia W.,	3 65
Clark, Thomas & Eli,	4 87	Hosley, Samuel,	2 00

Houghton, E. M.,	$ 1 62	Redfield, Geo. W.,	$ 9 29
Hovey, S. M.,	11 75	Robinson, Eliza A.,	5 00
Hovey, Chas. G.,	3 00	Robinson, Fannie E.,	1 83
Hoyt, H. H.,	11 72	Sabin, D. S.,	24 99
Ingram, Alonzo D.,	6 86	Sherman, O. L.,	36 34
Ingram, Chester,	5 47	Sherman, Nathan's	
Ingram, George,	2 00	Est.,	13 00
Jones, Harriet A. E.,	4 70	Shipman, J. W.,	2 00
Lamb, Chas. P.,	8 00	Shipman, Ezra O.,	2 00
Lamb, G. B.,	8 10	Shipman, J. N.,	1 22
Lincoln, O. L. & Wife,	6 00	Smith, Lewis,	11 34
Lincoln, E. R.,	19 94	Smith, Henry,	2 00
Merrifield, L. W.,	20 03	Staples, N. L.,	11 91
Merrifield, J. A.,	2 00	Stedman, G. D.,	27 94
Merrifield, A. M.,	7 65	Stedman, C. K.,	2 00
Merrifield, J. H.,	5 40	Stockwell, Anna,	1 62
Morse, F. J.,	34 18	Stoddard, Levi,	1 62
Morse, Thomas A.,	10 00	Stone, Henry B.,	2 00
Morse, Nelson,	23 05	Stratton, John S.,	2 00
Morse, Nelson & Bros.,	6 89	Timson, L. J.,	12 32
Morse, Ephraim,	10 29	Timson, A. L.,	3 00
Morse, Amherst,	9 00	Timson, Clark & Wife,	27 00
Morse, O. P.,	32 77	Tyler, Chas. E.,	9 47
Morse, O. P., Jr.,	11 50	Wheeler, E. P.,	11 48
Morse, Luke O.,	3 50	Wheeler & Morse,	7 29
Morse, Joshua,	2 03	Wheeler, Geo. R.,	3 22
Morse, Luke J.,	2 00	Wheeler, Charlotte A.,	6 89
Nash, J. W.,	9 07	Wheeler, John,	5 27
Nash, Cornelius,	2 65	Wheeler, H. H.,	2 92
Nash, Geo. W.,	3 00	Williams, Geo. B.,	45 77
Park, Chas. E.,	4 92	Williams, Abigail G.,	2 00
Perry, Martin,	1 62	Williams, Rosanna M.,	42 64
Pratt, R. P.,	4 86	Wood, A. & Sons,	20 14

SCHOOL DISTRICT No. 7.

Aldrich, Fanny M.,	$ 2 92	Cushing, Baxter C.,	$13 94
Blodgett, Joseph,	1 42	Davis, Hiram,	2 00
Bolles, Nelson & Mary,	1 42	Eddy, Oren,	2 00
Burroughs, Jarvis F.,	6 91	Gould, John,	6 86
Cook, C. M.,	4 05	Hall, Abby L.,	9 12

Hall, Henry,	$11 58	Rice, & Cowing,	$ 3 85
Hoyt, Hezekiah,	2 81	Snow, Ambrose,	3 49
Johnson, Mary,	1 42	Thorn, R. C.,	11 10
Leonard, C. R. & C.,	4 46	Tyler, Eli,	4 86
Leonard, Chandler,	2 00	Ware, William M.,	1 62
Lindsay, Willard,	15 13	White, Frank H.,	2 00
Lindsay, George,	3 00	White, F. H. and	
Miller, Henry W.,	8 89	Howe, Emma A.,	11 34
Miller, Joseph,	2 43	Wiswell, E. & I.,	1 22
Moran, James,	3 41		

School District No. 8.

Adams, H. W.,	$ 9 89	Knapp, Geo. W.,	$ 4 00
Ball, Horace,	3 00	Knapp, H. L.,	2 23
Bemis, Wm. L.,	10 10	Lamson, C. B.,	12 16
Bingham, W. E. and		Lamson, F. M.,	3 35
M. W.,	11 90	Lamson, D. B.,	2 67
Brooks, William & Wife,	4 64	Mason, Russell,	12 36
Bruce, Eli F.,	10 53	Moore, John M.,	9 08
Charter, James,	27 30	Morse, Emerson,	5 05
Charter, David's Est.,	1 83	Morse, Olin,	2 00
Dexter, J. W.,	15 39	Morse, B. E.,	9 70
Elmer, Chester W.,	11 34	Morse, Mary A.,	5 00
Fisher, J. H. & Wife,	4 84	Morse, Wm. H.,	23 88
Frost, Anna,	9 24	Morse, Alvin L.,	6 00
Frost, Wm. H.,	3 00	Morse, Joseph,	27 31
Hazelton, A. B.,	7 27	Morse, J. C.,	7 65
Hazelton, Eugene,	1 00	Perry, Chester E.,	4 05
Houghton, Elnathan,	2 00	Perry, John,	3 62
Houghton, M. N.,	14 34	Pickering, William,	40
Hubbard, Persis,	4 91	Sparks, C. E.,	13 34
Ingram, Porter,	2 00	Stratton, D. O.,	20 90
Ingram, Jonathan,	5 24	Walker, A. J.,	1 15
Ingram, Lydia,	3 24	White, Eli,	4 83
Ingram, Mason,	29 31	White, Henry T.,	2 00
Kelsey, Levi,	7 67	Worden, Avery,	3 83
King, Ezra & Wife,	5 15	Worden, John H.,	14 96

School District No. 9.

Amsden, A. L.,	$ 2 00	Mills, Huntly,	$ 3 83
Baker. Ransom & Wife,	49	Morse, Chas. E.,	8 08
Blodgett. R. T.,	81	Newton, R. M. & Wife,	17 22
Boynton, Manly,	1 22	Plimpton, S. H.,	61
Covey, P. C.,	9 48	Rand, Wm. R.,	3 04
Eager, Henry C.,	19 82	Redway, E. M.,	7 67
Eager, Walter W.,	2 00	Reed, D. S.,	8 47
Eddy, L. N.,	13 52	Rice, Hazelton,	21 23
Eddy, Jonathan,	13 70	Rutter, Philip,	2 03
Edwards, Abbott,	11 62	Saunders, Asa,	10 53
Field, Chas. K.,	5 27	Tenney, L. H.,	4 84
Flagg, H. W.,	18 67	Willis, Joseph,	6 48
Grout, Joel,	8 20	Willis, M. C.,	4 46
Holland, J. M.,	8 26	Wiswell E.,	8 10
Lyman, James,	21 63	Wiswell, I., *	8 10
Marcy, Rodney,	16 77	Wiswell, I., Jr.,	2 00
Mills, Alonzo H.,	2 00		

School District No. 10.

Adams, S. S.,	$23 84	Jones, Frank A.,	$ 8 27
Adams, J. O.,	11 72	Jones, John D.,	5 45
Adams, Horace,	13 34	Moore, Abigail,	3 50
Adams, P. W.,	2 03	Moore, Jonathan,	5 24
Adams, Asaph,	1 22	Morse, F. J. & L.	
Briggs, George and Wife,	7 47	Halladay,	41
		Sparks, Harlon E.,	11 72
Hunt, Edgar O.,	7 67	Thomas, A. J.,	2 70

School District No. 11.

Bailey, Zina G.,	$24 87	Stratton, Alonzo V.,	$ 4 73
Bailey, Chauncey B.,	8 10	Stratton, Asa,	7 86
Ingram, Orman & C. W.,	2 43	Stratton, E. M.,	6 86
Morse, Dolly R.,	7 70	Stratton, Charles,	2 00

Joint District No. 8, Newfane & Townshend.

Franklin, Polly,	$32 40	Wood, O. & A.,	$ 8 10
Franklin, O. E. & A. B.,	5 49		

Joint District No. 3, Newfane & Dummerston.

Betterly, Chester H.,	$23 25	Stone, Edmund,	$ 1 62
Betterly, James H.,	2 00		

Joint District No. 5, Newfane & Dummerston.

Brooks, William A., $ 5 65

Joint District No. 4, Newfane & Dover.

Holden, L. L.,	$ 2 61	Powers, L. C.,	$ 8 88
Johnson, Eliot,	7 29	Yeaw, William,	1 01

Total Town List, $3986 65

ADDENDA.

To list of school superintendents, page 193, should be added: 1867, D. I. Aldrich and R. M. Pratt.

To list of old inhabitants, page 221, the following should be added:

Samuel Bailey was a soldier of the Revolution, from its commencement to its termination. Came to Newfane from Marlboro, Mass., at an early date, and settled on the farm now owned by Harlon Sparks. Died about 1832. His son, David Bailey, was born in Massachusetts, June 14, 1786. Married Sarah Goodell, July 4, 1810. Died Oct. 14, 1867.

Pardon Perry, son of Joseph and Sabra Perry, was born in Newfane, Nov. 2, 1802. Married Sally Bridge, in 1826. Occupied the farm now owned by J. W. Dexter, at Pondville. Died Aug. 7, 1870.

Many of the dates in the sketch of the Morse family are taken from "Memorial of the Morses"; and for the correctness of those relating to persons not now resident of the town we have no other voucher.

ERRATA.

Page 36, tenth line, insert a comma after the word "children."
Page 53, third line from the bottom, for "1808," read *1838*.
Page 79, second line from the bottom should read "*three*," in place of "all."
Page 94, second stanza, seventh line, the last word should read "*longing*."
Page 136, seventh line from the bottom for "1866" read *1806*.
Page 156, second line from the bottom, for "1815," read *1805*.
Page 163, tenth line from the bottom, for "1804," read *1805*.
Page 187, tenth line from the bottom should read *A. S. Barnes*.
Page 223, ninth line from the top, for "1796," read *Nov. 21, 1795*.
Page 238, fifth line from the top should read, *Adams, James O*.

www.ingramcontent.com/pod-product-compliance
Lightning Source LLC
Chambersburg PA
CBHW031340230426
43670CB00006B/391